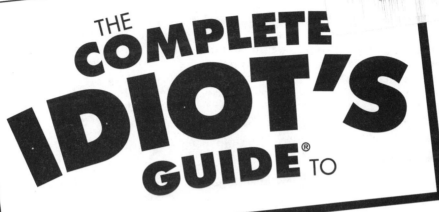

THE COMPLETE IDIOT'S GUIDE® TO

Programming Basics

by Clayton Walnum

ALPHA

A Pearson Education Company

To Lynn

Copyright © 2002 by Alpha Books

International Standard Book Number: 0-02-864286-4
Library of Congress Catalog Card Number: Available upon request.

04   03   02   8   7   6   5   4   3   2   1

Interpretation of the printing code: The rightmost number of the first series of numbers is the year of the book's printing; the rightmost number of the second series of numbers is the number of the book's printing. For example, a printing code of 02-1 shows that the first printing occurred in 2002.

Printed in the United States of America

Note: This publication contains the opinions and ideas of its author. It is intended to provide helpful and informative material on the subject matter covered. It is sold with the understanding that the author and publisher are not engaged in rendering professional services in the book. If the reader requires personal assistance or advice, a competent professional should be consulted.

The author and publisher specifically disclaim any responsibility for any liability, loss, or risk, personal or otherwise, which is incurred as a consequence, directly or indirectly, of the use and application of any of the contents of this book.

Publisher
Marie Butler-Knight

Product Manager
Phil Kitchel

Managing Editor
Jennifer Chisholm

Acquisitions Editor
Eric Heagy

Development Editor
Michael Koch

Production Editor
Katherin Bidwell

Copy Editor
Amy Lepore

Illustrator
Jody Schaeffer

Cover Designers
Mike Freeland
Kevin Spear

Book Designers
Scott Cook and Amy Adams of DesignLab

Indexer
Brad Herriman

Layout/Proofreading
Angela Calvert
Mary Hunt
Elizabeth Louden

Contents at a Glance

Contents

Introduction

If you've ever wondered how all that crazy stuff happens on your computer's monitor, this book is for you. Learning to program not only will dispel much of the mystery of what goes on inside your system's central processing unit (CPU), it will also make a great hobby, one that can keep you busy and amused for hours on end. More importantly, once you know about things like loops and objects, you can amaze your friends with your stunning intellect and cleverness. (Okay, maybe that's a *bit* of an overstatement.)

In any case, this book will provide you with all the knowledge you need to understand how computer programming works. Once you've mastered the basics presented here, you will have the knowledge to decide whether programming is for you and whether you'd like to take the next step.

Whom This Book Is For

This book is for anyone who wants to understand how programming works. Obviously, then, if you already use a programming language, you probably won't learn much here. However, if you've never had programming experience or you need a refresher on the basic techniques used in programming, this book is the perfect starting point. You need not have any experience with programming to enjoy this book. All you need is basic computer skills such as using a keyboard.

Software and Hardware Requirements

This book uses QBasic as the programming language. Because QBasic was one of the first versions of BASIC that Microsoft put out, it will run on just about any PC-compatible computer in existence.

As for the software, QBasic is available on DOS installation disks as well as on most Windows installation CD-ROMs. Just search the CD-ROM for "QBasic." I even understand, though you didn't hear it from me, that you can readily find QBasic for download in various places on the Internet. Do a search for "QBasic" on Google (www.google.com). I bet you can find all sorts of goodies, including tons of sample programs to study.

Extras ...

This book also features extra tidbits called *sidebars*. These asides are designed to supply you with extra information, tips, and cautions. Here's what you'll find ...

Cool Stuff

This is where you'll read about tricks and tips that can make programming more fun and convenient.

Danger Ahead!

This is where you'll find important information about problems you may run into as you write your programs.

Programmer Lingo

This is where you'll find definitions of the technical words you need to know as a programmer.

Point of Interest

This is where you'll read about interesting topics related to the discussion at hand.

Ready to Go?

That's about it. I see no point in delaying any longer your entry into the wonderful world of programming. To tell you the truth, I'm a little jealous. Although I've been programming since the early 1980s, I still remember the thrill I got the first time I wrote and ran a program. I hope you also find that thrill.

Acknowledgments

I would like to thank the many people who had a hand in getting this book from my head to the bookshelf. Special thanks go to Eric Heagy for keeping me busy, Michael Koch for polishing things up, and Kathy Bidwell and the production staff at Alpha books for putting out the book in time. As always, thanks also go to my family: Lynn, Christopher, Justin, Stephen, and Caitlynn.

Special Thanks to the Technical Reviewer

The Complete Idiot's Guide to Programming Basics was reviewed by an expert who double-checked the accuracy of what you'll learn here to help us ensure that this book gives you everything you need to know about programming basics. Special thanks are extended to Chris McGee.

Trademarks

All terms mentioned in this book that are known to be or are suspected of being trademarks or service marks have been appropriately capitalized. Alpha Books and Pearson Education, Inc., cannot attest to the accuracy of this information. Use of a term in this book should not be regarded as affecting the validity of any trademark or service mark.

Part 1

An Introduction to Programming

Before you can actually write a program, it helps to know what programs are and how they work. It also helps to know what tools you have to work with and what you use those tools for. In this part of the book, you learn how computers take the program code you write and turn it into the stuff you see on the screen. You also learn how to get started with the QBasic programming environment.

Programming 101

Okay, here you are—ready to step into the dark, unknown abyss of computer programming. Got your hard hat on? Before you get started with computer programming, it might help to have a bottle of Prozac on hand. No, not really. Programming isn't as weird and wild as you might think. You undoubtedly have some ideas about what a program is and how it works; otherwise, you wouldn't have bought this book to begin with. Although some of these ideas may be right on the money, others may be as crazy as the wombat Olympics.

Whatever your ideas about programming and wombats, this chapter gives you the skinny, the real poop, the absolute truth. After reading this chapter, you may find that your perceptions about programming are pretty solid, or you may find that you know as much about programming a computer as you do about driving the space shuttle. In either case, you'll be a better person for having spent time here. Um, before we get started, could you please pass the Prozac?

Psssst! Listen Up

We all like secrets. Well, except for secrets we know nothing about, of course. I know one you know nothing about, and I'm about to tip you off. Ready? Are you sure? Here it is: The computer-programming world has a well-kept secret. You won't hear programmers talking about it (which is, of course, why it's a secret). And if you've been using a computer for any time at all, you'll probably find this secret hard to believe. Nevertheless, it's as true as the sky is blue. So brace yourself. You're about to learn a shocking fact. Ready?

Computers are stupid.

It's true! Just how stupid are they? Computers are so stupid that they make monkeys look like physics professors—except on Fridays, when the monkeys like to dress up in funny outfits and play pranks on wombats. The fact is that a computer can do absolutely nothing on its own. Without programmers, computers are as useless as rubber razors. Computers can do only what they're told to do—and they're not even smart enough to complain about it. If you think for a minute, you'll realize this means that computers can only perform tasks that humans already know how to do. So why do we bother with computers? The great thing about computers is not that they're smart, but that they can pave roads in even the hottest weather ... No, wait! That's the highway department. What *computers* can do is perform endless calculations quickly and without getting bored and turning on reruns of *The Love Boat*.

Programmers are the people who tell computers what to do. You can always tell a programmer from a regular person because the programmer is standing over a computer and mumbling into its ear. Okay, so computers don't have ears. The point is that, when you use your computer, you're not actually programming it. For example, when you plop yourself down in front of a word processor and hack out a letter to Aunt Martha, who lives alone on Victoria Island with 18 cats, 2 dogs, and a wombat named Hank, you're not giving commands to the computer. You're only using the commands contained in the program. It's the computer program—which was written by a programmer—that actually tells the computer what to do.

Figure 1.1 shows how talented our artists are, and it illustrates the relationship between a computer user, a program, and a computer. Notice that there are no flowers or chocolates involved. This is because the relationship between a computer user and a computer usually isn't a romantic one (the key word here being "usually"). That's you, the computer user, way up at the top of the hierarchy (feeling dizzy?). You probably use your computer for many activities in addition to word processing, such as organizing data in a spreadsheet, keeping track of information in a database, and maybe even playing games. In all these cases, you execute a program, which in turn provides instructions to the computer.

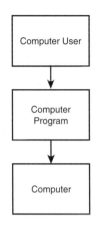

Figure 1.1

As a computer user, you're on top of the heap.

The bottom line is that if you want to give commands directly to your computer, you must learn to write programs. You can't just whisper in its microphone, and you can't flatter it with flowers and chocolates.

What's in It for You?

Good question. Another good question is, "Why do wombats even *have* an Olympics?" But I digress. There can be as many reasons for you to learn to program as there are purchases on my last credit card statement. Only you know what attracts you to programming. Here are some of the reasons that may be going through your mind:

➤ You're looking for a fun and rewarding hobby.

➤ You want to be able to write the programs you really need—the ones you can't always find at the software store.

➤ You want to learn more about how computers work.

➤ You have to learn programming for school or work.

➤ You want to impress your friends.

➤ Some misguided person gave you this book as a gift, and you don't want to hurt his or her feelings.

These all are legitimate reasons. You may have a better one, but whatever your reason, once you get started with programming, you'll find that it can be both fascinating and addictive. Your spouse or significant other, however, may ban computers from your home and burn this book after he or she realizes just how addictive computer programming can be. Consider yourself warned.

Looks Like Greek

Did you ever build a model airplane? When you opened the box, you found that the instructions were missing and half the pieces were broken. So you returned it, got another one, and opened that box. Inside you found—*voilà!*—a list of numbered instructions. By following the instructions in the order in which they were presented, you put your model together piece by piece. When you finally reached the last instruction, your model was complete—except, of course, for those few parts that are always left over.

Programmer Lingo

A **computer program** is a list of instructions that the computer follows from beginning to end. A computer programmer writes this list of instructions using one of the many computer languages.

A *computer program* is much like that list of instructions, except the instructions in a computer program don't tell you what to do. They tell the computer what to do.

Still, a computer program is nothing more than a list of commands. The computer follows these commands, one by one, until it reaches the end of the program. Unlike when you built your model, however, the computer, after finishing with its program, will have no leftover pieces. Computers are stupid, not sloppy.

Each line in a computer program is a single command that the computer must obey. If it doesn't obey, you're probably trying to program my six-year-old and not your computer. Each command does only a very small task, such as printing a name on the screen or adding two numbers. When you put hundreds, thousands, or even hundreds of thousands of these commands together, your computer can do wonderful things: balance a checkbook, print a document, or draw pictures.

Programmer Lingo

Machine language is the only language your computer really understands. Machine language consists of nothing but a lot of numbers, which are very difficult (if not impossible) for humans to understand. Programming languages enable people to write programs in an English-like language that is then changed into machine language so the computer can understand it.

Parlez-Vous BASIC?

Computers don't understand English. They're stupid, remember? They can't even understand Pig Latin. They're *really* stupid. Computers understand only one thing—*machine language,* which is entirely composed of numbers. Unfortunately, many human minds deal poorly with numbers. That's especially true if you're taking a course in advanced calculus, but that's another story. Imagine, for example, a human language in which the numbers 10, 12, 14, 15, and 26, have the following significance:

10	is
12	how
26	hello
14	wombat
15	your

Now, imagine walking up to a friend and saying "26, 12 10 15 14?" Your friend wouldn't know what to say. (If your friend answers "32 65 34," he spends way too much time with computers.) If you expect your friend to respond, you'd better use the words "Hello, how is your wombat?" Conversely, if we mere mortals have any hope of making sense of machine language, we have to change it into something we can understand, something that has as little to do with numbers as a mosquito has to do with insect repellent. That's where computer languages come in.

In this book, you'll be fiddling around with a computer language called QBasic. QBasic programs are a dialect of a computer language called BASIC, which stands for beginner's all-purpose symbolic instruction code. BASIC was developed not to help computers but to help people make sense out of the numerical nonsense that machines delight in. QBasic replaces many of the numbers used by machine language with words and symbols that we lowly humans can more easily understand and remember.

Now, wait a minute. Computers understand only numbers, right? A BASIC program uses words and symbols (and a few numbers) so that people can understand the program. How, then, can the computer understand and run BASIC? Now you know why computer programmers whisper to their computers. Okay, so you don't know.

The truth is that, when you load a language like QBasic, you are also loading an interpreter, which is a special program that can take the words and symbols from a BASIC program and convert them into machine language that the computer can understand. Without QBasic's interpretation of your programs, your computer wouldn't have the slightest idea what to do with the program.

Point of Interest

QBasic is only one of many versions of the BASIC language. Older versions of DOS (pre-5.0) came with a version of BASIC called GW-BASIC. There was also a more advanced version of QBasic called QuickBasic, and you can go down to your local software store right now and buy Visual Basic. (While you're there, pick me up a copy of Baldur's Gate II. I'll pay you on Thursday. No, really.) All these software packages enable you to create computer programs with BASIC, but they all implement the BASIC language slightly differently.

Programmer Lingo

A **compiler** changes your program into an executable file (for example, WORD.EXE or SIMCITY.EXE). An executable program is actually a machine language program that's ready for your computer to read and understand. Not every computer programming language includes a compiler, although most do.

Point of Interest

Because a language such as QBasic uses an interpreter to translate your program into machine language as the program runs, you cannot run such a program without the interpreter. To run a QBasic program, for example, you must first load the program into the QBasic interpreter and then select the interpreter's Run command. Many modern versions of BASIC, however, now use compilers to change BASIC programs into executable files, which can be run directly.

There are all kinds of computer languages, including Pascal, C++, FORTRAN, COBOL, Modula-2, BASIC, and Swahili. Well, not that last one. All computer languages have one thing in common: They can be read by humans and therefore must be converted to machine language before the computer can understand them.

Some languages, such as BASIC, convert the program to machine language one line at a time as the program runs. Other languages, such as Pascal, use a *compiler* to convert the entire program all at once before any of the program runs. In any case, all programming languages must be converted to machine language for the computer to understand the program.

Getting Down to the Nitty-Gritty

Now that you know something about computer programs, how do you go about creating one? Writing a computer program, though not particularly difficult, can be a long and tedious process— much like writing a term paper for school or a financial report for your boss. You start out with a basic idea of what you want to do and write a first draft. After reading over the draft and resisting the urge to throw the pages into the fireplace, you go back to writing—polishing your prose until it glows like the top of Uncle Walter's head. Over the course of the writing process, you may write many drafts before you're satisfied with the document you've produced. You may also go through a bag of Oreos and a gallon of milk. This is why writing reports can make you fat.

Writing a computer program requires development steps similar to those you use when writing a paper or report, so make sure you have Oreos by your side and milk in the fridge. The following list outlines these steps:

1. Type the program using QBasic's editor.
2. Save the program to disk.
3. Run the program and see how it works.

4. Fix programming errors.

5. Go back to step 2.

As you can see, most of the steps in the programming process are repeated over and over again as errors are discovered and corrected. Even experienced programmers seldom write programs that are error-free. Programmers spend more time fine-tuning their programs than they do initially writing them, which is why they eat so many gummy bears and drink so much Coke. All that rewriting saps their energy and lowers their blood-sugar levels.

This fine-tuning is important because we humans are not as logical as we'd like to think. Moreover, our minds are incapable of remembering every detail required to make a program run perfectly. Heck, most of us are lucky if we can remember our telephone numbers. Only when a program crashes or does something else unexpected can we hope to find those sneaky errors that hide in programs. Computer experts say that there's no such thing as a *bug*-free program. After you start writing full-length programs, you'll see how true this statement is.

Programmer Lingo

Bugs are programming errors that stop your program from running correctly. Bugs are also nasty creatures with spindly legs and crunchy shells that make you scream when they leap out of shadows. This book doesn't deal with the latter type of bug, however, so we won't mention them here. Oh yeah, I guess I just did. By the way, the term "bug" came into existence when someone found an actual insect inside a computer. Apparently, the insect had done some nasty things to the computer's circuits. Really!

Squashing That Panic Attack

Panic attacks are a common phenomenon for people who program computers. This is because computers like to sneak up behind people and yell things like, "Watch out for that wombat!" Seriously though, after reading all that's involved in writing and running a computer program, you might be a little nervous. After all, you bought this book because it promised to teach you computer programming. No one warned you about such mysterious topics as machine language, interpreters, compilers, and program bugs. So, is programming easy or not?

Errr … yes and no.

It's very easy to write a computer program by forcing a programmer to write you one, especially if you're holding his gummy bears hostage. Luckily for those of us who don't have a live-in programmer we can threaten, it's also pretty easy to learn to write simple programs with a language like QBasic. The QBasic language is logical, English-like, and easy to understand. With only minimal practice, you can write many useful and fun programs with QBasic. All you need is the time to read this book and the ambition to write a few programs of your own. In fact, what you'll learn in this book is enough programming for just about anyone who's not planning to be a professional programmer.

However, if you want to make programming a career, you have much to learn that's not covered in this introductory book. For example, consider a word-processing program like Microsoft Word, which took dozens of programmers many years to write. To write such complex software, you must have intimate knowledge of how your computer works and a remarkable tolerance for gummy bears. Additionally, you must have spent many years learning the intricacies of professional computer programming.

Still, there's a lot you can do with QBasic, whether you're interested in writing utilities, simple applications, or even games. And, once you get the hang of it, you'll discover that programming in BASIC is not as difficult as you may have thought.

After all, computers may be stupid, but you're not.

The Least You Need to Know

➤ Computers are stupid and can do only what they are told to do.

➤ There are many reasons to learn to program; if nothing else, programming is a rewarding hobby.

➤ A computer program is nothing more than a list of commands.

➤ There are many computer languages. In this book, you will learn about a language called BASIC.

➤ Before a computer can run a program, the program must be converted to machine language. This conversion is done by an interpreter or a compiler.

➤ Depending on what you want to do, programming can be very easy or very complicated.

Chapter 2

Introducing the Programmer's Toolbox

In This Chapter

➤ Learning about code editors

➤ Understanding compilers

➤ Finding problems with debuggers

➤ Introducing integrated development environments

If you've ever had a handyman come over to your house and fix stuff (you know, a sticky door, a broken step, or that freaking dining room light fixture that hangs down so low that you crack your head on it every time you try to clear the table), you've probably noticed that Mr. (Ms.?) Fix-It carries around a hefty set of tools with which to do his (her?) job. Programmers are no different. Well, they're a little different. Programmers can't hang their tools from a belt. Believe me, I know. The last time I tried to hang a computer monitor from a tool belt, I ended up with my pants around my ankles. Anyway, the point is that a programmer needs tools, too, and in this chapter, you get a look at some of these tools. Tighten your belts!

Typing It Up

Programmers consider themselves to be artists, just like musicians and novelists. And just as a musician writes a song or a novelist writes a book, programmers write programs. This is, of course, an actual physical process in which the programmer types on a keyboard. And, golly-gee, what a coincidence, most computers have a keyboard! Unfortunately, you can type on your computer's keyboard all day, but you still won't be writing a program until you're typing text into a specific kind of application called a source-code editor.

Depending on the language, a source-code editor can be as simple as Windows Notepad or as complex as Visual Studio's built-in editor. Most programming languages, however, use source-code files that are nothing more than plain text. For this reason, you can often get by with a stripped-down editor like Windows Notepad. For example, Figure 2.1 shows a short C# (Microsoft's newest programming language) program typed into Notepad.

Figure 2.1

A simple C# program in Windows Notepad.

```
MyProg.cs - Notepad                                          _ □ X
File  Edit  Search  Help
using System;

namespace ConsoleApplication1
{
    /// <summary>
    /// Summary description for Class1.
    /// </summary>
    class Class1
    {
        static void Main(string[] args)
        {
            //
            // TODO: Add code to start application here
            //
        }
    }
}
```

Although you can write C# programs using a simple text editor like Notepad, the language comes with its own built-in editor that provides all kinds of conveniences, including displaying language elements in different colors, automatic indenting, search and replace, and much more. Figure 2.2 shows the same C# program in the built-in editor provided with the language.

Point of Interest

A third-party product is a product that's manufactured by a company not associated with the company that manufactures the product with which the third-party product is used. Yow! That's a mouthful and a half. Here's an example: If you had your own company that made a source-code editor called Way Cool VB Editor that was designed as a tool for Microsoft's Visual Basic .NET, Way Cool VB Editor would be considered a third-party product.

To make your choices even wider, many third-party companies provide standalone source-code editors that can be used with a variety of programming languages. Such editors are often very expensive but provide every possible feature and convenience you can imagine. I even once heard of a third-party source-code editor that would automatically refill the programmer's bowl of corn chips. Er ... okay, I'm lying about that one.

As with Microsoft's new C# language, most full-fledged programming languages come with built-in editors. The language you'll be using for most of the examples in this book is QBasic. In spite of the fact that QBasic is ancient, it still comes with its own text editor. Figure 2.3 shows QBasic's source-code editor in action.

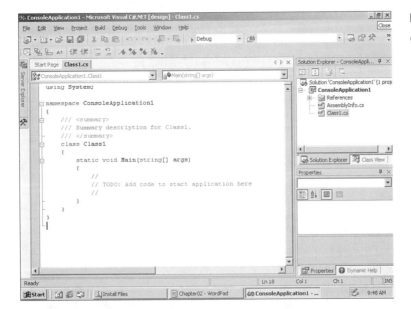

Figure 2.2

C#'s built-in editor.

Figure 2.3

QBasic's built-in editor.

Using a One-Line-at-a-Time Translator

Once you write your program's source code, you can't just demand that your computer run it. Well, you can, but it won't do any good, and you'll look pretty goofy yelling orders at your computer's monitor. As you learned in Chapter 1, "Programming 101," your program's source code has to be changed into a format the computer can understand.

In general, this happens in one of two ways. The first way is through the use of an interpreter. This is a person who stands behind you and yells orders at the computer on your behalf. Actually, an *interpreter* is a piece of software that reads through your program one line at a time, executing each command. The process looks something like this:

1. Read a line of source code.
2. Convert the line to machine language.
3. Pass the machine language instruction to the computer for execution.
4. Go back to step 1 until the interpreter has read all lines of source code.

Programmer Lingo

An **interpreter** is a piece of software that executes program source code one line at a time.

An interpreter must convert your program's source code to machine language at the same time it's running the program. As a result, your program's user can't use the program unless he also has the interpreter. What a pain! Also, the process of converting and running a program all at the same time bogs things down a bit. For this reason, interpreted programs run much slower than those that have been converted to machine language with a compiler.

QBasic uses an interpreter to run programs, so its programs are slower than those created by, say, Visual Basic, which comes with a compiler. (A newer version of QBasic, called QuickBasic, comes with a compiler, too.) To access QBasic's interpreter, you simply choose the Start command, as shown in Figure 2.4.

Figure 2.4

Starting QBasic's interpreter.

Consulting a Full-Service Translator

In many cases, interpreters are as much a roadblock as they are a bumpy road. Sure, for your purposes (learning the basics of computer programming), an interpreted language works just fine. QBasic runs plenty fast enough—especially on today's high-octane computers—to demonstrate everything you need to know.

Professional programmers, however, often need to squeeze every microsecond of speed out of a computer, so they cannot tolerate the slow-downs caused by interpreters. The big boys use a piece of software known as a *compiler* to convert source code to machine language. A compiler converts an entire source-code file to machine language, storing the results in an executable file, which is the file you, the user, run to start the application. Conceptually, the process goes something like this:

1. Read a line of source code.

2. Convert the line to machine language.

3. Store the machine-language instructions in the program's executable file.

4. Go back to step 1 until the compiler has read all lines of source code.

Programmer Lingo

A **compiler** is a piece of software that converts an entire source-code file into machine language, which is stored in an executable file.

Notice that nowhere in this process is a line of code executed. Compilation is a conversion process and nothing more. All the results of the compilation get stored in a disk file for later execution. Because the entire conversion has been saved to disk ahead of time, the program's user can simply run the executable file. He doesn't need to have the compiler, which is purely a development tool. Moreover, the program runs as fast as the machine allows it to. No slow-downs here!

Compilers are usually standalone programs that a programmer can run directly. Many modern development environments, however, link their tools to a unified user interface. This makes compilers work a lot like interpreters, except for the fact that the compiler produces an executable file.

For example, Microsoft's new Visual Basic .NET language comes as part of a development environment called Visual Studio .NET. When you want to compile and test a Visual Basic .NET program, you can select a Run command, as shown in Figure 2.5. Visual Studio then compiles the program into an executable file and runs the executable file.

Figure 2.5

Starting Visual Basic .NET's. compiler

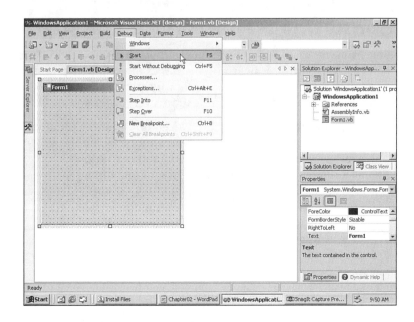

Soliciting the Help of Debuggers

Writing a full-size program is a meticulous process and, like all meticulous processes, is error prone. No programmer on the planet has ever written a perfect program of reasonable length, so it follows that there is not a single bug-free program on the planet.

Programmer Lingo

A **debugger** is a piece of software that enables you to explore, in slow motion, what's going on in your program. In a typical debugging session, you would execute each line of source code one at a time and watch the results.

Some bugs, however, are worse than others. For example, what would you rather have on your arm, a ladybug or a wasp? The same is true of computer programs, except, of course, programs don't have arms, which is why they have a tough time buying shirts.

More to the point, some program bugs lie dormant in the code, requiring just the right conditions to rear their ugly heads. Others are more obvious, and although it would be great to be able to get rid of all the errors in a program, only the more obvious ones are likely to be found.

So, how does one find these errors? One way is to run the program and then scream bloody murder when the screen goes blank and your letter of complaint to the Society for the Propagation of Immense Mosquitoes flies off to digital heaven. A more reasonable way is to take out a piece of software called a *debugger*.

The earliest program debuggers did little more than enable you to run a program a line at a time, pausing between each line so that you could see the results. These days, full-featured debuggers can do everything from a simple program trace to displaying the contents of memory and much more. Figure 2.6 shows debugger windows in the new Visual Studio .NET.

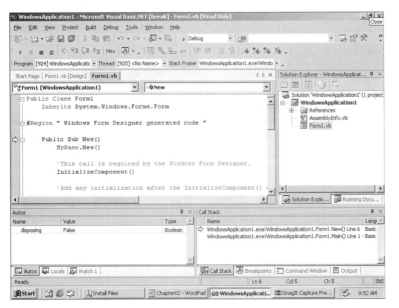

Figure 2.6

Starting Visual Basic .NET's debugger windows.

Believe it or not, in spite of its age, QBasic comes with its own debugger. This debugger isn't anywhere near as powerful as the ones that come with today's programming packages, but it can perform all the basic tasks needed to find errors in a program. Figure 2.7 shows QBasic's Debug menu, which holds the debugger's commands. You'll learn more about the QBasic debugger and the debugging process in Chapter 15, "Lookin' for Creepy Crawlies."

Figure 2.7

QBasic's Debug menu.

Putting It All Together

Back in the day, the process of writing and compiling a program was very much a literal set of steps that the programmer had to perform by typing commands at the DOS prompt. The process went like this:

1. Write the source code with a text editor.
2. Save the source code to a file.
3. Run a compiler to produce object-code files from each source-code file.
4. Run a linker to produce the final executable file from the various object-code files.

Programmer Lingo

A **linker** is a piece of software that takes the various files produced by a compiler and links them together to create an application's final executable file.

Today, these steps haven't really changed much, but all the tools programmers used to run "by hand" are now often merged into a single software package called an integrated development environment (IDE). In many cases, even the steps required to build a program have been merged.

For example, Visual Studio, which is the most popular IDE today, can perform these last three steps all with a single click of a button. The fact that, up to this point, I haven't even mentioned something called a *linker* (see step 4) is a result of this tight tool integration. Although a compiler and a linker are really different tools, most people just think of the entire process as "compiling a program," with no mention of a linker.

Cool Stuff

Even with advanced development environments like Visual Studio, you can still do your programming the old fashioned way—writing, compiling, and linking your programs by typing commands at a DOS prompt. With all the conveniences of an advanced IDE, though, I don't know why you'd want to do that.

Some IDEs differentiate between compilation and linking by having a command that can simply compile a source-code file (a good way to find syntax errors) or build the application, which is the entire process of compiling and linking. Because IDEs are pretty smart, the build process will compile source code only if there have been changes. Otherwise, the build command simply does a link, as long as the executable file isn't up-to-date.

The screen shots in this chapter have shown you the IDEs for both Visual Studio .NET (which includes the languages Visual Basic .NET, Visual C# .NET, and Visual C++ .NET) and QBasic. In both of these development environments, all the tools you need are available from each IDE's menus.

The Least You Need to Know

➤ Depending on the language, a source-code editor can be as simple as Windows Notepad or as complex as Visual Studio's built-in editor.

➤ Most programming languages use source-code files that are nothing more than plain text.

➤ Many programming languages come with their own built-in editors that provide all kinds of conveniences, including displaying language elements in different colors, automatic indenting, search and replace, and much more.

➤ Many third-party companies provide standalone source-code editors that can be used with a variety of programming languages.

➤ An interpreter converts your program's source code to machine language at the same time it's running the program.

➤ A compiler converts an entire source-code file to machine language all at once, storing the results in an executable file.

➤ A debugger is a piece of software that enables you to explore, in slow motion, what's going on in your program.

➤ Today, programming tools are often merged into a single software package called an integrated development environment (IDE).

Chapter 3

Crankin' It Up with QBasic

In This Chapter

➤ Running QBasic

➤ Giving commands to QBasic

➤ Loading, saving, and printing programs

➤ Typing program text

➤ Editing program text

➤ Finding words or phrases in a program

Now that you have a general idea of what a computer program is and how it works, it's time to load up QBasic and get to work. In this chapter, you learn about the QBasic programming environment and how to write your first program. If you've used word processors before, this chapter covers a lot of familiar ground. If you have no experience with text editing, however, you should study carefully the discussions that follow. After all, you can't write a program until you know how to type it in!

Where Is QBasic?

In the old days, the most common computer operating system was MS-DOS, which stands for most skunks don oval slippers. (If you believe that, close this book now; you have no hope of becoming a programmer.) Actually, MS-DOS stands for Microsoft disk operating system. This operating system, just like any other program, was software installed on your computer. It may have already been installed when you bought your computer, or you may have installed it yourself. In either case, the QBasic programming language came with it.

Point of Interest

If Microsoft Windows was installed on your computer when you bought it and you can't find a Windows installation disk, call the company from which you bought the computer and ask where your copy of QBasic is.

Now (almost) everyone uses Microsoft Windows, and all that MS-DOS stuff is as archaic as dinosaur footprints. However, QBasic still remains a very useful language for learning to program, if for no other reason than it's free and almost everyone has it. Yep, that's right. Even though you're running Microsoft Windows, you still have a copy of QBasic. You just have to find it. Let me give you a hand.

First, take out your Microsoft Windows installation CD-ROM. After you have the CD-ROM, look in the Tools\oldmsdos directory. You should see two files named qbasic.exe and qbasic.hlp. Just copy those files to a directory named QBasic on your computer's hard disk, and you're ready to go! If you have a hard time locating these files, go to your Start menu, select the Search item, and then select For Files and Folders. When the search window appears, use it to search the CD-ROM and your hard disks for the qbasic.exe file.

Loading QBasic

Before you can run a QBasic program or write programs of your own, you must load QBasic. This is no different from having to load a word processor before writing a document—except with QBasic, you'll never feel obligated to write a letter to weird Uncle Henry. QBasic actually includes its own word-processing program, which you will use to write your programs. To load QBasic, go to your QBasic directory and double-click the QBasic application file. When you do, click the OK button on the little window that appears, and you'll see the screen in Figure 3.1.

Figure 3.1

QBasic when it first appears.

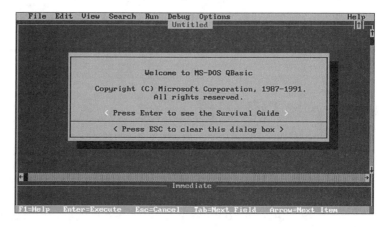

The welcome dialog box enables you to look at QBasic's Survival Guide (a brief help screen) by pressing Enter or by clicking the "Press Enter to see the Survival Guide" text line with your mouse. To get rid of the dialog box and get started with QBasic, press your keyboard's Esc key or use your mouse to click on the "Press ESC to clear this dialog box" text line.

When you close the welcome dialog box, you'll see QBasic's main window, as shown in Figure 3.2.

Menu bar   Edit window

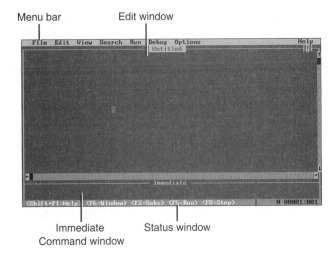

Figure 3.2

QBasic's main window.

Immediate
Command window   Status window

QBasic's main window comprises several smaller windows and a menu, each labeled in Figure 3.2 and listed here:

➤ **Menu bar**   You can access QBasic's various commands from here.

➤ **Edit window**   You type and view your programs in this window.

➤ **Immediate command window**   Any programming commands that you type in this window are performed immediately by the computer rather than being added to your program. You'll learn about immediate commands in Chapter 5, "Computer-Style Arithmetic." However, you might as well know now that commands like "Bring me Michelle Pfeiffer" don't work worth a darn.

➤ **Status window**   The status window shows the keys you can press to access certain commands and gives a quick description of any highlighted menu command. It also shows the line and column position of the text cursor.

Now that you know how the QBasic main screen is set up, let's take a closer look at this powerful programming environment.

Exploring QBasic's Menu Bar

Computers are stupid and so is QBasic. You can sit at your desk and stare at QBasic's main screen as long as you like, but until you give it a command, it'll just sit and stare back. Worse, you'll always be the first to blink.

As in many computer programs, you can use your keyboard or your mouse to give commands to QBasic by selecting entries from the menu bar at the top of the screen. To select commands with your keyboard, first press the Alt key. Notice that the first letter of each menu title lights up, and a black box appears around the File menu title. The black box indicates the menu that will open when you press Enter.

Cool Stuff

You can open any menu instantly by holding down the Alt key while pressing the first letter of the menu's title. For example, to open the File menu, press Alt+F. This type of keystroke is called a shortcut key.

To select the menu you want, use the left and right arrows to move the black box. When the box is on the menu you want, press Enter to open the menu.

When the menu appears, use the up- and down-arrow keys to highlight the command you want. Press Enter to activate the highlighted command.

Using a mouse to select menu commands is a little easier. Place the mouse pointer over the menu title and click the left mouse button. When the menu drops down, click the command you want to issue.

Don't fret about what all the menu commands do. You'll learn most of them later. For now, how about using the File menu to have a little fun?

Loading a QBasic Program

Before you can run a QBasic program, the program must be loaded. This doesn't mean you should force your program to chug-a-lug a quart of Smirnoff's; it means you must bring the program's text file (called the source code) into QBasic's editor window.

Source code is the program text that you type into an editor. With compiled languages, a program's source code no longer is needed after the program is compiled. Still, programmers usually save their source code so that they can make changes or additions to the program. Programmers also save their source code so that they can impress their friends and attract members of the opposite sex with their cleverness.

You load a source-code file with the Open command of the File menu, as shown in Figure 3.3.

When you select the Open command, you'll see a dialog box similar to the one shown in Figure 3.4.

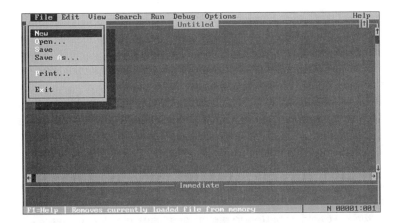

Figure 3.3

Select the Open command.

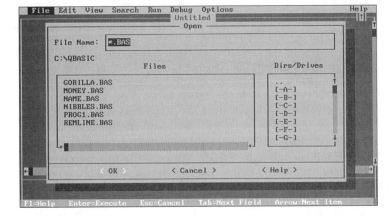

Figure 3.4

The Open dialog box.

As with menus, you can select files from this dialog box with either your keyboard or your mouse. To use your keyboard, type the name of the file you want to load and press Enter. If you want to avoid typing the filename, press Tab to move the cursor to the Files list box. Use the up- and down-arrow keys to highlight the file you want and press Enter to load the file.

You can select any button at the bottom of the dialog box by pressing your keyboard's Tab key until the blinking text cursor is on the button and then pressing Enter.

To select a file using your mouse, double-click the file you want in the Files list box. To double-click a file, place your mouse pointer over the file's name and then click the mouse's left button twice quickly. You can also select the file by clicking the file once to highlight it and then clicking the OK button at the bottom of the dialog box.

If you change your mind about opening a file, just select the Cancel button.

Of course, right now, you don't have any programs to load, so you'll just have to take all of this on faith!

25

Point of Interest

Tabbing is the process of using your computer's Tab key to move from one part of a dialog box to another. Most dialog boxes contain many parts—including text-entry fields and buttons—that you must access in one way or another. If you have a mouse, you can just click the field or button you want to access. Keyboard users, on the other hand, can use the Tab key to move to the next field or button in the dialog box. When you get to the last field or button, pressing Tab moves you back to the first.

Controlling the Edit Window

By now, you've probably noticed that QBasic's edit window has a couple of extra controls. Along the right side and bottom of the window are scroll bars that enable you to view the parts of a program that are offscreen. You can scroll the program up or down one line at a time in the edit window by clicking the scroll bar's up or down arrow. Likewise, you can scroll left or right one line by clicking the horizontal scroll bar's arrows.

To scroll up or down a full page, click in the vertical scroll bar above or below the scroll thumb. Scrolling horizontally works the same way, except you click in the horizontal scroll bar. Finally, you can move instantly to any place in a program by placing your mouse cursor over the appropriate scroll thumb (the little box inside the scroll bar), holding down the left mouse button and moving the scroll thumb to the position you want.

To scroll a program from the keyboard, use the keyboard's arrow keys or the Page Up and Page Down keys.

Typing Programs

You're reading this book either because you want to learn to program or because somebody is reading your copy of *People* magazine. In any case, to write QBasic programs, you have to learn to use QBasic's editor. This section teaches you just that.

To start a new program, you must have an empty edit window. To open one, select the New entry of the File menu; this opens an empty window named Untitled. It is into this window that you'll type the commands that make up your QBasic program.

Before typing a new program, however, you should give the empty window an appropriate name. (Names like Adrian, Samantha, and Guido the Man are out.) To name your program, first select the Save As item of the File menu. You'll then see a dialog box similar to the one in Figure 3.5.

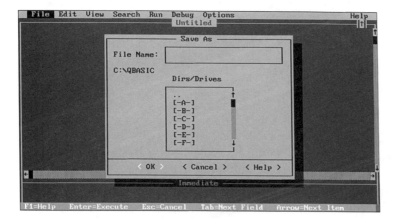

Figure 3.5

The Save As dialog box.

When the Save As dialog box appears, type the filename PROG1.BAS into the File Name edit box. Then press Enter on your keyboard or click the dialog's OK button with your mouse. When you do, the name of the window changes to PROG1.BAS.

Now that you have a newly named program window, you can type your program. Type the word **cls** (note the lowercase) and press Enter. What happened? If you typed the letters correctly, QBasic changed them from lowercase to uppercase. This is because CLS is a QBasic *keyword*, a word that is part of the QBasic language. (For those who are curious, CLS is the command to clear the screen.) Whenever QBasic recognizes a keyword, it automatically makes it all capital letters.

Point of Interest

All your BASIC programs should use the file extension .BAS (short for BASIC—get it?) because that's the extension QBasic expects programs to have. Moreover, that's the extension used by other programmers.

Now type the following text line exactly as it is shown here—be sure you include all punctuation (and the misspelled words!):

```
input Whatis yourr name"; Name$
```

When you press Enter, you see the dialog box in Figure 3.6.

27

This is a syntax error dialog box—QBasic's way of telling you that you're not as smart as you think you are. Just as with human languages such as English, computer languages have rules that dictate how sentences (or, in this case, commands) must be constructed. In the line you just typed, you didn't follow the rules, so QBasic complained.

To fix the line so that QBasic can understand it, you must add a quotation mark immediately before the word "What":

Programmer Lingo

A **keyword** is a word that is part of a programming language. Keywords, also known as reserved words, cannot be used as anything else in a program.

1. Press Enter to get rid of the syntax error dialog box.

2. Use the left-arrow key to move the flashing text cursor under the letter W in the word "What."

3. Type a quotation mark (") and press the down-arrow key to move from the line.

Figure 3.6

QBasic showing a syntax error.

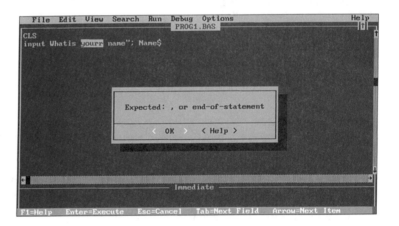

Now QBasic recognizes the command. In addition, it changed the word "input" to all capital letters because INPUT, like CLS, is a QBasic keyword. However, just because QBasic can now make sense of the line doesn't mean the line is correct. It only means that the line follows QBasic's syntax rules. You still have two misspelled words: "Whatis" and "yourr."

QBasic's text editor enables you to correct typing mistakes easily. First, use the arrow keys to position the flashing text cursor under the space between the words "yourr" and "name." Now press the Backspace key. Presto! The extra letter vanishes, and the rest of the line moves to the left to fill in the space you deleted.

You still have a mistake in the line, though. There should be a space between the words "What" and "is." Luckily, you can add characters to a line as easily as you can delete them. Use the arrow keys to position the blinking text cursor under the "i" in the word "Whatis" and then press the spacebar. When you do, a space character appears at the text cursor's position, and the rest of the line moves to the right.

Finish typing the program by adding the following lines. Remember to type them exactly as they're shown. To indent the line that starts with the word PRINT, start by typing two spaces.

```
FOR X = 1 TO 200
  PRINT Name$; " ";
NEXT X
```

Your screen should now look like Figure 3.7.

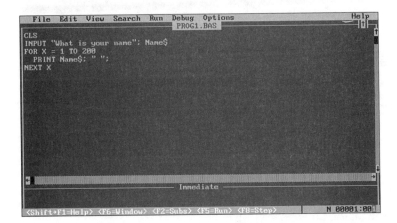

Figure 3.7

QBasic and your new program.

Soon you'll run the program and see what it does. First, however, you should save your program to disk so that if anything goes wrong when you run it, you won't lose your work. (It's possible for a programming error to lock up your computer, forcing you to restart it. It's also possible for a programming error to infuriate you enough to throw your computer out the nearest window. In either case, you'll be glad you saved your program first.)

To save your program, select the Save item of the File menu. After you select this command, your program is safely stored on your disk under the name PROG1.BAS (or whatever you named the program).

To run the program, select the Start command from the Run menu or press Shift+F5. This program first asks you to enter your name. Type your name and press Enter. You should then see a screen similar to the one in Figure 3.8.

To get back to QBasic, press any key—as it says at the bottom of the screen.

Congratulations! You've just written and run your first QBasic program. Pat yourself on the back, go get a snack, and brag until everyone in your household is thoroughly annoyed.

Figure 3.8

Your running program.

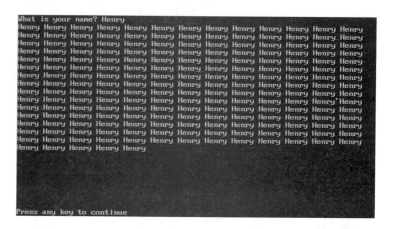

Printing a Program

If you have a printer connected to your system, you can print a hard copy of your program. Although you don't have to print your programs, you might want to have a copy on paper to file away. Also, it's often easier to find programming errors on paper than onscreen. More importantly, printing programs uses up ink and paper, which makes it look like you're actually accomplishing something. (Of course, wasting paper also kills trees, so you might want to examine your priorities—or recycle the printouts of your unfinished novel by printing on the reverse side.)

How about printing the program you just wrote? To print, select the Print item of the File menu. You'll see the dialog box shown in Figure 3.9.

Figure 3.9

The Print dialog box.

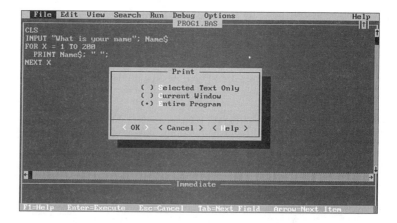

The Print dialog box contains several printing options. You can print selected text only (you'll learn to select text later in this chapter), text shown in the current window only, or the entire program.

When the Print dialog box first appears, it assumes you want to print the entire program, so that option is already selected for you. (Nothing like a mind-reading computer, eh?) However, you can change the option easily. From your keyboard, use the up and down-arrows to move the selection marker (the dot) to the option you want and then press Enter. To use your mouse, click the option you want and then click the OK button.

Onscreen buttons are used in many computer programs to enable you to make selections in dialog boxes. Buttons in computer programs work much like buttons in real life, the difference being that you push onscreen buttons by clicking your mouse, and you push real buttons with your finger. (Some computers let you push onscreen buttons with your finger, too. In the future, most computers will work this way.) In QBasic, buttons are usually at the bottom of a dialog box and are a pair of angle brackets containing commands like OK or Cancel. They don't look as cool as the buttons you see in Windows. (QBasic is old, remember?)

For now, select the Entire Program option and press Enter. The Print dialog box vanishes from the screen, and your program prints on your printer. You now can annoy people further with your bragging—they'll especially enjoy you waving the newly printed program in their faces while saying "na na nana na."

Cool Stuff

QBasic includes an online help system. If you aren't sure how to do something, check the Help menu. This menu provides access not only to help for QBasic but also to full instructions for using the help system. To see these instructions, select the Using Help command of the Help menu or press Shift+F1. Many dialog boxes contain a Help button that lets you get instant help about the dialog box.

Cutting, Copying, and Pasting

Every text editor worthy of the name enables you to select text blocks and manipulate them in various ways. QBasic's editor also provides you with these handy functions. You can find the text-editing functions in the Edit menu, shown in Figure 3.10.

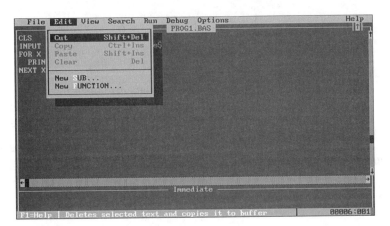

Figure 3.10

QBasic's Edit menu text.

Point of Interest

You can access edit functions directly from the keyboard, without using the Edit menu, by pressing the keys shown in the Edit menu. For example, to cut a block of text, press Shift+Del. To Paste the cut text back into your program, press Shift+Ins. Once you learn these shortcut keys, you can select editing functions quickly and conveniently.

Before you can use editing functions, you must select the text that those functions will manipulate. Figure 3.11 shows what a selected block of text looks like.

Figure 3.11

Selected text.

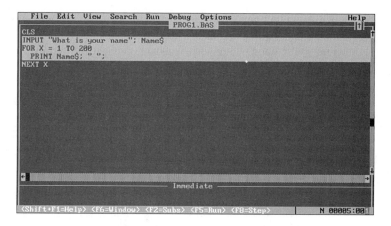

As with most functions, you can select text using either your keyboard or your mouse. You can also select text by pointing to it with your little finger and saying "Select this text," followed immediately by the magic words "Please," "Thank you," and "Shala-bama-dingo." Unfortunately, this latter method rarely works.

To select text from the keyboard, first use the arrow keys to place the blinking text cursor anywhere on the first line of the text block. Then hold down the Shift key and press the down-arrow key to highlight the lines in the block. Each time you press the down arrow, you highlight another line of text.

To select text with your mouse, place the mouse pointer on the first line you want to select, hold down the left mouse button, and drag the mouse pointer to the last line in the block.

Try selecting some text now. Using either the keyboard or mouse technique, select the middle three lines of your program's text. After selecting the text, open the Edit menu. The Cut, Copy, and Clear menu commands are now enabled. The Cut command removes the highlighted text from the screen and places it into QBasic's clipboard (a special text buffer from which you can later paste the text back into a different location in your program). The Copy command also places the selected text into the clipboard, but it does so without removing the text from the screen. Finally, the Clear command removes the selected text from the screen but does not place it into the clipboard.

Danger Ahead!

When you select the Clear entry of the Edit menu, any text you have highlighted is deleted forever—so use this command with care.

For now, select the Copy command. When you do, the Edit menu closes, and you're back at QBasic's edit window. Everything looks the same, except a copy of the highlighted text is now stored in QBasic's clipboard.

To use the clipboard, first deselect the selected text block by pressing any arrow key on your keyboard or by clicking your left mouse button. (Actually, you should click your *mouse's* left mouse button. If *you* have a left mouse button, consult a surgeon immediately and have it removed.) Look at the Edit menu again. Because there is no longer a text block selected, the Cut, Copy, and Clear entries are no longer enabled. However, the Paste entry is enabled. This tells you that there is text in the clipboard. In this case, it's the text you just copied. Close the Edit menu, place the blinking text cursor on the first blank line below your program, and select the Paste command. The text you copied is pasted into your program at the text cursor's location, as text shown in Figure 3.12.

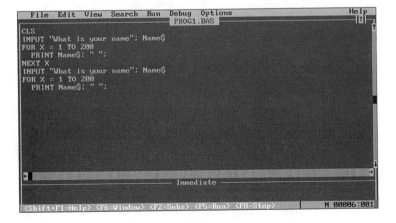

Figure 3.12

After pasting text into your program.

Cool Stuff

If you select the Paste command when you have a text block highlighted onscreen, the text in the clipboard replaces the highlighted text. Similarly, if you start typing when you have a text block highlighted, whatever you type replaces any and all of the highlighted text.

Before moving on to the next section, restore your program to its original state; you can do this either by deleting the extra lines you just pasted into it or by reloading the PROG1.BAS file. To delete a line, place the text cursor on the line and press Ctrl+Y text.

Searching and Replacing

In a small program like the one you just wrote, it's easy to find specific words or phrases. For example, if you want to find the keyword INPUT, just look at the screen and there it is. However, in large programs, finding text visually is tougher than chasing an angry bear up a tree. Luckily, QBasic includes search commands. These commands are, of course, found in the Search menu, shown in Figure 3.13.

Figure 3.13

QBasic's Search menu.

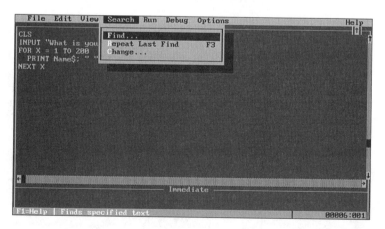

As you can see, the Search menu contains three entries: Find, Repeat Last Find, and Change. To find the next occurrence (starting at the text cursor's location) of any word or phrase, select the Find item of the Search menu. You'll see the dialog box in Figure 3.14.

When the Find dialog box appears, the word at the text cursor's location appears in the Find What edit box. If this is the word you want to find, just press Enter to start the search. If you want to look for a different word or phrase, type it into the Find What edit box and press Enter. If you don't want to search for a word or phrase, you might want to ask yourself why the heck you're staring at the Find dialog box.

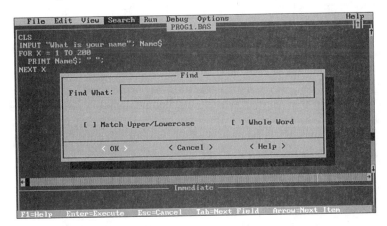

Figure 3.14

The Find dialog box.

Try the Find command now by following these steps:

1. Press Ctrl+Home to place the blinking text cursor at the beginning of your program.

2. Select the Find item of the Search menu. The Find dialog box appears.

3. In the Find What edit box, type the word **name** and press Enter. QBasic finds and highlights the first occurrence of the word "name."

4. To find other occurrences of this word, select the Repeat Last Find entry of the Search menu or just press F3. Each time you select this command, QBasic finds another occurrence of the word "name."

Notice that QBasic doesn't care whether the word or phrase contains upper- or lowercase letters. Any match is okay. You can make the search case sensitive by checking the Match Upper/Lowercase option box. (Option boxes look like a pair of square brackets and are used to turn various options on or off.) When this option is selected, the search finds only words that match exactly, including the case of the letters.

To select an option box from the keyboard, follow these steps:

1. Press your keyboard's Tab key until the blinking text cursor is in the option's check box.

2. Tab to the option box and then press the spacebar to toggle (turn on or off) the option.

3. To toggle an option box with your mouse, place your mouse pointer over the option and click the left mouse button.

In addition to checking for case, you can also tell QBasic's search function to find only whole words. For example, suppose you're looking for the word "red" in your program. You select the find function, type in **red**, and press Enter. To your surprise, the first word the computer finds is "Fred." This is because the word "red" is part of "Fred." If you want to find only the complete word "red," you must check the Whole Word option box. Then the search function will ignore words that happen to contain the letters "red."

Now, suppose you've completed a program, and for some reason, you've decided you want to change all occurrences of the word "Name" to "FirstName". You could go through the entire program, line by line, and change each occurrence of the word yourself. However, in a large program, this task would take a lot of time—and make you madder than a hornet in a mason jar. Worse, you're almost certain to miss some occurrences of the word you want to change. A better way to tackle this problem is to use the Search menu's Change command. When you select this command, you see the dialog box in Figure 3.15.

Figure 3.15

The Change dialog box.

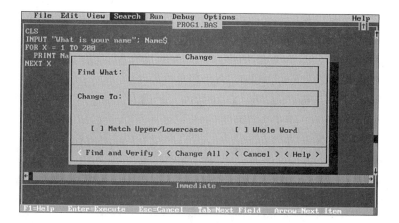

The Change dialog box looks much like the Find dialog box, except it has two edit boxes (boxes into which you can type text) instead of one and has different buttons at the bottom. To use the Change function, type the word you want to find into the Find What edit box. Then press Tab to move the text cursor to the Change To edit box and type the replacement text.

You then must select one of the buttons at the bottom of the dialog box. If you select the Find and Verify button, each time QBasic finds the target text, it'll ask whether you want to change it. If you select the Change All button, QBasic makes all the changes without further input from you. The Find and Verify button is often the best way to perform this type of global change—it ensures that only the words you want to change get changed.

To get a little experience with the Change function, use it to change all occurrences of "Name" in your program to "FirstName." If you need help, you can follow these numbered steps:

1. Select the Change entry of the Search menu. The Change dialog box appears.

2. Type the word **Name** into the Find What edit box.

3. Press the Tab key. The text cursor moves to the Change To edit box.

4. Type the word **FirstName**.

5. Press Tab. The text cursor moves to the Match Upper/Lowercase option box.

6. Press your spacebar to select the Match Upper/Lowercase option.

7. Press Tab until the text cursor is on the Change All button.

8. Press Enter to select the Change All button and change all occurrences of "Name" to "FirstName". A box appears containing the message "Change complete."

9. Press Enter to remove the message box.

After you complete this change, your program should still run properly—for reasons you won't understand until later in this book. But, understand it or not, go ahead and run the program by pressing Shift+F5. Cool, huh? And the best news is that you're now ready to move on to Chapter 4, "Places Where Numbers Live," where you'll really start learning about programming. If you'd like to take a break, you can exit QBasic by selecting the Exit command of the File menu.

The Least You Need to Know

➤ To run QBasic, change to the directory that contains its files and double-click the QBasic application file.

➤ To load a program file, select the Open item of the File menu.

➤ To save a program file to disk, use the Save or Save As item of the File menu.

➤ To start a new program, select the New item of the File menu.

➤ To print a program, select the Print entry of the File menu.

➤ You can view offscreen portions of a program by using the edit window's scroll bars. From your keyboard, you can scroll a program with the Page Up, Page Down, and arrow keys.

➤ QBasic changes all keywords to uppercase, regardless of how you type them. Keywords are the reserved words that make up a computer language.

➤ QBasic can find syntax errors and warn you about them. However, it can't find all possible errors in your program.

➤ To run a program, select the Start item of the Run menu or press F5 on your keyboard.

➤ Using the QBasic editor, you can cut, copy, and paste text much like you would with a text editor. These editing commands are located in the Edit menu, but you can also select them by using shortcut keys.

➤ The QBasic editor lets you find and replace words or phrases in your programs. The Find and Replace commands are in the Search menu.

➤ To exit QBasic, select the Exit entry of the File menu.

Part 2
The Absolute Basics

This is where you'll start writing real programs. Along the way, you'll discover the basic programming techniques that every computer language must support, including storing values, performing mathematical operations, and deciding what parts of a program should run based on the data the program is currently evaluating.

Chapter 4

Places Where Numbers Live

In This Chapter

➤ Understanding computer memory

➤ Using binary numbers as codes

➤ Creating variables

➤ Displaying output on the screen

➤ Setting a variable's value

➤ Using different types of data

I don't know whether anyone has told you this or not, but the only thing you can store in your computer's memory is numbers. What's even more incredible is that the only numbers you can store are 0 and 1. You may find this fact absolutely mind boggling when you think about doing things with your computer like balancing a budget or playing *Might & Magic*. How can your computer do so much with only two freakin' numbers?! In this chapter, you'll discover this amazing secret.

A Comfy Home for Numbers

Your computer is stuffed to overflowing with something called memory—at least, with the amount of memory in today's computers, you would think the computer would be overflowing. But all that memory in your computer fits into just a few circuits, each of which can fit easily in the palm of your hand. What's important to us at this point in our discussion of computer programming is not the physical size of memory but what it actually contains.

Imagine a long row of tiny boxes, a row so long that you can't even see the end. Now imagine that each of these boxes holds one of two things, a 0 or a 1. Congratulations! You now know everything about what your computer memory looks like, conceptually speaking. No kidding! The absolute truth is that your computer's memory is filled with nothing more than millions, and maybe even billions, of 0s and 1s.

What you don't know, however, is how your computer uses this huge row of 0s and 1s to do all the cool stuff it does. That, as you've no doubt guessed, is where things get tricky.

Yes and No

With only two numbers to work with, your computer can do nothing more than say, in its mysterious electronic language, "yes" or "no." If the computer looks into one of its tiny boxes and sees a 0, it says "no." If it sees a 1, it says "yes." Easy, right? If you think about it, by saying just "yes" or "no," you can say just about anything you want. How? By grouping a bunch of yes's and no's together.

Suppose, for example, you need to hold a conversation with a friend, but you can answer only by placing pennies in boxes. A box with a penny means "yes," and a box without a penny means "no." Unfortunately, your conversation will require four answers: "yes," "no," "maybe," and "Please pass the pizza." What to do? You make an agreement that "yes" means yes, "no" means no, "yesno" means maybe, and "yesyes" means you get a slice of pizza. Tricky but effective!

There's only one problem. To say "yesno" or "yesyes," you need two boxes. So now, when your friend asks a question that requires "yes" as an answer, you drop a penny into the right-hand box. When you need to answer "no," you leave the right-hand box empty. When you need to say "maybe," you put a penny in the left-hand box but leave the right-hand box empty. Finally, when you get hungry, you put a penny in both boxes. You are now using binary numbers to hold a meaningful conversation. Just think of a penny as a 1 and no penny as a 0, and you've got it.

Imagine how many questions you could answer if you had a few million boxes to respond with. Mathematically speaking, every time you add a box, you double the number of possible answers. That is, when you have only one box, you have only two possible answers, but when you have two boxes, you can have four answers. Three boxes equals eight answers. This continues as high as you need it to, and the number of possible answers gets huge very quickly. With only 16 boxes, you can respond to your friend with over 64,000 possible answers!

A Secret and Handy Code

This is how computers get so much mileage out of those lowly 0s and 1s. The people who design computers and the people who program them came up with a set of codes by grouping those 0s and 1s together. For example, they agreed that the value 01000001 is the code for the letter "A," 0100010 is the code for the letter B, and so on. There are similar codes for every character in our alphabet as well as for numbers and punctuation.

Because these 0s and 1s ended up in groups of eight, the computer scientists decided to name the grouping a *byte*. Where did this goofy name come from? Well, one of those little boxes that can hold a 0 or 1 was, and still is, called a bit, meaning a tiny piece. But, as it turns out, the word "bit" is also the past tense of "bite." Get it? If you think that's goofy, consider the fact that computer scientists also named a group of four bits a *nybble*—really, I am not making this up.

Point of Interest

If you think it's a bizarre idea to communicate with people using just two values like 0 and 1, maybe you should think back to the days of Morse code. Using a telegraph machine and dots and dashes, you could send any message you wanted, including the entire contents of an encyclopedia if that was what you needed to do. So you can see that computers, as amazing as they are, aren't even doing anything new!

Bits As Regular Numbers

In most cases, computer programs don't deal with single bits. Usually, computer programs deal with, at minimum, bytes and more often with various groupings of bytes. The thing to know about values like 01000001 is that they can be expressed in our own number system, just by converting between the binary number system (based on the number 2) and our decimal number system (based on the number 10) number system. The mechanics of performing such a conversion is beyond the scope of this book. It's enough for you to know that a byte (8 bits) can represent any number between 0 and 255. Here are some examples:

    00000000 = 0

    00000001 = 1

    00100101 = 37

    10000000 = 128

    11111111 = 255

You don't have to memorize these values. I've only shown them so you can see how binary numbers can represent decimal numbers. From now on in this book, we won't be too concerned with binary numbers; rather, we'll only deal with the decimal numbers represented by groups of bits and bytes.

Working with Variables

Now, because we're going to group our bits eight at a time, let's say that each little box in your computer's memory represents a byte, which, from a programming point of view, is a better way of looking at things. You can think of your computer's memory as millions of little boxes, each holding a single value from 0 to 255, and forget all those 0s and 1s. Each little box is numbered, starting at zero. The actual number of boxes in your computer depends on how much memory you have installed. So your computer's memory now looks something like Figure 4.1.

Figure 4.1

Your computer's memory.

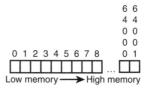

When you put information into your computer, a little guy named Benny grabs the data and runs away with it, giggling. Okay, I'm lying. Actually, your computer stuffs the data into one of those little boxes that make up its memory. But in which box should the value be stored, and how can you refer to that box in a way that makes sense in a program? This is where variables come in.

Variables are really just memory boxes with names. Because you, the programmer, supply the names, you can name your variables almost anything you want, making your programs easier to read and understand. You could even name a variable Benny, though why you'd want to is a mystery.

When you first create a variable in a QBasic program, the memory box it represents contains a zero. Later in your program, you can store values into the memory box by referring to its name. For example, to keep track of the score in a game, you might have a variable named score. Whenever the player's score changes, you can put the new score value into the variable named score. In this way, you've set aside a little piece of memory that contains data you need in your program.

You must follow certain rules when creating variable names. Every computer language has these rules, and although the rules from one language to another are similar, they aren't the same. In the case of QBasic, a variable name must be no longer than 40 characters. Also, the name must start with a letter. The other characters can be letters, numbers, or a period. You can't use spaces in a variable name, but you can use a period to separate words in the name if you need to.

Because QBasic isn't case sensitive, you can use any combination of upper- or lower-case letters in a variable name—the variable names Benny, benny, and BENNY all mean the same thing to QBasic. However, this isn't the case for all languages. C++, for example, thinks of Benny, benny, and BENNY as all different names because C++ is a case-sensitive language. The last rule for variable names is the same in every language: You can't use a keyword as a variable name.

Here are some valid QBasic variable names:

```
Total
Money.Spent
name23
AMOUNT
```

Here are some invalid QBasic variable names:

```
3456
current_balance
Date Paid
PRINT
```

Now, if you were programming in C++, the second name (current_balance) in the preceding list would be okay for a variable name because you can use the underscore character in C++.

Getting Values into Memory

Now that you can name the boxes that make up your computer's memory, how can you put numbers into those boxes and take them out again? Let's face it; your computer wouldn't be of much use if you didn't have a way of getting data in and out of it. For example, to understand computer *input* and *output*, let's say you want to type that letter to weird Uncle Henry. Your first task is to get the characters that make up the letter into your computer's memory where you can manipulate them. You can't just dictate the letter as you would to a secretary. Computers have really terrible ears. You have to use one of the computer's input devices—in this case, the keyboard—to type your letter, placing it into memory one character at a time. Each one of these characters fits perfectly into one of those little boxes in memory.

When you finish typing and editing your letter, you need a way to get it out of the computer's memory so that Uncle Henry can read it. You could call Uncle Henry and have him fly in and read the letter on your computer screen, but that kind of defeats the purpose of writing a letter. Besides, Uncle Henry hates to fly, remember? You need another kind of device—an output device—to which you can send the letter to get it into a form that is useful. You probably want to use a printer, but you might also save your letter onto a disk and send the disk to Uncle Henry. Then he could just load the letter into his computer's memory and read it onscreen. In any case, your printed letter or the file on the disk will contain all the characters you loaded into the little boxes in your computer's memory.

The process of moving data in and out of a computer is called, appropriately enough, *input* and *output* (or I/O, for short). There are all kinds of input and output, but you only need to know a couple to get started with QBasic and to explore the way computers use numbers.

Programmer Lingo

Input devices, such as your keyboard and your mouse, transfer data from you to your computer. **Output devices,** such as printers and monitors, transfer data from the computer back to you. Some devices, such as disk drives, are both input and output devices.

Point of Interest

Interactive programs allow two-way communication between the user and the computer. For example, the computer might output a question to the user by printing the question onscreen. The user might then answer the question by typing on his or her keyboard.

Most input and output is controlled by the program that is currently running. If you load a program that doesn't use the keyboard, the program will not notice your keystrokes—no matter how much you type. Likewise, if a program wasn't designed to use your printer, you have no way of accessing the printer when running that program.

Obviously, then, if it's up to a program to control your computer's input and output, every programming language must contain commands for input and output. In fact, a programming language without I/O commands would be about as useful to you as a book of matches would be to a fish. By providing commands for putting data into the computer and getting data back out again, a computer language allows you to create interactive programs.

QBasic, like any other computer language, features several commands for controlling input and output. The two commands you must learn to try out simple I/O are PRINT and INPUT. In this section, you'll get up to speed on these handy commands.

Look! It's on the Screen!

The PRINT command enables you to make text appear on the computer's screen. You might want to do this to ask the user a question, or you might print text on the screen to show the user a piece of information he asked for. Suppose you want to print a simple message on the screen. Here's a short QBasic program that shows you how to do this:

```
CLS
PRINT "Hi, there!"
PRINT "What's a nice person like you"
PRINT "doing with a computer like this?"
```

Load QBasic and type the program exactly as you see it, including all the spaces and punctuation. The program is called HITHERE.BAS, so after you type it, you should save it under this name. (You learned to save program files in Chapter 3, "Crankin' It Up with QBasic," remember?) This is just about the simplest computer program you can write. Here's a line-by-line explanation:

1. The CLS command clears the computer's screen.

2. The PRINT command displays "Hi, there!"

3. The PRINT command displays "What's a nice person like you".

4. The PRINT command displays "doing with a computer like this?"

When you run HITHERE1.BAS, you see this output on the screen:

```
Hi, there!
What's a nice person like you
doing with a computer like this?
```

As you can see, each PRINT command creates a single line of text onscreen. The text that the command prints is the text you place after the word PRINT. This text, called a *string literal,* must be enclosed in quotation marks. The "Press any key to continue" message (which isn't shown here) comes from QBasic, not from the program.

> **Programmer Lingo**
>
> A **string** is a group of text characters. A **string literal** is text that you want the computer to use exactly as you type it. You tell the computer that a line of text is a string literal by enclosing the text in quotation marks.

Now It's in Memory!

Now you know how to use QBasic to ask a computer user a question, which is one form of output. But how can you get the user's answer into your program and thus into your computer's memory? You could have the user write you a memo, but that's too slow. As you may have guessed, QBasic has a command, called INPUT, that can get both *numeric values* and text from the user.

To get input into your programs, you need to use the INPUT command. INPUT commands and variables go together like Abbott and Costello: You must follow every INPUT command with the name of a variable. QBasic stores the input in the variable.

Suppose you're writing a program that needs to know the number of cars in a parking garage. Suppose also that when the user runs the program, the first thing he or she must do is input the current car count. This part of the program might look something like this:

```
CLS
PRINT "Please enter the number of cars"
INPUT cars
PRINT "You have"; cars; "cars"
```

Programmer Lingo

Numeric values are values that can be used in mathematical operations. Text, on the other hand, is made up of alphabetic characters, numeric characters (not values), and other symbols (such as punctuation) that you need to write words and sentences in English (or any other language for that matter). The stuff you're reading in this book is text.

Here's a line-by-line explanation of the program:

1. The CLS command clears the screen.

2. The PRINT command asks the user for the number of cars.

3. The INPUT command accepts the user's response. The program stores the number in the variable cars.

4. The PRINT command displays the string literal "You have", the value stored in the variable cars, and the string literal "cars".

Type the program into QBasic and run it. When you see a question mark on the screen, this is your cue to input a value to the program. Type any number you like and press Enter. Your screen should resemble the following output. Notice that, in this example, the 3 appears in bold and represents the number you would type:

```
Please enter the number of cars
? 3
You have 3 cars
```

Where did that question mark come from? The INPUT command puts the question mark on the screen to tell the user to input something into the program. The word cars following the INPUT command is a variable name. This name is used to identify the little box in memory where the response is stored. Suppose you type the number 8 in response to the program. Your computer's memory might look something like Figure 4.2.

Figure 4.2

Your computer's memory with the variable cars.

```
                                        6 6
                            c           4 4
                            a           0 0
                            r           0 0
        0 1 2 3 4 5 s 7 8               0 1
        [ ][ ][ ][ ][ ][ ][8][ ][ ] ... [ ][ ]
```

In this figure, QBasic has assigned the variable cars to memory location 6 and has placed the value 8 into that location. You don't have to worry about where QBasic puts variables in memory. QBasic handles all that for you.

How about that last line in the program? Pretty fancy-looking PRINT command, wouldn't you say? This shows how powerful the PRINT command can be. In this case, the PRINT command displays not only string literals but also the value stored in the variable cars. See the semicolons? By using semicolons, you can build a line of text from different elements. In the PRINT command above, the line of text displayed on-screen comprises three elements: the string literal "You have", the variable cars, and the string literal "cars". The semicolons tell the PRINT command to place each of these elements one after the other on the same line.

Notice that QBasic can easily tell the difference between the string literal "cars" and the variable cars. Now you know why the quotation marks are so important. In fact, without the quotation marks, QBasic would interpret each word following the PRINT command as a variable rather than as a string.

Numeric and String Variables

Variables can exist as many different types. For now, you can think of variables as holding either numeric values or (strings of) text. Numeric values hold numbers, of course, and text values hold words. You can't store text in a variable that's supposed to hold a numeric value, and you can't store a numeric value in a variable that's supposed to hold text.

In QBasic, to create a variable for holding text, just add a dollar sign ($) to the variable's name, as shown in this short QBasic program:

```
CLS
PRINT "Please enter the number of cars"
INPUT cars$
PRINT "You have "; cars$; " cars"
```

Here's the familiar line-by-line explanation:

1. The CLS command clears the screen.

2. The PRINT commands asks the user for the number of cars.

3. The INPUT command asks the user to type an answer. The program stores the text the user types in the string variable cars$.

4. The PRINT command displays a combination of regular text and the value stored in cars$.

When you run the program, you are asked to enter the number of cars. In this case, however, whatever you type is treated as text, not as a numeric value. This means you can type **Three** or **3**. Figure 4.3 shows what the running program looks like.

Danger Ahead!

You can never store text in a numeric variable. If you try to, most languages, including QBasic, will give you an error message. In the case of QBasic, the error message is "Redo from start." This poorly written message is really trying to say, "Please reenter your input." In other words, QBasic is giving you another chance to input a valid value.

Figure 4.3

The running car program using your string variable.

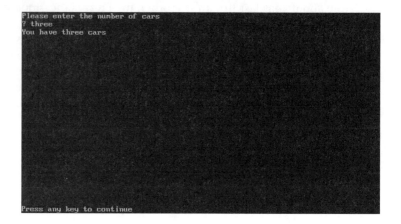

Note that numbers entered as text cannot be used as numeric values. That is, they cannot be used in mathematical calculations.

Look at the last line of this program. The first string literal ("You have ") ends with a space, and the second string literal (" cars") starts with a space. If you remove these spaces, the text string printed on your screen looks something like this snippet:

You havethreecars.

Why didn't you have this problem with the first version of this program? Because that version used a numeric variable. When QBasic prints a numeric variable, it always leaves space for a negative sign in front of the value. If the value is positive, all you see is the extra space because QBasic doesn't print the positive sign. However, if the value is negative, you'll see the negative sign. Run the first version again, and this time enter a negative number like –3. You'll see the screen in Figure 4.4.

Figure 4.4

A negative sign fills the space between the string and the variable.

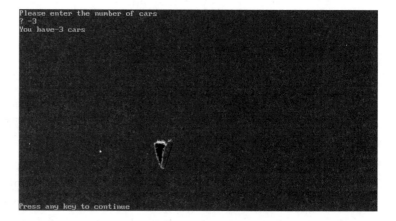

You can't have a negative number of cars in your garage (at least, not in this universe), so you don't have to worry about the negative sign in this program.

50

In addition to the space for a negative sign, QBasic always places a space after a numeric variable. However, string variables are never printed with extra spaces, so to make the output look right, you have to add spaces wherever necessary (unless, of course, you want the strings to run together).

Danger Ahead!

Spelling a variable name incorrectly creates program bugs that are difficult to find. For example, suppose you have in your program a variable named `Total.Numbers`. As you type the lines of your program, you accidentally spell this variable as `TotalNumbers`. To QBasic, `Total.Numbers` and `TotalNumbers` are different variables, each with their own value.

What's a Nice Integer Like You Doing Here?

When you use numeric variables and string variables, you are using variables of two different data types. Numeric variables can hold only numbers, and string variables can hold only text strings. What you haven't learned is that numeric variables can be divided into many other data types, including integers, long integers, single precision, and double precision.

Cool Stuff

Although numeric variables can hold only numbers and string variables can hold only text strings, that doesn't mean a string variable can't hold a character that represents a number. For example, when assigned to a numeric variable, the number 3 represents a value that can be used in arithmetic operations. However, the character 3 assigned to a string variable is just a text character—no different from any other text character such as A or Z. Although a string variable can hold number characters, those characters cannot be used directly in mathematical operations.

Until now, you've been concerned only with giving your numeric variables appropriate names; you haven't worried about what type of value they hold. You can ignore a variable's data type because QBasic can determine data types on its own. But what if you want to be sure that a variable always contains a certain type of data, no matter what type of assignment operation it's involved in? For example, what if you want to add two floating-point numbers, but you want to store the result as an integer? What are floating-point numbers and integers, anyway?

An *integer* is any whole number such as 23, 76, –65, or 1,200. Notice that none of these numbers contains a decimal portion. Notice also that none of them is smaller than –32,768 or greater than 32,767. A QBasic integer must fall into this range. The truth is that this isn't a very big range for an integer value. Today's modern programming languages allow integers that represent truly huge numbers, so huge that it's not likely you'll ever need anything larger.

What if you need to use a number that doesn't fit into the integer range? You can use a long integer. A long integer resembles an integer in that it can hold only a whole number. However, the range of a QBasic long integer is much larger: –2,147,483,648 to 2,147,483,647, to be exact. Unless you're trying to calculate the national debt or count the number of times Elizabeth Taylor has been married, you're not likely to need values larger than these.

Numbers that contain a decimal portion are called *floating-point* or real numbers. Like integers, they come in two flavors. In QBasic, a single-precision floating-point number is accurate to six decimal places (for example, 34.875637). A double-precision floating-point number, on the other hand, is accurate to 14 decimal places (for example, 657.36497122357638). Floating-point numbers in QBasic can be very tiny or incredibly large. Other computer languages have similar types of numerical values, although the values they can hold vary depending on the language and the system on which the language runs.

Danger Ahead!

When writing a program, you may be tempted to make all your integer variables long integers and all your floating-point variables double-precision. When you do this, you no longer need to worry about whether your values go out of range. However, this technique has two drawbacks. First, long integers and double-precision numbers take up more memory than their smaller counterparts. Second, your computer takes longer to access and manipulate these larger values, so using them can significantly slow down your programs. Use long integers and double-precision values only when you really need them.

Remember when you learned about string variables? You learned that to create a variable of this data type, you had to add a dollar sign to the variable's name. The various numeric data types also have suffixes that tell QBasic the type of data the variable holds. To specify a particular data type in QBasic, you only have to add the appropriate suffix to the variable's name. The following table shows the various data types and their corresponding suffixes.

Type	Suffix	Example
Integer	%	total%
Long integer	&	count&
Single precision	!	value!
Double precision	#	weight#
String	$	name$

Point of Interest

Like a variable, a constant has a data type. The difference is that the data type is implicit. For example, 10 is an integer, 23.7564 is a single-precision floating-point number, and "Alexander" is a string. You can tell what the data type is just by looking at the value, and so can your computer language.

Here's a version of the cars program that uses an integer variable named cars%:

```
CLS
PRINT "Please enter the number of cars"
INPUT cars%
PRINT "You have"; cars%; "cars"
```

Now that you know how computers store numbers, you're ready to do something useful with those numbers. In the next chapter, you learn how to make your computer perform arithmetic.

The Least You Need to Know

➤ Your computer's memory holds nothing but 0s and 1s.

➤ Because these 0s and 1s ended up in groups of eight, the computer scientists decided to name the grouping a "byte."

➤ A byte (8 bits) can represent any number between 0 and 255.

➤ Variables are just memory boxes with names.

➤ The process of moving data in and out of a computer is called I/O.

➤ QBasic's PRINT command displays text on the computer's screen.

➤ QBasic's CLS command clears the computer's screen.

➤ A string is a group of text characters.

➤ The INPUT command accepts a value from the user and stores it in a variable.

➤ A numeric variable can hold only numeric values. A string variable can hold only text.

➤ Numeric variables can be divided into many other data types, including integers, long integers, single-precision floating point, and double-precision floating point.

➤ An integer is any whole number. In QBasic, an integer must fall into the range from −32,768 to 32,767. The range of a QBasic long integer is −2,147,483,648 to 2,147,483,647.

➤ Numbers that contain a decimal portion are called floating-point or real numbers.

Computer-Style Arithmetic

It wasn't that long ago that all computer classes in colleges were part of the math department. This may even still be true in some schools. This unfortunate circumstance led to a common misunderstanding that, in order to program a computer, you have to be some sort of math genius. While this may be true of some types of programming (such as writing 3D games), most programming requires very little math, just the same old addition, subtraction, multiplication, and division you do every day of your life.

Moreover, when you're writing a program, you won't have to wear down pencils adding long columns of numbers or fry your brain trying to figure out 35,764 divided by 137. The computer can do the calculations for you. If you know how to use the basic arithmetic operations to solve simple problems, you know all the math necessary to write a computer program. Computer programming is more logical than mathematical. It's just a matter of common sense. (If you have trouble remembering to come in out of the rain, computer programming may not be for you.)

Still, you can't avoid math entirely. Heaven knows that your humble author has tried. Computers, after all, are number-crunching machines that like nothing better than spitting out the results of hundreds, thousands, or even millions of calculations. It's ι to you, the wise programmer, to give the computer the commands it needs to perform these calculations. In this chapter, you'll learn to do just that.

Using Basic Arithmetic

In Chapter 4, "Places Where Numbers Live," you learned about variables—the little boxes in memory in which your program stores numbers. Unlike a constant such as the number 3, variables can represent almost any value—except maybe the number of times I had to call technical help about that software I just installed! Variables are extremely valuable entities. Because variables represent numbers, you can use them in mathematical operations.

For example, suppose you run a small video store, and you want to know how many tapes you have. You might think to yourself, "I've got 20 copies of *Fun-Loving Vixens*, 50 copies of *The Sixth Cents*, and 10 copies of *Cooking with Madonna*. So, I've got 80 videotapes." If you want to use the computer to solve this mathematical problem, you could load QBasic and type PRINT 20+50+10 into the immediate-command window. The computer would print the answer: 80. Just as in school, the + symbol means addition in a computer program.

There's a better way, however, to solve the videotape problem—one that works with any number of videotapes. This new method uses variables in mathematical operations. As you've learned, you can call a variable just about anything you like. (Yes, you can even call a variable late.for.dinner.) Names such as vixens, cents, and cooking are completely acceptable. Beginning to see the light? Look over the TAPES1.BAS program that follows:

```
CLS
PRINT "Enter number of Fun-Loving Vixens"
INPUT vixens
PRINT "Enter number of The Sixth Cents"
INPUT cents
PRINT "Enter number of Cooking with Madonna"
INPUT cooking
tapes = vixens + cents + cooking
PRINT "Total number of tapes: ";
PRINT tapes
```

This program asks you how many copies you have of each videotape. As you type your answers, the computer zaps those answers into the variables vixens, cents, and cooking. Then the program adds the variables and plunks the total into another variable called tapes. Finally, the program displays the number contained in tapes. Now you know the following two things:

1. You have 80 videotapes in your store.

2. With movie titles like these, you'll be out of business faster than you can say, "Cooking with *whom?*"

The following lines show the output from the program. The bold represents what the user entered:

```
Enter number of Fun-loving Vixens
? 20
Enter number of The Sixth Cents
? 50
Enter number of Cooking with Madonna
? 10
Total number of tapes:  80
```

By using a program similar to this one, you can get a new tape total anytime you like. Just provide your program with new counts for each movie.

Guess what? You just used math in a computer program. It didn't hurt a bit, did it?

Raising the Arithmetic Bar

Of course, computers can do more than add. They can perform any basic arithmetic operation. Most languages even have functions for figuring out things like square roots and absolute values. If you don't know what a square root or an absolute value is, don't hit the panic button; you still won't have trouble programming your computer. Just don't plan to write an algebra tutorial anytime soon.

Let's assume your videotape store is still thriving, despite its horrible selection. Suppose you now want to find the total value of your inventory as well as the average cost per tape. To find the total value of your inventory, multiply each title's price by the number of copies you own. Perform this calculation for all titles and then add these amounts together to get the total value. To find the average value per tape, divide the total value by the total number of tapes. In QBasic, you could calculate these totals using a program similar to this:

```
CLS
PRINT "How much is Vixens?"
INPUT price
PRINT "How many Vixens do you have?"
INPUT quantity
total.num.tapes = quantity
total.value = price * quantity
PRINT "How much is Sixth Cents?"
INPUT price
PRINT "How many Sixth Cents do you have?"
INPUT quantity
total.num.tapes = total.num.tapes + quantity
total.value = total.value + price * quantity
PRINT "How much is Cooking?"
INPUT price
PRINT "How many Cooking do you have?"
```

```
INPUT quantity
total.num.tapes = total.num.tapes + quantity
total.value = total.value + price * quantity
average.value = total.value / total.num.tapes
PRINT
PRINT "The total value of all tapes is:"
PRINT "$"; total.value
PRINT "The average value is:"
PRINT "$"; average.value
```

Here is the output from the program. The numbers that appear in bold represent the values you theoretically provided:

```
How much is Vixens?
? 29.95
How many Vixens do you have?
? 12
How much is Sixth Cents?
? 34.95
How many Sixth Cents do you have?
? 23
How much is Cooking?
? 14.98
How many Cooking do you have?
? 8

The total value of all tapes is:
$ 1283.09
The average value is:
$ 29.8393
```

This program is a bit longer than the first one, but it still uses only basic arithmetic. It's longer because it performs more calculations than the first example.

What's going on here? This program first asks you for the price and quantity of each tape you have in stock. The program then calculates the total value of all the tapes in your store as well as your average value per tape. If you look at the program carefully, you'll see something strange about total.num.tapes. Specifically, what the heck does the line total.num.tapes = total.num.tapes + quantity do? How can the same variable be on both sides of an equation? Why do I keep asking these dumb questions?

First, you have to stop thinking that the equals sign (=) always means "equals." It doesn't. In QBasic arithmetic operations, this symbol actually means "takes the value of," which makes it an *assignment operator*. (Even in programming, however, the equals sign still can mean "is equal to," as you'll learn later in this book.)

You also must understand that most programming languages, including QBasic, interpret statements from right to left. So, in the line `total.num.tapes = total.num.tapes + quantity`, `total.num.tapes` and `quantity` are added first and then the result of the addition is assigned back to `total.num.tapes`—that is, the result is stored in `total.num.tapes`, wiping out the value that was there previously.

Confused? How about an example? Suppose `total.num.tapes` is equal to 7 and `quantity` is equal to 3. When the computer sees the line `total.num.tapes = total.num.tapes + quantity`, it adds 7 to 3 and pops the value 10 into `total.num.tapes`. Using this method, you can add values to a variable that already holds a value. You'll do this often in your programs.

Programmer Lingo

An **assignment operator** is used to assign a value to a variable. In QBasic, the assignment operator is an equals sign, but other computer languages may use different assignment operators. In Pascal, for example, the assignment operator is a colon followed by an equals sign (`:=`).

As you can see, a QBasic program uses an asterisk (*) to represent multiplication, not an x as you might expect. This is typical of most computer languages. The forward slash character (/) represents division because the computer keyboard doesn't have a division symbol. You could try painting a division symbol on one of your keys, but you'll still have to use the slash character in your programs.

Table 5.1 displays all the QBasic arithmetic operators.

Table 5.1   QBasic Arithmetic Operators

Operator	Name	Use
+	Addition	Sum values
−	Subtraction	Subtract values
*	Multiplication	Multiply values
/	Division	Divide values
\	Integer division	Determine the whole number result of division
^	Exponentiation	Raise a value to a power
MOD	Modulus	Determine the remainder of division

Table 5.2 shows some examples of mathematical operations using the arithmetic operators.

Table 5.2 Mathematical Examples

Operation	Result
5+8	13
12–7	5
3*6	18
10/3	3.333333
10\3	3
2^3	8
10 MOD 3	1

Cool Stuff

When you use regular division, denoted by the forward slash character (/), you are performing the type of division you learned in school. You may end up with a result like 2 (as in the operation 4/2) or a result like 2.4 (as in the operation 12/5).

When you use integer division, denoted by the backslash character (\), your answer will always be an integer because QBasic drops any part of the result that lies to the right of the decimal point. This means that, with integer division, the operation 12\5 results in 2 rather than 2.4.

The MOD operator performs division, too, but it only gives you the remainder of the division. For example, 4 goes into 14 three times with a remainder of 2, so the operation 14 MOD 4 yields a result of 2. As a beginning programmer, you probably won't have a lot of use for this operator.

Finally, the exponentiation operator (^) is used to raise numbers to a power. When you raise a number to a power, you multiply the number times itself the number of times indicated by the exponent (the number after the ^ character). For example, 10^2 is the same as 10 * 10, which equals 100. The operation 5^3 is the same as 5 * 5 * 5, which equals 125.

Me First! Me First!

Another curious line in the last program is `total.value = total.value + price * quantity`. This program line is similar to the line that calculates the total number of tapes, but it contains both an addition and a multiplication operation. This brings up the important topic of operator precedence or, as it's more commonly known, the order of operations.

If you were to add `total.value` to `price` and then multiply the sum by `quantity`, you'd get an incorrect result. Operator precedence dictates that all multiplication must take place before any addition. So, in the preceding line, `total.value` is calculated by first multiplying `price` times `quantity` and then adding that product to `total.value`.

Don't forget about operator precedence; if you do, your calculations won't be accurate, and your programs won't run correctly. Not adhering to the rules of operator precedence can also affect your home life: Broken programs make for grumpy programmers, and grumpy programmers are no fun to have around.

The order of operations for QBasic is exponentiation first; then multiplication, division, integer division, and MOD; and finally, addition and subtraction. This is typical for most programming languages. Operations of the same precedence are evaluated from left to right. For example, in the expression `3 * 5 / 2`, 3 is first multiplied by 5, which gives a result of 15. This result is then divided by 2, giving a result of 7.5. Table 5.3 summarizes the QBasic operator precedence.

Point of Interest

When writing a program line that contains many arithmetic operations, you may want to use parentheses to more clearly indicate the order of operation. For example, the formula `total.value = total.value + (price * quantity)` is easier to read than the formula `total.value = total.value + price * quantity`. Both formulas, however, yield the same result.

Table 5.3   QBasic Operator Precedence

Order	Operator	Name
1	^	Exponentiation
2	* / \ MOD	Multiplication, division, integer division, and modulus
3	+ -	Addition and subtraction

You can change operator precedence by using parentheses. For example, suppose you wanted the addition in the line total.value = total.value + price * quantity to be calculated before the multiplication. You could rewrite the line as total.value = (total.value + price) * quantity. Any operation enclosed in parentheses is performed first. Consequently, total.value and price are added first, and the sum is then multiplied by quantity.

The Least You Need to Know

➤ Computer programming is more a logical task than a mathematical one.

➤ You use variables to hold values, and you can assign a new value to a variable any time you want.

➤ QBasic can handle all regular arithmetic operations, such as addition, subtraction, multiplication, and division.

➤ The equals sign (=) enables you to assign values to variables.

➤ The order in which QBasic evaluates arithmetic expressions follows the standard rules of operator precedence (order of operations).

Chapter 6

Decisions the Computer Way

In This Chapter

➤ Changing program flow with branching

➤ Making decisions with IF, ELSE, and ELSEIF

➤ Comparing values with relational operators

➤ Programming with logical operators

So far, you've learned some of the very basic (or is that BASIC?) skills you need to program a computer. For example, you now know what programs are and generally how they work. You also know how computers store data and how your programs can give the computer the appropriate data to store. You can even do a little math with your computer.

In this chapter, you learn how your programs can analyze data to decide what parts of your program to execute. Until now, your programs have executed their statements in strict sequential order, starting with the first line and working line by line to the end of the program. Now it's time to learn how you can control your program's flow—the order in which the statements are executed—so that you can do different things based on the data your program receives.

If the idea of computers making decisions based on data seems a little strange, think about how you make decisions. For example, suppose you're waiting for an overtime basketball game to get over so you can watch your favorite TV show. You turn on the TV and check what's on. Then you choose one of the following two actions:

➤ If basketball game is over, you settle in to watch your show.

➤ If the basketball game isn't over, you turn off the TV and whine about sports preempting your favorite show.

In either case, you've made a decision based on whether or not there is a basketball game still going on.

Computers use this same method to make decisions (except that they never complain and don't give a darn how long a basketball game runs). You will see the word if used frequently in computer programs. Just as you might say to yourself, "If the basketball game is over, I'll watch my show," a computer uses IF to decide what action to take.

A Digital Road Map

Program flow is the order in which a program executes its code. Your programs so far in this book have had sequential program flow. The truth is, almost all program code executes sequentially. However, virtually every program reaches a point at which a decision must be made about a piece of data. The program must then analyze the data, decide what to do about it, and jump to the appropriate section of code. This decision-making process is as important to computer programming as pollen is to a bee. Virtually no useful programs can be written without it.

Programmer Lingo

Unconditional branching occurs when a program branches to a new location in the code without analyzing data and making a decision. An unconditional branch occurs every time your program encounters that branch instruction. **Conditional branching** occurs when the program branches based on a decision of some type. This type of branching may or may not occur based on the results of the decision.

When a program breaks the sequential flow and jumps to a new section of code, it is called *branching*. When this branching is based on a decision, the program is performing *conditional branching*. When no decision-making is involved and the program always branches when it encounters a particular branching instruction, the program is performing *unconditional branching*.

To continue with the sports example, suppose you turned on the TV and saw that the game was over, but decided to complain about overtime sports anyway. Because the poor TV network was destined to be the focus of your wrath whether or not the game preempted your show, your complaining is unconditional. No matter what, after checking the TV, you complain.

It's Simply a Matter of Choice

Most conditional branching occurs when the program executes an IF...THEN statement, which compares data and decides what to do next based on the result of the comparison. If the comparison works out one way, the program performs the statement following the THEN keyword. Otherwise, the program does nothing and drops to the next program line. This gives each comparison two possible outcomes.

Simple IF...THEN *Statements*

You've probably seen programs that print menus on the screen. To select a menu item, you often type its selection number. When the program receives your input, it checks the number you entered and decides what to do. Here's a QBasic program that illustrates how this type of menu selection might work:

```
CLS
PRINT
PRINT "    MENU"
PRINT "-----------"
PRINT " 1. Red"
PRINT " 2. Green"
PRINT " 3. Blue"
PRINT
INPUT "Your selection: ", choice%
PRINT
IF choice% = 1 THEN PRINT "You chose red."
IF choice% = 2 THEN PRINT "You chose green."
IF choice% = 3 THEN PRINT "You chose blue."
```

The output of the program would look like this:

```
    MENU
-----------
 1. Red
 2. Green
 3. Blue

Your selection: 2

You chose green.
```

The preceding program prints a menu and lets you enter a menu selection. The program then uses a series of IF...THEN statements to compare the value you entered with the acceptable menu choices. See the equals signs in the IF...THEN statements? These are not assignment operators; they are *relational operators* that enable you to compare two or more values. Look at the first IF...THEN statement in the program. If this line were written in English, it would read "If the value of the variable choice% equals 1, then print ..." The other IF...THEN statements in the program have similar meanings.

Programmer Lingo

Relational operators such as the equals sign enable you to compare two pieces of data. By comparing variables to constants, for example, you can check variables for specific values. The most common relational operator is the equals sign, which checks whether two expressions are equal. However, there are also relational operators for such relationships as less than, greater than, and not equal to. (You'll see these operators later in this chapter.) When you use relational operators to compare two values, you are writing a conditional expression, which is an expression that is either true or false.

A simple IF...THEN statement includes the keyword IF followed by a *Boolean* expression—an expression that evaluates to either true or false. You follow the Boolean expression with the keyword THEN and, finally, with the statement you want executed if the Boolean expression is true.

Programmer Lingo

A **Boolean** expression is an expression that evaluates to either true or false. For example, the expression 3 + 4 = 7 is true, whereas the expression 6 + 1 = 9 is false. A Boolean expression usually compares a variable to a constant or to another variable, such as num + 1 = 7 or num1 − 10 = num2.

How do IF...THEN statements work? Let's say that when you execute the preceding program, you type the value 1. When the program gets to the first IF...THEN statement, it checks the value of choice%. If choice% equals 1 (which it does, in this case), the program prints the message "You chose red" and then drops down to the next IF...THEN statement. This time, the program compares the value of choice% with the number 2. Because choice% doesn't equal 2, the program ignores the THEN part of the statement and drops down to the next program line, which is another IF...THEN statement. The variable choice% doesn't equal 3 either, so the THEN portion of the third IF...THEN statement is also ignored. The program ends at this point because there are no more program lines left.

Suppose you enter the number 2 at the menu. When the program gets to the first IF...THEN statement, it discovers that choice% is not equal to 1, so it ignores the THEN part of the statement and drops down to the next program line, which is the second IF...THEN statement. Again, the program checks the value of choice%. Because choice% equals 2, the program can execute the THEN portion of the statement; the message "You chose green" is printed onscreen. Program execution drops down to the third IF...THEN statement, which does nothing because choice% doesn't equal 3.

Point of Interest

The conditional expression in an IF...THEN statement, no matter how complex it is, always evaluates to either true or false. If the expression evaluates to true, the THEN portion of the statement is executed. If the expression evaluates to false, the THEN portion is not executed. True and false are actual values: True equals any nonzero value, and false equals 0. Consequently, the statement IF 1 THEN PRINT "True!" prints the message "True!", but the statement IF 0 THEN PRINT "False!" does nothing. In the first statement, the value 1 is considered true, so the THEN part of the statement is executed. In the second statement, the 0 is considered false, so the THEN portion of the statement is ignored.

Complex IF...THEN *Statements*

The previous program demonstrates the simplest IF...THEN statement. This simple statement usually fits your program's decision-making needs just fine. Sometimes, however, you want to perform more than one command as part of an IF...THEN statement. To perform more than one command, press Enter after THEN, write the commands you want to add to the IF...THEN statement, and end the block of commands with the END IF keyword. Here is a revised version of the menu program that uses this technique:

```
CLS
PRINT
PRINT "    MENU"
PRINT "-----------"
PRINT " 1. Red"
PRINT " 2. Green"
PRINT " 3. Blue"
PRINT
INPUT "Your selection: ", choice%
PRINT

IF choice% = 1 THEN
   COLOR 4
```

```
      PRINT "You chose red."
   END IF

   IF choice% = 2 THEN
      COLOR 2
      PRINT "You chose green."
   END IF

   IF choice% = 3 THEN
      COLOR 1
      PRINT "You chose blue."
   END IF

   COLOR 7
```

Cool Stuff

Notice that some program lines are indented. By indenting the lines that go with each IF block, you can more easily see the structure of your program. This program also uses blank lines to separate blocks of code that go together. The computer doesn't care about the indenting or the blank lines, but these features make your programs easier for you—or another programmer—to read.

The output for the program looks like this:

```
   MENU
   - - - - - - - - - - -
   1. Red
   2. Green
   3. Blue

Your selection: 1

You chose red.
```

What's happening in the program? Suppose you run the program and enter the number 2. When the program gets to the first IF…THEN statement, it compares the value of choice% with the number 1. Because these values don't match (or, as stuffy programmers say, the statement doesn't evaluate to true), the program skips over every program line until it finds an END IF statement, which marks the end of the block of code that goes with the IF.

This brings the program to the second IF…THEN statement. When the program evaluates the conditional expression, it finds that choice% equals 2, and it executes the THEN portion of the IF…THEN statement. This time, the THEN portion is not just one command but two. The program changes the text color to green (the color selected from the menu) and then prints the message. Finally, the program reaches END IF, which marks the end of the IF…THEN statement.

This brings the program to the last IF…THEN statement, which the program skips over because choice% doesn't equal 3. The last line of the program is a COLOR statement without an IF. This command changes the text back to its original white color.

You might think it's a waste of time for the program to evaluate other IF…THEN statements after it finds a match for the menu item you chose. You'd be right. When you write programs, you should always look for ways to make them run faster; one way to make a program run faster is to avoid all unnecessary processing. But how, you may ask, do you avoid unnecessary processing when you have to compare a variable with more than one value?

One way to keep processing to a minimum is to use QBasic's ELSEIF clause. Before you learn about ELSEIF, however, let's look at the simpler version, ELSE. This keyword enables you to use a single IF…THEN statement to choose between two outcomes. Virtually all programming languages have some form of the ELSE clause. When the IF…THEN statement evaluates to true, the THEN part of the statement is executed. When the IF…THEN statement

Point of Interest

When you want to set up a multiline IF statement, you must end the first program line of the statement after THEN. This is the signal to QBasic that all the following commands, up to the next END IF, are part of the IF block.

evaluates to false, the ELSE portion is executed. When the IF…ELSE statement evaluates to neither true nor false, it's time to get a new computer. Here's a program that demonstrates how ELSE works:

```
CLS
INPUT "Please enter your name: ", name$
PRINT
IF name$ = "Fred" THEN
  PRINT "Hi, Fred!"
ELSE
  PRINT "Hello, stranger."
END IF
```

Here is the output for this program:

```
Please enter your name: Fred

Hi, Fred!
```

When you run this program, you're asked to enter your name. If you enter the name Fred, the program recognizes you and gives you a personal hello. Otherwise, the program considers you a stranger and treats you accordingly. (If you like, you can personalize the program by changing all occurrences of Fred to your name.) As you can see, the ELSE clause is executed only when the IF…THEN statement is false. If the IF…THEN statement is true, the program ignores the ELSE clause.

This program also demonstrates how to compare strings. Strings are compared just as numerical values are: by using the equals sign, which, in the case of an IF…THEN statement, is a relational operator. You will compare strings often in your programs, especially programs that require text input from the user. By using string comparisons, you can catch an incorrect response to a prompt and print an error message onscreen to inform the user of the incorrect entry.

ELSE provides a default outcome for an IF...THEN statement. A default outcome doesn't help much, however, in an IF...THEN statement that must associate program code with more than two possible outcomes (as in the preceding menu program). Suppose you want the previous program to recognize your friends' names, too. No problem. First, get some friends; then use QBasic's ELSEIF keyword, as shown here:

```
CLS
INPUT "Please enter your name: ", name$
PRINT
name$ = UCASE$(name$)
IF name$ = "FRED" THEN
  PRINT "Hi, Fred!"
ELSEIF name$ = "SARAH" THEN
  PRINT "How's it going, Sarah?"
ELSEIF name$ = "TONY" THEN
  PRINT "Hey! It's my man Tony!"
ELSE
  PRINT "Hello, stranger."
END IF
```

The output for the program looks like this:

Please enter your name: **sarah**

How's it going, Sarah?

Cool Stuff

When you need to get string input from the user, it's often a good idea to change the input to all uppercase or all lowercase. This enables the program to recognize a word no matter in which case the user types it. For example, in the previous program, the user's input is modified to uppercase before it is compared to the names in the IF and ELSEIF clauses. With this method, Fred can type his name any way he likes: Fred, fred, FRED, or even fRed. One of your goals as a programmer should be to make your programs as easy to use as possible. Allowing the user to enter a string in any form is one way to do this.

In the program, you're asked to enter a name. This time, however, the program uses an IF…THEN statement with a series of ELSEIF clauses to check the name entered against the names the program can recognize. When the program finds a match, it skips over any remaining ELSEIF and ELSE clauses. If the program finds no match—that is, if the user hasn't entered the name Fred, Sarah, or Tony—the ELSE clause executes and provides a default response. This default ensures that, no matter what the user types, he or she will receive a greeting.

Here is a new version of the menu program that uses ELSEIF and ELSE clauses. You should now know enough about computer decision-making to figure out how it works:

```
CLS
PRINT
PRINT "    MENU"
PRINT "-----------"
PRINT " 1. Red"
PRINT " 2. Green"
PRINT " 3. Blue"
PRINT
INPUT "Your selection: ", choice%
PRINT

IF choice% = 1 THEN
   COLOR 4
   PRINT "You chose red."
ELSEIF choice% = 2 THEN
   COLOR 2
   PRINT "You chose green."
ELSEIF choice% = 3 THEN
   COLOR 1
   PRINT "You chose blue."
ELSE
   PRINT "Invalid selection!"
END IF

COLOR 7
```

Here's the output for the program:

```
    MENU
-----------
 1. Red
 2. Green
 3. Blue

Your selection: 2

You chose green.
```

How Do You Compare?

The preceding programs in this chapter used only the equals operator to compare values. You'll often need to compare values in other ways. You might, for example, want to know if a value is less than or greater than another value. In this case, you use relational operators.

Single Comparisons

All computer languages, including QBasic, feature an entire set of relational operators that you can use in IF...THEN statements and other types of comparisons. These operators include not only the equals sign (=) but also not equal to (< >), less than (<), greater than (>), less than or equal to (<=), and greater than or equal to (>=). The relational operators are summarized in Table 6.1.

Table 6.1   Relational Operators

Operator	Meaning	Examples
=	Equals	3=(4-1) or "FRED"="FRED"
<>	Not equal to	5<>(3+3) or "FRED"<>"SAM"
<	Less than	3<23 or "A"<"B"
>	Greater than	41>39 or "BART">"ADAM"
<=	Less than or equal to	5<=6 or "ONE"<="ONE"
>=	Greater than or equal to	10>=10 or "THREE">="TWO"

The following program demonstrates the use of the less-than operator:

```
CLS
INPUT "Enter a number no larger than 50: ", number
PRINT
IF number < 10 THEN
  PRINT "Your number is less than 10."
ELSEIF number < 20 THEN
  PRINT "Your number is greater than 9 and less than 20."
ELSEIF number < 30 THEN
  PRINT "Your number is greater than 19 and less than 30."
ELSEIF number < 40 THEN
  PRINT "Your number is greater than 29 and less than 40."
ELSEIF number < 50 THEN
  PRINT "Your number is greater than 39 and less than 50."
ELSEIF number = 50 THEN
  PRINT "Your number is 50."
ELSE
  PRINT "Your number is out of the acceptable range."
END IF
```

The output for the program looks like this:

```
Enter a number no larger than 50: 60

Your number is out of the acceptable range.
```

When you run the program, it asks you to enter a number no larger than 50. After you type the number, the program determines the number's range and prints a message informing you of this range. This program doesn't just demonstrate the use of the less-than operator; it keeps you off the streets by having you do a lot of typing. More important, however, this program further illustrates the way a block of IF and ELSEIF clauses work.

Suppose you type the number 9 when you run the program. When the program gets to the IF clause, it compares 9 to 10 and discovers that 9 is less than 10. (And to think you paid thousands of dollars for a machine to tell you that.) The IF clause then evaluates to true, and the program prints the message "Your number is less than 10."

Look at the block of ELSEIFs that go along with the IF. Isn't 9 also less than 20? Moreover, isn't 9 also less than 30, 40, and 50? Why then, when you enter the number 9, don't you also see the messages associated with all of these ELSEIFs in addition to the message associated with the IF?

The answer to this question has to do with the way the IF...ELSEIF block works. Once an IF or ELSEIF evaluates to true, the program skips the rest of the statements in the block—or, as programmers say, the program branches to the next statement after the block. In the case of the preceding program, there is no statement after the block so the program simply ends.

Point of Interest

When using relational operators with strings, the value of each letter in a string is relative to its alphabetic order. In other words, the letter A is less than the letter B, the letter B is less than the letter C, and so on. When comparing lowercase letters and uppercase letters, however, the lowercase letters have a greater value than their uppercase counterparts. Therefore, a is greater than A, and b is greater than B. Finally, just as when you organize words into alphabetical order, when a program compares strings, the letters on the left have greater significance than those on the right. For example, Mick is less than Mike to QBasic.

Your Computer As Spock

A single comparison in an IF…THEN statement often isn't enough to determine whether data matches your criteria. How can you be sure, for example, that the user will enter a number within a specific range? One way would be to offer the user large sums of money. Although this may ensure that data is entered properly, it requires you to stay by the computer at all times to make sure you're getting your money's worth. Hardly practical. A better way to ensure that data is in the correct range is to use logical operators in your IF…THEN statements.

Let's say that the user is asked to enter a number between 10 and 50, inclusive. To discover whether a number is within this range, you must check not only that the number is greater than or equal to 10 but also that the number is less than or equal to 50. To help handle these situations, most computer languages feature *logical operators*—in the case of QBasic, these operators are AND, OR, and NOT—that can be used to combine expressions in an IF statement.

Programmer Lingo

Logical operators, including AND, OR, and NOT, enable you to evaluate more than one condition in a single IF statement. They're called logical operators because they use computer logic to join two or more Boolean expressions into a larger Boolean expression. (Remember that Boolean expressions always evaluate to true or false.)

The AND operator requires all expressions to be true for the entire expression to be true. For example, the expression (3+2=5) AND (6+2=8) is true because the expressions on both sides of the AND are true. The expression (4+3=9) AND (3+3=6) is not true, however, because the expression on the left of the AND is not true. Remember this when combining expressions with AND: If any expression is false, the entire expression is false.

The OR operator requires only one expression to be true for the entire expression to be true. For example, the expressions (3+6=2) OR (4+4=8) and (4+1=5) OR (7+2=9) are both true because at least one of the expressions being compared is true. Note that in the second case, both expressions being compared are true, which also makes an OR expression true.

The NOT operator switches the value of (or negates) a logical expression. For example, the expression (4+3=5) is not true; however, the expression NOT (4+3=5) is true. Take a look at the following expression:

(4+5=9) AND NOT (3+1=3)

Is this expression true or false? If you said true, you understand the way that logical operators work. The expressions on either side of the AND are both true, so the entire expression is true. If you said false, you must write this entire chapter 10 times on the blackboard.

Of course, you wouldn't write expressions like (4+5=9) AND NOT (3+1=3) in your programs. They would serve no purpose because you already know how the expressions evaluate. However, when you use variables, you have no way of knowing in advance how an expression may evaluate. For example, is the expression (num < 9) AND (num > 15) true or false? You don't know without being told the value of the numerical variable num. By using the logical operators in your IF…THEN statements, though, your program can do the evaluation and, based on the result—true or false—take the appropriate action.

The following program demonstrates how logical operators work. When you run the program, it asks you to enter a number between 10 and 50. If you type a number that is out of that range, the program lets you know. Although this program is similar to the previous one, it works very differently. After the user types a number, the program uses a single IF…THEN statement to determine whether the number is within the acceptable range. If the number is out of range, the program prints an error message and ends.

```
CLS
INPUT "Enter a number between 10 and 50: ", number
PRINT
IF (number < 10) OR (number > 50) THEN
   PRINT "The number"; number; "is out of range!"
ELSE
   PRINT "The number"; number; "is in range."
END IF
```

Danger Ahead!

In many cases, an IF…THEN statement containing several expressions joined by logical operators is confusing to understand. It is sometimes necessary to add parentheses not only to organize the expressions but also to be sure that the expressions are evaluated in the proper order. For example, look at the following IF…THEN statement:

IF ((num > 10) AND (num < 20)) OR (NOT CHOICE) THEN...

Because expressions inside parentheses are evaluated first, the outermost parentheses around the ANDed expressions ensure that the AND is evaluated before the OR. In addition, expressions with parentheses are evaluated from the inside out. In other words, num>10 and num<20 are evaluated before the AND, and the AND is evaluated before the OR. Without the extra parentheses in the preceding IF…THEN statement, you wouldn't know which expressions went with the AND and which with the OR.

The output for the program looks like this:

```
Enter a number between 10 and 50: 35

The number 35 is in range.
```

The Infamous GOTO

Most of this chapter has been dedicated to conditional branches. If you recall, however, programmers can also use unconditional branches. This type of branching can be accomplished by using the GOTO instruction, which forces program execution to branch to a specific line number or label. Because line numbers in most programs are now obsolete, you don't have to worry about how to use them—you never will need them. You may, however, want to use labels (although even that is unlikely).

The following is a QBasic program that uses the GOTO instruction to branch to a specific place in the program. The destination of the branch is marked by the label lessthan.

```
  CLS
  INPUT "Please enter a number: ", number
  PRINT
  IF number <= 100 THEN GOTO lessthan
  PRINT "Your number is greater than 100."
  END
lessthan:
  PRINT "Your number is less than or equal to 100."
```

Here is the output for the program:

```
Please enter a number: 132

Your number is greater than 100.
```

In the program, notice that when the label's name follows the GOTO, it doesn't include a colon; however, the actual label in the program does include a colon. Notice also that this program uses the command END to stop the program's execution. You haven't seen this command before. Although it is not often used in programs, there may be times when you find it useful. Since the END statement is a command just like PRINT or INPUT, you can have as many as you like in a program. After all, there may be more than one place in your program where you need to stop program execution. As you can see in the program, the END keyword doesn't mark the actual end of the program. Rather, it tells QBasic to stop executing statements.

Point of Interest

Although the GOTO statement may seem like a handy thing to have around, it has been so misused in the past that most programmers avoid it like nuclear waste. Overuse of GOTO can turn a program into a tangled, unreadable mess. A modern, structured language like QBasic has no need for the GOTO instruction. It is included in QBasic only to keep the language compatible with earlier versions of BASIC. This is the last time you will see the GOTO instruction in this book. Start developing good habits now and never use GOTO in your programs.

As soon as you understand all this stuff about computer decision-making, you'll be 90 percent of the way to becoming a programmer. Making decisions is, after all, one of the most important things a program does. It's safe to say that there's not a single worthwhile program on the planet that doesn't use IF...THEN statements or something similar.

The Least You Need to Know

➤ The order in which a program executes its statements is known as program flow.

➤ When a computer jumps to a new location in the code, it's called branching.

➤ To compare data and perform a decision, you use IF...THEN statements.

➤ To perform several decisions in an IF statement, you can add ELSE and ELSEIF clauses.

➤ Multiline IF statements end with the END IF keyword.

➤ To compare data, programs use relational operators, including equals (=), does not equal (<>), less than (<), greater than (>), less than or equal to (<=), and greater than or equal (>=).

➤ To evaluate multiple expressions in an IF...THEN statement, you can use the logical operators (AND, OR, and NOT).

Chapter 7

Do It Again and Again

In This Chapter

➤ Understanding program looping

➤ Using FOR...NEXT, WHILE, and DO loops

➤ Knowing when to use each type of loop

If there's one thing a computer is an absolute expert at it's performing repetitive operations. It doesn't matter if you want something done once or you want it done a million times. Your computer will go at the task with mindless ease, never getting bored and never once uttering a single complaint. Consider, for example, a disk file containing 10,000 names and addresses. If you tried to type labels for all those people, you'd have aching fingers in no time. A computer, on the other hand, can spit out all 10,000 labels tirelessly.

Every computer language must have some form of looping command to instruct a computer to perform repetitive tasks. Looping is the process of executing a block of statements repeatedly. Starting at the top of the block, the statements are executed until the program reaches the end of the block, at which point the program goes back to the top and starts over. The statements in the block can be repeated any number of times, from once to forever. QBasic features three types of looping: FOR...NEXT loops, WHILE loops, and DO loops. In this chapter, you learn to use these powerful programming techniques.

Around and Around We Go

The most often used loop in programming is probably the FOR...NEXT loop, which instructs a program to perform a block of code a specified number of times. You could, for example, use a FOR...NEXT loop to instruct your computer to print those 10,000 address labels. Because you don't currently have an address file, however, let's say you want to print your name on the screen six times. Here's one way to do this:

```
CLS
INPUT "Please enter your name: ", name$
PRINT
PRINT name$
PRINT name$
PRINT name$
PRINT name$
PRINT name$
PRINT name$
```

The program output looks like this:

```
Please enter your name: Shawn

Shawn
Shawn
Shawn
Shawn
Shawn
Shawn
```

See all those PRINT statements in the program? As a computer programmer, whenever you see program code containing many identical instructions, a little bell should go off in your head. When you hear this little bell, you should say to yourself, "Hmmmm. This looks like a good place for a loop."

Having many lines in your program that contain identical instructions makes your program longer than necessary and wastes valuable memory. It also shows poor programming style. Unless you want your programming friends to snicker behind your back, learn to replace redundant program code with program loops.

The preceding program can be streamlined easily by using a FOR...NEXT loop, and here's how:

```
CLS
INPUT "Please enter your name: ", name$
PRINT
FOR x = 1 TO 6
  PRINT name$
NEXT x
```

The output of this second version is identical to the first (except a different name was entered); now the program is shorter and contains no redundant code. The output looks like this:

```
Please enter your name: Justin

Justin
Justin
Justin
Justin
Justin
Justin
```

Cool Stuff

To produce programs that are tightly written, shorter, and faster, always try to replace repetitive program code with program loops.

Look at the program line beginning with the keyword FOR. The loop starts with this line. The word FOR tells QBasic that you're starting a FOR…NEXT loop. After the word FOR is the loop-control variable x. The *loop-control variable,* which can have any legal numerical-variable name, is where QBasic stores the current loop count. See the number after the equals sign? QBasic uses this number to begin the loop count.

When the FOR loop begins, QBasic places the number 1 in the variable x. The program then drops down to the next line and prints the user's name. The line NEXT x tells QBasic to *increment* (increase by one) the loop-control variable and start again at the top of the loop. So, x becomes 2, and the program returns to the FOR line. The program then compares the value in x with the number following the keyword TO. If the loop count (in x) is less than or equal to the number following TO, the program executes the loop again. This process continues until x is greater than 6.

Programmer Lingo

A **loop-control variable** holds the current loop count. When the value of this variable reaches the requested loop count, the loop ends.

Whew! Got all that? Or did you fall asleep halfway through? If you just woke up, rub the fuzzies from your eyes and read the preceding paragraph a couple times to make sure it sinks in. If you still can't stay awake, take a nap.

Suppose you want to modify the program to print your name 10 times. What would you change? If you answered, "I'd change the 6 in the FOR line to 10," you win the Programmer of the Week award. If you answered, "I'd change the light bulbs in the back hall," you must turn in your copy of QBasic to the programming police.

Programmer Lingo

In computer programs, variables are often incremented and decremented. When you **increment** a variable, you add some value to it. When you **decrement** a variable, you subtract some value from it. If the value of the increment or decrement is not explicit, it's assumed that the value is 1. For example, the statement "The program increments the variable num by 5" means that num is increased in value by 5. On the other hand, the statement "The program increments num" usually means that num is increased by 1.

Watch Your Step on This Ride

The previous example of a FOR…NEXT loop increments the loop counter by 1, but suppose you want a FOR…NEXT loop that counts from 5 to 50 by fives. You can do this by adding a STEP clause to your FOR…NEXT loop, as shown in this example:

```
CLS
INPUT "Please enter your name: ", name$
PRINT
FOR x = 5 TO 50 STEP 5
  PRINT name$
  PRINT "Loop counter value: ", x
NEXT x
```

Figure 7.1 shows the program's output.

Figure 7.1

Counting by fives.

```
Please enter your name: Stephen

Stephen
Loop counter value:         5
Stephen
Loop counter value:        10
Stephen
Loop counter value:        15
Stephen
Loop counter value:        20
Stephen
Loop counter value:        25
Stephen
Loop counter value:        30
Stephen
Loop counter value:        35
Stephen
Loop counter value:        40
Stephen
Loop counter value:        45
Stephen
Loop counter value:        50

Press any key to continue
```

When you run this program, you're asked to enter your name. The program then prints both your name and the current value of the loop variable 10 times. Besides showing how to use the STEP clause, this program also shows how you can place more than one command in the body of a FOR...NEXT loop. You can, in fact, have as many statements as you like between the FOR and NEXT.

Look closely at the FOR...NEXT loop in the previous program. Unlike the other programs, this loop doesn't start counting at 1. Rather, the loop variable begins with a value of 5. Then, thanks to the STEP 5 clause, the loop variable is incremented by 5 each time through the loop. x goes from 5 to 10, from 10 to 15, and so on up to 50, resulting in 10 loops.

Here's a program that shows how you can use the STEP clause to count backward. (Well, the STEP clause won't help you count backward, but it'll help your computer!)

```
CLS
INPUT "Please enter your name: ", name$
PRINT
FOR x = 50 TO 5 STEP -5
  PRINT name$
  PRINT "Loop counter value: ", x
NEXT x
```

Figure 7.2 shows the output for the program.

Programmer Lingo

The body of a loop comprises the commands performed each time through the loop. In a FOR...NEXT loop, for example, these are the statements between the FOR line and the NEXT line.

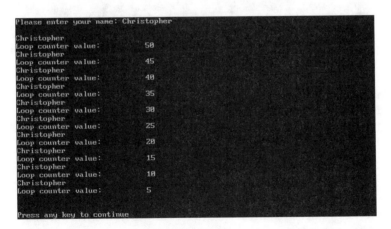

Figure 7.2

Counting backward by fives.

Notice that the loop limits are in reverse order; that is, the higher value comes first. Notice also that the STEP clause uses a negative value, which causes the loop count to be decremented (decreased) rather than incremented. Finally, notice that, no matter how hard you try, you can't train a penguin to play chess. This has little to do with computing, but it is nevertheless one of the great mysteries of the cosmos.

Where We'll Stop, Nobody Knows

Just as with most numerical values in a program, you can substitute variables for the constants in a FOR...NEXT loop. In fact, you'll probably use variables in your loop limits as often as you use constants, if not more. Here's how to do this:

```
CLS
INPUT "Please enter your name: ", name$
INPUT "Please enter the print count: ", count
PRINT
FOR x = 1 TO count
  PRINT name$
  PRINT "Loop counter value: ", x
NEXT x
```

Figure 7.3 shows the program's output.

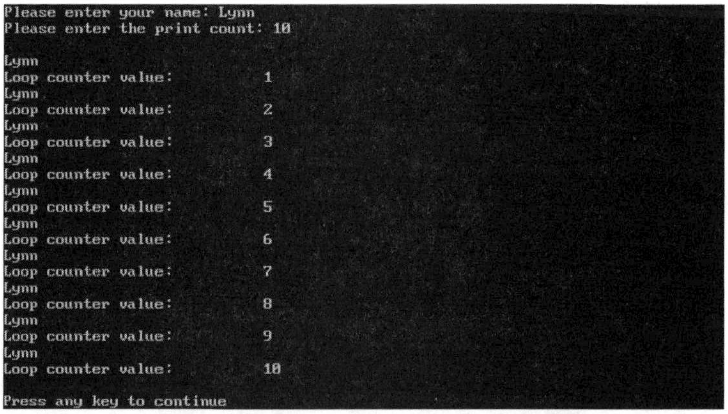

Figure 7.3

Using variables in FOR...NEXT *loops.*

```
Please enter your name: Lynn
Please enter the print count: 10

Lynn
Loop counter value:          1
Lynn
Loop counter value:          2
Lynn
Loop counter value:          3
Lynn
Loop counter value:          4
Lynn
Loop counter value:          5
Lynn
Loop counter value:          6
Lynn
Loop counter value:          7
Lynn
Loop counter value:          8
Lynn
Loop counter value:          9
Lynn
Loop counter value:         10
Press any key to continue
```

When you run this program, you're asked to enter your name and the number of times you want it printed. The program then prints your name the requested number of times. As you can see in the program lines, you can have the program print your name any number of times because the loop's upper limit is contained in the variable count; count gets its value from you at the start of each program run.

Using variables in FOR...NEXT loops makes your programs more flexible and produces a powerful programming construct. As you'll soon see, you can use variables with other types of loops, too. In fact, you can use a numerical variable in a program in most of the places where a numerical value is required. You can even use numerical variables as ice-cream topping, but they tend to stick to the roof of your mouth.

Getting Dizzy Yet?

Another type of loop you can use in your programs is the WHILE loop. Unlike a FOR...NEXT loop, which loops the number of times given in the loop limits, a WHILE loop continues executing until its control expression becomes true. The control expression is a Boolean expression much like the Boolean expressions you used with IF statements. In other words, any expression that evaluates to true or false can be used as a control expression for a WHILE loop. Here's a program that shows a WHILE loop in action:

```
CLS
num = 1
WHILE num <> 0
   INPUT "Please enter a number: ", num
WEND
PRINT
PRINT "Looping is finished."
```

Figure 7.4 shows the program's output.

```
Please enter a number: 2
Please enter a number: 6
Please enter a number: 45
Please enter a number: 3
Please enter a number: -5
Please enter a number: 7
Please enter a number: 0

Looping is finished.




Press any key to continue
```

Figure 7.4

Using a WHILE loop.

How does the WHILE loop in the program work? First, the loop variable num is set to 1. Then, at the start of the WHILE loop, the program compares the value in num with the literal value 0. If these two values don't match, the expression evaluates to false, and the program executes the body of the loop, which in this case is a single INPUT statement. This statement gets a number from the user and stores it in the variable num. The program then comes to the WEND keyword (which stands for WHILE END). This tells QBasic that it has reached the end of the loop and must now go back and check the value of num again.

If the user entered a value other than 0, the two values in the loop's control expression again don't match, and the INPUT statement executes again. If the values do match, the control expression

Programmer Lingo

A **loop-control expression** is a Boolean expression that determines whether a loop should continue or end. In a WHILE loop, when the control expression becomes false, the loop ends. As long as the control expression is true, the loop continues.

evaluates to true, the loop ends, and the program branches to the first statement after WEND, which in this case is a PRINT statement.

Notice how the program sets the variable num to 1 before the WHILE loop starts. This is important because it ensures that the value in num starts at a value other than 0. If num did happen to start at 0, the program would never get to the INPUT statement within the WHILE loop. Instead, the loop's control expression would immediately evaluate to true, and the program would branch to the PRINT statement. Mistakes like this make programmers gnash their teeth and answer the phone with, "What do you want, clown?"

Danger Ahead!

Always initialize (set the starting value of) any variable used in a WHILE loop's control expression. Failure to do so may result in your program skipping over the loop entirely. Initializing a variable means setting it to its starting value. In QBasic, all numeric variables are automatically initialized to 0. If you need a variable to start at a different value, you must initialize it yourself.

Nearing the End of the Ride

Most languages, including QBasic, also feature some form of the DO loops. A DO loop is much like a WHILE loop, except a DO loop evaluates its control expression at the end of the loop rather than at the beginning. So the body of the loop—the statements between the beginning and end of the loop—is always executed at least once. In a WHILE loop, the body of the loop may or may not ever get executed. The following sample program shows how a DO loop works:

```
CLS
DO
   INPUT "Please enter a number: ", num
LOOP UNTIL num = 0
PRINT
PRINT "Looping is finished."
```

Figure 7.5 shows this program's output.

Figure 7.5

Using a DO loop.

```
Please enter a number: 4
Please enter a number: 3
Please enter a number: 6
Please enter a number: 7
Please enter a number: 2345
Please enter a number: -756
Please enter a number: 4.576
Please enter a number: 0

Looping is finished.




Press any key to continue
```

When you run the program, you're asked to enter a number. As long as you enter a number other than 0, the program continues to loop. When you finally enter 0, the loop ends.

Notice that you don't need to initialize the loop-control variable num before entering the loop; num gets its value from the INPUT statement that comes before the loop's control statement is executed. So if you've got a headache from gnashing your teeth, try changing your WHILE loops to DO loops. The variable num always holds a valid value when the program reaches the LOOP UNTIL portion of the loop, where num is compared with 0.

The DO loop actually has two forms: one that ends with LOOP UNTIL and one that ends with LOOP WHILE. LOOP UNTIL allows a loop to continue until the control expression becomes true. LOOP WHILE allows a loop to continue until the control expression becomes false. For example, in the previous program, the loop continues until num equals 0. You could reverse this logic by using a LOOP WHILE rather than a LOOP UNTIL. In this case, the last line of the loop would read LOOP WHILE num <> 0, which forces the loop to continue as long as num doesn't equal 0.

Cool Stuff

Different looping methods work best in different programming situations. Although experience is the best teacher, you should keep some things in mind when selecting a looping construct. When you want a loop to run a specific number of times, the FOR...NEXT loop is usually the best choice. When you want a loop to run until a certain condition is met, the WHILE or DO loops work best. Remember that the body of a DO loop is always executed at least once because the control expression is checked at the bottom of the loop. A WHILE loop, on the other hand, is not guaranteed to execute at all because its control expression is evaluated first, at the top of the loop.

One Last Spin

You've learned a lot about program looping in this chapter, and you're probably not sure how or why you would use these techniques. The following three programs give you the chance to broaden your experience with the three looping constructs. When you run any of the programs, you're asked to enter a string that contains the word "loop." After you enter the string, the program uses one of the looping techniques to find and mark the location of the substring "loop" in the string you entered.

All three programs yield the output shown in Figure 7.6, but each uses a different looping technique to get the job done.

Figure 7.6

Testing loop techniques.

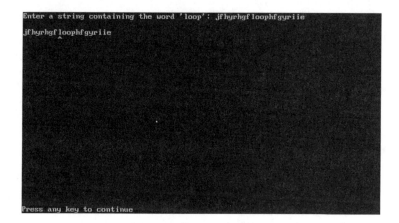

Be sure you understand these programs before you move on to the next chapter. Looping is a valuable tool to use when writing programs. You'll use it more than a cat uses a litter box.

Program 1

```
CLS
INPUT "Enter a string containing the word 'loop': ", s$
PRINT

location = 0
FOR x = 1 TO LEN(s$)
  IF MID$(s$, x, 4) = "loop" THEN location = x
NEXT x

IF location = 0 THEN
  PRINT "Word 'loop' not found."
ELSE
  PRINT s$
  FOR x = 1 TO location - 1
    PRINT " ";
  NEXT x
  PRINT "^"
END IF
```

After clearing the screen, Program 1 asks the user to enter a string containing the word "loop." It then initializes the variable location, which holds the location of the substring loop to 0. A FOR...NEXT loop is then executed. This loop's limit is from 1 to the length of the string that the user entered.

Within the loop, the string function MID$ uses the loop-control variable x as the starting location at which to check for the requested substring. By using this variable, MID$ starts its string comparisons at the first character and moves forward through the string a character at a time, looking for the substring loop. When the IF statement evaluates to true (when MID$ finds the substring), the variable location is set to the value of the loop variable x. The FOR...NEXT loop continues until it reaches the end of the string.

If location is still 0 when the loop finishes, the substring was not found. The program then prints an error message. If location is greater than 0, the program prints the contents of s$, which is the string the user entered. The program then uses another FOR...NEXT loop to print enough spaces to place the cursor immediately beneath the first character of the substring "loop," at which point it prints a caret marking the substring's location.

Point of Interest

The value of a FOR...NEXT loop's loop-control variable should never be changed directly by your code. Except in rare circumstances, FOR...NEXT loops should always be allowed to run their full cycle. If a loop is not working the way you expect it to, make sure you're not accidentally changing a loop-control variable in your code.

Program 2

```
CLS
INPUT "Enter a string containing the word 'loop': ", s$
PRINT

x = 1
WHILE (MID$(s$, x, 4) <> "loop") AND (x < LEN(s$))
  x = x + 1
WEND

IF x = LEN(s$) THEN
  PRINT "Word 'loop' not found."
ELSE
  PRINT s$
  FOR i = 1 TO x - 1
    PRINT " ";
  NEXT i
  PRINT "^"
END IF
```

Program 2 works much like Program 1. The difference is that this version of the program uses a WHILE loop to locate the substring. After the user enters his string, the loop counter x is initialized to 1 to ensure that the program gets into the WHILE loop. The loop's control expression uses the logical operator AND to make two comparisons.

In the first comparison, MID$ checks for the substring. The second comparison ensures that the loop won't continue beyond the length of the string, which would happen if the user's string did not contain the word "loop."

When the WHILE loop ends, the variable x contains the location of the substring if the string was found or the length of s$ if the substring wasn't found. The results of the search are printed using similar code to that found in Program 1.

Point of Interest

New programmers are infamous for creating WHILE and DO loops that never end. For example, if you write a WHILE loop whose control expression can never become true, your loop will loop forever. When this happens, it'll look to you as though your program has "locked up" your machine (your computer has stopped dead in its tracks and will accept no input). But really, your program is looping frantically with no hope of ever moving on. The only way out of this predicament is to press Ctrl+Break to terminate the program. If pressing Ctrl+Break shows that your program was in the middle of a WHILE or DO loop when it got hung up, it's time to check the loop's control expression for conditions that cannot possibly be met.

Program 3

```
CLS
INPUT "Enter a string containing the word 'loop': ", s$
PRINT

x = 0
DO
  x = x + 1
LOOP UNTIL (MID$(s$, x, 4) = "loop") OR (x = LEN(s$))

IF x = LEN(s$) THEN
  PRINT "Word 'loop' not found."
ELSE
  PRINT s$
  FOR i = 1 TO x - 1
    PRINT " ";
```

```
   NEXT i
   PRINT "^"
END IF
```

Program 3 works much like Program 2, except it uses a DO loop rather than a WHILE loop to search through the user's string. In this version of the program, the loop continues until the substring is found or until the loop counter x is equal to the length of the string the user entered. In the latter case, the substring is not in the string, so an error message is printed. Otherwise, the user's string is displayed, and the location of the substring is marked.

Just like the expressions used in IF statements, the control expressions used in WHILE and DO loops can be built using the logical operators AND, OR, and NOT. However, the more complex a control expression becomes, the more likely it is that the expression doesn't mean what you think it means. Try to keep loop-control expressions as simple as possible and study them carefully to be sure they represent the logic you want.

Point of Interest

As mentioned previously, each type of looping construct works best in different circumstances. For example, a FOR...NEXT loop should be used only for loops that always execute from the starting limit to the ending limit. If you find yourself needing to get out of a FOR...NEXT loop before the loop has run its course, you should probably be using a WHILE loop or DO loop.

The Least You Need to Know

➤ Computer programs perform repetitive operations with loops, such as FOR...NEXT loops, WHILE loops, and DO loops.

➤ To perform a set of commands a specific number of times, you use a FOR...NEXT loop.

➤ A STEP clause in a FOR...NEXT loop makes the loop-control variable count up or down.

➤ Numeric variables can be substituted for loop limits in a FOR...NEXT loop.

➤ A WHILE loop repeats until its loop-control expression evaluates to true.

➤ A DO loop always executes at least once because its control expression is at the bottom of the loop rather than at the top.

➤ The DO loop has two forms. In the first form—the DO...UNTIL loop—the loop continues until the control expression becomes true. In the second form—the DO...WHILE loop—the loop continues until the control expression becomes false.

Part 3

Taking the Next Step

With the very basics out of the way, you're now ready to explore stuff like input and output, which comes in many forms. For example, in this part of the book, you'll learn how to display text on the screen and how to save data to, and get data from, a file.

Chapter 8

Saying It with Text

In This Chapter

➤ Joining strings

➤ Using string lengths

➤ Handling substrings

➤ Converting strings and numbers

Although we all love to see pictures of spectacular sunsets or snow-covered mountain ranges, when it comes to computers, you mostly have to settle for words and numbers. And, until you can figure out a way to write a letter using images of sunsets or balance your checkbook with a range of photographed mountains, that's the way things will stay. The truth is that, even if you're running a graphical user interface like Windows, most information displayed on your computer screen is in text form.

Because text displays are so important in computing, all programming languages feature a number of functions and commands that manipulate text. These functions enable you to join two or more strings into one, find the length of a string, extract a small portion of a string, or convert numbers to strings or strings to numbers. In this chapter, you'll learn to use many of QBasic's string-handling functions.

'Til Death Do They Part

You'll often have two or more strings in your programs that you must combine into one. For example, you may have a user's first name and last name in two separate strings. To get the user's entire name into a single string, you have to *concatenate* (join together end to end) the two strings. Use QBasic's concatenation operator, which looks like an addition operator, to handle this string-handling task. To join three strings, for example, type the following:

```
string1$ + string2$ + string3$
```

Programmer Lingo

Concatenation is the process of joining two or more strings end to end to create one large string. QBasic performs concatenation with the plus sign (+), which acts as the string-concatenation operator.

Simply joining the strings, however, is not a complete program statement; you also must tell QBasic where to store the new string. To do this, use QBasic's assignment operator, the equals sign (=). The assignment operator for strings works just like the assignment operator for numeric variables. For example, to make the string variable insult$ equal to the text string Your face could stop Big Ben, use the following command:

```
insult$ = "Your face could stop Big Ben"
```

To see how all this works, look at this program:

```
CLS
INPUT "Enter your first name: ", first$
INPUT "Enter your last name: ", last$
name$ = first$ + " " + last$
PRINT
PRINT "Your full name is: "; name$
```

When you run the program, you are asked to type your first name and then your last name. The program then prints your full name onscreen. It's not the fact that your name is displayed that makes this program interesting—you already know how to use a PRINT statement to display output. What's interesting is that the final output is in a single string, name$, not in the two original name strings, first$ and last$. This single string is created by using QBasic's string assignment operator (=) and string concatenation operator (+) to join the two original name strings.

The preceding program delivers the following output:

```
Enter your first name: Freddy
Enter your last name: Kruger
Your full name is: Freddy Kruger
```

Do you see something different about the INPUT commands in the program? Look at the INPUT command in the second line. Do you see the comma separating the prompt from the input variable first$? The comma here, instead of the usual semicolon, tells

QBasic not to print the question mark that usually appears when you use an INPUT command. This technique enables you to create any type of prompt you need. Pretty tricky, eh?

The Long and Short of It

Every string has a length: the number of characters contained in that string. For example, the string Why did the chicken cross the road? has a length of 35 because it contains 35 characters. (Spaces are characters, too.) The string Because the farmer was chasing him with a hatchet! has a length of 50. Theoretically, a string can have any length from 0 to infinity. In QBasic, however, a string is much more conservative and can be any length from 0 to 32,767 characters.

Programmer Lingo

A **null string** is a string that contains 0 characters. How can a string contain 0 characters? Easy! When you assign a string variable to an empty string, you get a string with a length of 0, as shown in the following example: string1$ = "". Notice that there are no characters between the quotation marks. This creates an empty, or null, string. At first, you may think creating a null string makes about as much sense as drinking from an empty glass. But sometimes you may want to initialize a string variable to a null string so that you'll know the string doesn't contain old data.

Sometimes in your program you may need to know the length of a string. For example, you might want to calculate the position of a string onscreen in which the position of one string depends on where a previous string ends. To find the length of a string variable, use QBasic's LEN function, as in the following:

```
length% = LEN(string1$)
```

Here, the function's single argument, string1$, is the string for which you want the length. The LEN function returns the length of the string as a numerical value that can be used anywhere you can use a numeric value.

Notice that the previous paragraph refers to a string variable called string1$. Why is there a number after the name? The number is actually part of the variable's name and is required because string$ is the name of a QBasic function. Remember: You

can't use QBasic function names or keywords as variable names, so you must change (or add) at least one character to set the variable name apart from the keyword or function name.

What the heck is a function, anyway? A *function* is simply a command that performs a specific task and then sends a result (returns a value) back to your program. (The result returned from a function is called a *return value*.) For example, in the previous paragraph, you learned that LEN is a function that calculates the number of characters in a string. After doing this calculation, LEN sends the number of characters back to you so you can use it in your program. Usually, you assign a function's return value to a variable.

QBasic features two types of functions. The first type includes QBasic's built-in functions such as LEN, ABS (absolute value), and SQR (square root). QBasic boasts dozens of built-in functions that you can use in your programs. QBasic also lets you write your own functions, which usually comprise several program lines that perform a specific task.

Here's a revised version of the previous program, one that uses the LEN function:

```
CLS
INPUT "Enter your first name: ", first$
INPUT "Enter your last name: ", last$
name$ = first$ + " " + last$
PRINT
PRINT "Your full name is "; name$
length% = LEN(name$)
PRINT "The length of your name is"; length%
```

The following is the output from the program:

```
Enter your first name: James
Enter your last name: Bond

Your full name is James Bond
The length of your name is 10
```

Cool Stuff

In this program, you don't have to use the variable `length%`. You could rewrite the last two lines as one, like this:

```
PRINT "The length of your name is"; LEN(name$)
```

This method demonstrates how you can use functions in the same way you use numbers or numeric variables.

Bits and Pieces

Just as you can concatenate strings to create a larger string, you can separate strings into smaller strings called *substrings*. You might think that because you use the plus sign to perform concatenation, you would use the minus sign to extract substrings. If you try this, however, you'll annoy QBasic and embarrass yourself in front of your friends. The truth is that the minus sign serves no purpose when working with strings. Instead, QBasic has several special string-handling functions that were created especially to extract whatever portion of a string you need. These string-handling functions are LEFT$, RIGHT$, and MID$.

The LEFT$ function returns a specified number of characters in a string, beginning with the left-most, or first, character of the string. This is similar to what happens when the hatchet-wielding farmer catches up with his runaway chicken—except cutting a substring from another string is a lot less messy than separating a chicken from its head.

Programmer Lingo

A **substring** is a portion of a larger string. For example, the string Twitdum is a substring of Seymour Twitdum.

To use LEFT$, you might type a command such as the following:

```
string2$ = LEFT$(string1$, 7)
```

This function call has two arguments. The first argument is the string from which you want to extract a substring; the second argument is the number of characters, counting

99

from the first character in the string, that you want to include in the substring. So, the example

```
string2$ = LEFT$(string1$, 7)
```

returns the first seven characters of the variable string1$. If string1$ was the phrase Yabba Dabba Do, LEFT$ would return the string Yabba D.

The function RIGHT$ returns a specified number of characters in a string, starting from the rightmost, or last, character of the string. So, the statement

```
string2$ = RIGHT$(string1$, 7)
```

Danger Ahead!

When you call a function such as LEFT$, be certain you have the function's arguments in the right order. A function call such as s$ = LEFT$(n$, 5) works just fine, but the function call s$ = LEFT$(5, n$) stops a QBasic program dead in its tracks.

returns the last seven characters of the variable string1$. If string1$ was the phrase QBasic rocks heavily!, this call to RIGHT$ would return the string eavily!.

Finally, the function MID$, which has two forms, allows you to extract text from any position in a string. In fact, you can use MID$ to do anything you can do with LEFT$ and RIGHT$—and much more. In other words, if you can remember only one string-handling function, MID$ is the one to remember. If you can't remember even one string-handling function, forget QBasic and join the bikini-gazers at the beach.

In the first form of MID$, you supply as arguments the source string (the string from which you will cut your substring) and a starting position. The function then returns a substring consisting of all the characters from the starting position to the end of the string. One example is the following program statement:

```
string2$ = MID$(string1$, 7)
```

In this case, if string1$ was I'd rather be at the beach, string2$ would be equal to ther be at the beach. (The "t" in "rather" is the seventh character in string1$.)

In the second form of MID$, you supply as arguments the source string, a starting position, and the length of the substring you want. The function then returns a string composed of all the characters from the starting position up to the requested length. Assuming that string1$ still equals I'd rather be at the beach, the statement

```
string2$ = MID$(string1$, 7, 4)
```

would make string2$ equal to ther.

Cool Stuff

Although LEFT$ and RIGHT$ are handy functions, you can replace any call to them (when you use a function, you "call" it) with a call to MID$. For example, the following two function calls produce exactly the same results:

```
string2$ = LEFT$(string1$, 8)
```

and

```
string2$ = MID$(string1$, 1, 8)
```

Likewise, the next two function calls also produce the same results:

```
string2$ = RIGHT$(string1$, 8)
```

and

```
string2$ = MID$(string1$, LEN(string1$)-7)
```

To get a little practice with substrings, try this program:

```
CLS
INPUT "Enter a string: ", string1$
string2$ = LEFT$(string1$, 5)
string3$ = RIGHT$(string1$, 5)
string4$ = MID$(string1$, 3, 5)
PRINT
PRINT "The first five characters are ";
PRINT "'"; string2$; "'"
PRINT "The last five characters are ";
PRINT "'"; string3$; "'"
PRINT "Five characters from the middle are ";
PRINT "'"; string4$; "'"
```

When you run the program, you are asked to enter a string. Type anything you like, as long as the text is at least seven characters long and doesn't contain words that make people blush. After you enter the string, the program extracts several substrings and displays them onscreen.

Here is a typical program run:

```
Enter a string: This is a test.

The first five characters are 'This '
The last five characters are 'test.'
Five characters from the middle are 'is is'
```

Look at the PRINT commands near the end of the program. Notice how some end with a semicolon? When you end a PRINT command with a semicolon, the next PRINT command following it begins printing on the same line as the first PRINT command. Because the first PRINT in each pair of PRINT commands ends with a semicolon, each pair prints only a single line of text.

Point of Interest

When you run the previous program, try entering a string that's less than five characters in length. Because the LEFT$ and RIGHT$ string-handling functions assume a string length of at least five characters and the function MID$ assumes a string length of at least seven characters, you might expect the program to drop dead if you give it a string shorter than it expects. But the following program output shows what really happens. QBasic's functions are smart little devils. If you give them values that don't make sense, they usually can still figure out how to handle the situation. Despite QBasic's cleverness, you should watch out for this kind of error. The following output shows what happens if you enter a string with fewer than five characters:

```
Enter a string: rat

The first five characters are 'rat'
The last five characters are 'rat'
Five characters from the middle are 't'
```

A Textual Scavenger Hunt

Now that you know how to extract a substring from a larger string, you may wonder how you can find the exact substring you want. Suppose, for example, you have a string containing a list of names, and you want to find the name Twitdum. The function INSTR (which stands for "in string") was created for just this task. (Well, actually, it was created to find any string, not just Twitdum.)

Like the function MID$, INSTR (notice that there's no dollar sign after INSTR) has two forms. One form of INSTR enables you to find the first occurrence of a substring by providing the function with the source string (the string to search through) as well as the substring for which to search. For example, the following line finds the position of the substring Twitdum in string1$:

```
P% = INSTR(string1$, "Twitdum")
```

When you find the position of the string, simply use MID$ to extract the actual string. (If INSTR cannot find the requested substring, it returns a value of 0.) In the previous example of Twitdum, you'd use MID$ to extract the substring like this:

```
string2$ = MID$(string1$, P%, 7)
```

After finding the first occurrence of a substring, you may want to search the rest of the string for another occurrence. After all, your name list might contain more than one Twitdum. To continue searching, you use the second form of the INSTR function. This second form takes as arguments not only the string to search and the substring for which to search but also the starting position of the search.

You could use the value returned in P% to continue searching the string, as in the following:

```
P% = INSTR(P% + 1, string1$, "Twitdum")
```

Notice that the starting position, which is the function's first argument, is P% + 1, not just P%. If you used P%, the function would find the same substring it just found. An error like this in your program can be very hard to detect.

The following program demonstrates how all this substring-search stuff works. This program requires no input. Just run it and compare its output with the program listing:

```
CLS
string1$ = "SmithTwitdumFreemanTwitdumRothTwitdum"
position% = INSTR(string1$, "Twitdum")
PRINT "The first occurrence of ";
PRINT "'"; MID$(string1$, position%, 7); "' ";
PRINT "is at position"; position%
position% = INSTR(position% + 1, string1$, "Twitdum")
PRINT "The second occurrence of ";
PRINT "'"; MID$(string1$, position%, 7); "' ";
PRINT "is at position"; position%
position% = INSTR(position% + 1, string1$, "Twitdum")
PRINT "The third occurrence of ";
PRINT "'"; MID$(string1$, position%, 7); "' ";
PRINT "is at position"; position%
```

103

After clearing the screen, this program sets the string variable string1$ to a list of names. Then the program uses the INSTR function to find the position of the first occurrence of the substring Twitdum, which is stored in the integer variable position%. Three PRINT commands then display the substring and its position, using the MID$ function and the value of position%.

Next, the INSTR function finds the position of the second occurrence of the substring—this time using the form of INSTR that specifies the starting position for the search. In this example, the starting position is position% + 1. Again, the PRINT commands display the substring and its position.

The third occurrence of the substring is located and displayed in the same way. If the source string contained more than three occurrences of Twitdum, you could find them in exactly the same way that the program found the first three.

Programmer Lingo

A **delimiter** is a character used to separate words in a string. For example, the delimiter in the string Fred,Sam,Otis,Hal is a comma.

Here is the output from the program:

```
The first occurrence of 'Twitdum' is at position
6
The second occurrence of 'Twitdum' is at
position 20
The third occurrence of 'Twitdum' is at position
31
```

Another way to use the string functions presented in this chapter is to separate words in a string. To do this, you have to know the character between the words. This character, which can be anything you like, is called a *delimiter*. In most sentences, the delimiter is the space character. The following is a program that asks you to type a string containing three words separated by spaces. After you enter the string, the program uses the string-handling functions to find and separate the words into different strings:

```
CLS
PRINT "Enter a string containing three ";
PRINT "words separated by spaces."
INPUT string1$
pos1% = INSTR(string1$, " ")
word1$ = LEFT$(string1$, pos1% - 1)
pos2% = INSTR(pos1% + 1, string1$, " ")
word2$ = MID$(string1$, pos1% + 1, pos2% - pos1% - 1)
word3$ = RIGHT$(string1$, LEN(string1$) - pos2%)
PRINT
PRINT "Your three words are ";
PRINT "'"; word1$; ",' '"; word2$; ",' and '"; word3$; ".'"
```

The first four lines of the program clear the screen, print a prompt, and ask the user to enter a string consisting of three words separated by spaces. In the fifth line, the program finds the location of the first space character and stores its position in the integer variable pos1%. In the sixth line, the program uses the LEFT$ function to extract the first word from the string by using the location of the space minus 1 as the length of the substring. (For example, if the first word in the string is muskrat, the first space will be at position 8. The length of muskrat is then 8 – 1, or 7.)

In the seventh line, the program finds the location of the second space character, and the eighth line uses the function MID$ to extract the second word from the string. The start of the second word is located at pos1% + 1, which is the position of the first character after the first space. The length of the word is calculated by subtracting the location of the first space from the location of the second space minus 1. (If you find these calculations a little confusing, run through each program step on a piece of paper. You'll see that the math is really very simple. It's just difficult to describe in English.)

The program extracts the third word using the RIGHT$ function. The number of characters to extract from the right of the string is calculated by subtracting the position of the second space from the length of the string. Finally, the last three lines of the program print the program's output, which displays the three words that were extracted from the main string.

Here is the program's output:

```
Enter a string containing three words separated by spaces.
? One Two Three

Your three words are 'One,' 'Two,' and 'Three.'
```

The previous program is the most complicated program you've confronted. Study it carefully to be sure you understand the way the various functions determine the location of each word in the string. Also review how each word is then extracted into a separate string variable. When you understand this program, you're well on your way to being a programmer.

Please realize that this program isn't nearly as complicated as it may seem from reading its description. Describing even fairly simple programming ideas in English—especially mathematical and logical concepts—often requires a lot of words. If you don't understand how the program works, get a pencil and a piece of paper. Then start at the top of the listing and work each program line out on paper. By playing computer and writing the results of each command down in black and white, you'll quickly see how the program works—without words getting in the way.

Danger Ahead!

When concatenating strings, it's easy to forget that you might need to separate the strings with some sort of delimiter. For example, when joining a first name to a last name, you'll end up with a string like GaryGilbert if you forget to add a space between the two names.

105

You can use the techniques you learned in this program to do all sorts of useful things in your other programs. You might, for example, want to write a program that counts the number of words in a document. To do this, you'd need to look for the spaces that separate words. You could also use string-handling techniques to take a group of words, extract them from a document, and sort them into alphabetical order. You're not ready to write these kinds of programs yet, of course, but by the time you get to the end of this book, you will be.

A Capital Idea

As you know, alphabetic characters in programs can be typed in either uppercase or lowercase letters. Sometimes you might want your strings to be displayed all in one case or the other. Most programming languages provide functions for switching from lowercase to uppercase or vice versa. To change all characters in a string to either uppercase or lowercase, use QBasic's handy UCASE$ (which stands for "uppercase") and LCASE$ (which stands for "lowercase") functions.

To see how UCASE$ and LCASE$ work, try the following revised version of the previous program:

```
CLS
PRINT "Enter a string containing three ";
PRINT "words separated by spaces."
INPUT string1$
pos1% = INSTR(string1$, " ")
word1$ = LEFT$(string1$, pos1% - 1)
pos2% = INSTR(pos1% + 1, string1$, " ")
word2$ = MID$(string1$, pos1% + 1, pos2% - pos1% - 1)
word3$ = RIGHT$(string1$, LEN(string1$) - pos2%)
PRINT
PRINT "Your three words are ";
PRINT "'"; word1$; ",' '"; word2$; ",' and '"; word3$; ".'"
word1$ = UCASE$(word1$): word2$ = UCASE$(word2$)
word3$ = UCASE$(word3$)
PRINT "Your three words in uppercase are ";
PRINT "'"; word1$; ",' '"; word2$; ",' and '"; word3$; ".'"
word1$ = LCASE$(word1$): word2$ = LCASE$(word2$)
word3$ = LCASE$(word3$)
PRINT "Your three words in lowercase are ";
PRINT "'"; word1$; ",' '"; word2$; ",' and '"; word3$; ".'"
```

When you run this program, be sure the three words in your string include both uppercase and lowercase letters. After you type the string, the program displays the three words the way you typed them, followed by the same words in uppercase and then lowercase letters. The following is the program's output:

```
Enter a string containing three words separated by spaces.
? Tom Dick Harry

Your three words are 'Tom,' 'Dick,' and 'Harry.'
Your three words in uppercase are 'TOM,' 'DICK,' and 'HARRY.'
Your three words in lowercase are 'tom,' 'dick,' and 'harry.'
```

One point of interest in the program is in the following line:

```
word1$ = UCASE$(word1$): word2$ = UCASE$(word2$)
```

This line demonstrates how you can save space by putting short statements together on a single line and simply separating the statements with a colon. However, as handy as this technique may be, you should not overuse it; it may make your programs hard to read. Place multiple statements on a single line only when they are short and closely related in some way.

Numbers to Strings

You probably remember that there's a big difference between numerical values and text strings, even if the text string contains numeric characters. Numerical values, such as the number 5 or the integer variable number%, can be used in mathematical operations. Strings, however, cannot. Luckily, most programming languages include a function for converting strings that contain digits to numerical values. In QBasic's case, the function VAL (which stands for "value") does this type of conversion. You can also change numerical values into strings with the STR$ function (STR stands for "string"). This is something you might want to do with the result of a calculation.

To convert a number string into a numerical value, use the VAL function:

```
number = VAL(string1$)
```

The variable string1$ is the string you want to convert to a numerical value. Keep in mind that VAL can convert only string characters that represent numbers: digits, decimal points, and minus signs. The following statement makes number! equal to 3.4:

```
number! = VAL("3.4Apples")
```

Because the characters that compose the word "Apples" are not numerical characters, VAL can do nothing with them and ignores them. If VAL cannot convert the string at all, as in the case of number! = VAL("Apples"), it returns a value of 0.

You should also know that VAL ignores spaces in strings and that it understands number strings in scientific notation form. Table 8.1 shows a summary of the results of the VAL function when it is used with different strings. (If you don't know about scientific notation, don't worry. Just be aware that the last example in the table shows a string using this number form.)

107

Table 8.1   VAL **Function Results**

Function Call	Result
VAL("34")	34
VAL("56.23")	56.23
VAL("23.6&HYG")	23.6
VAL("2 3 4")	234
VAL("-76")	–76
VAL("764,345")	764
VAL("0")	0
VAL("SJuHGd")	0
VAL("HFGYR345")	0
VAL("nine")	0
VAL("3.4D+4")	34000

Danger Ahead!

The fact that VAL returns a 0 when it cannot convert a string to a numerical value can lead to problems in your programs. Problems arise because 0 is a perfectly valid numerical value. For example, both of the expressions number = VAL("0") and number = VAL("Apples") return a value of 0; the value is really only valid, however, for the first example. Be aware of this possible ambiguous outcome when using VAL in your programs.

Converting strings to numerical values is only half the story. You may also need to go the other way and convert a numerical variable into a string. You might, for example, want to convert a numerical value to a string so you can add it to a text document. You can do this conversion by calling the STR$ function, which looks like this:

```
string1$ = STR$(number)
```

Here, number is the numerical value you want to change into string form. For example, the program statement

```
string1$ = STR$(34.45)
```

makes `string1$` equal to the string "34.45."

The following program demonstrates the VAL and STR$ functions:

```
CLS
INPUT "Enter the first number: ", number1$
INPUT "Enter the second number: ", number2$
number1 = VAL(number1$)
number2 = VAL(number2$)
number3 = number1 + number2
result$ = STR$(number3)
PRINT
PRINT "The result of summing ";
PRINT number1$; " and "; number2$;
PRINT " is"; result$; "."
```

Point of Interest

When the function STR$ converts a numerical value into a string, it always reserves a space for the value's sign. Strings created from positive numbers always have a leading space, and strings created from negative numbers always begin with a negative sign.

When you run the program, it requests two numbers that are input as strings. The strings are converted into numerical values so that they can be used in an addition operation. The result of this operation, a numerical value, is converted into a string before it's printed.

Specifically, the program first clears the screen and requests two string values from the user. These strings are stored in the string variables `number1$` and `number2$`. After the strings are entered, the VAL function converts them into numerical values that are stored in the variables `number1` and `number2`. The two values are then added, and the result is stored in the variable `number3`. Next, the STR$ function converts the numerical value in `number3` to the string `result$`. Finally, the last few lines print a message to the user, displaying the string in `result$`.

When you run the program, make sure the strings you enter are composed of valid number characters. Otherwise, the program may print incorrect results. The following lines show the program's output:

```
Enter the first number: 23.5
Enter the second number: 65.23

The result of summing 23.5 and 65.23 is 88.73.
```

Guess what? You're now a master of string handling. Cool, eh? The next step is a little mystery that goes by the name of "array." You'll solve that mystery in the next chapter.

The Least You Need to Know

➤ To join strings together, use the plus sign (+) operator.

➤ The equals sign (=) is used to assign strings to variables in the same way it's used to assign numerical values to variables.

➤ The number of characters contained in a string is the string's length.

➤ The LEN function returns the length of a string.

➤ Programmer's call a portion of a string a substring.

➤ The functions LEFT$, RIGHT$, and MID$ allow you to extract substrings from other strings.

➤ The function INSTR returns the position of a substring within a string.

➤ You can use the functions LCASE$ and UCASE$ to convert strings to lowercase and uppercase, respectively.

➤ The function VAL converts number strings to numerical values, whereas the function STR$ converts numerical values to strings.

Chapter 9

Fancier Places Numbers Live

In This Chapter

➤ Learning about arrays

➤ Processing arrays with loops

➤ Understanding numerical and string arrays

➤ Using DATA and READ to initialize arrays

Most of the variables you use in your programs will be simple values that you can access with a variable name. For example, when you need to keep track of a score in a game, you might use an integer variable called score. When the score changes, you place a new value in score, and when the game's over, you display the value of score so that the player can see how well he did.

Until now, you've learned about various types of numerical variables, including integers, long integers, single-precision variables, and double-precision variables. You also know about string variables, which can hold text. Now that you have a good understanding of these data types, it's time to explore one last data type, a handy data structure called an array. Think about that variable named score. What if you have four players in your game? Keeping track of those four scores is the perfect use for an array.

A Clever Solution to a Tricky Problem

Often in your programs, you'll want to store many values that are related in some way. Suppose you're writing that game I mentioned in this chapter's introduction, and you want to keep track of each player's score. One way to do this is to give each player a variable in your program, as shown in the following:

```
CLS
INPUT "Enter Chris's score: ", score1
INPUT "Enter Stephen's score: ", score2
INPUT "Enter Justin's score: ", score3
INPUT "Enter Caitlynn's score: ", score4
PRINT
PRINT "PLAYERPLAYERS' SCORES"
PRINT "----------------"
PRINT "Chris:"; score1
PRINT "Stephen:"; score2
PRINT "Justin:"; score3
PRINT "Caitlynn:"; score4
```

When you run the program, you're asked to enter scores for each of four players. After you enter these scores, they're displayed on the screen:

```
Enter Chris's score: 140
Enter Stephen's score: 154
Enter Justin's score: 207
Enter Caitlynn's score: 125

PLAYERPLAYERS' SCORES
----------------
Chris: 140
Stephen: 154
Justin: 207
Caitlynn: 125
```

Nothing too tricky going on here, right?

Now examine the listing. Remember when you learned to keep an eye out for repetitive program code? (Well, I wouldn't suggest actually keeping an eye out. Eyeballs tend to dry out quickly and are easily knocked off your desk.) How about all those INPUT statements in the program? The only real difference between them is the name of the variable used to store the input value. If you could find some way to make a loop out of this code, you'd need only one INPUT line to input all the data and only one PRINT line to display the averages for all four players. You could, in fact, use a FOR...NEXT loop that counts from 1 to 4.

But how can you use a loop when you're stuck with four different variables? The answer is an array. An *array* is a variable that can hold more than one value. When you first studied variables, you learned that a variable is like a box in memory that holds a single value. Now, if you take a bunch of these boxes and put them together, what do you have? (No, the answer isn't "a bunch of variables smooshed together.") You'd have an array. For example, to store the scores for your four players, you'd need an array that can hold four values. You could call this array `scores`. You could also call this array `These.are.the.players.scores`, but who wants to do all that typing?

Now you have an array called `scores` that can hold four player scores, but how can you retrieve each individual score from the array? You could run out on your front lawn in a tutu, wave rooster feathers over your head, and shout praises to the gods of computing. However, an easier way—and one that doesn't amuse the neighbors quite so much—is to add something called a subscript to the array's name.

A *subscript* is a number that identifies the box in which an array value is stored. For example, to refer to the first score in your `scores` array, you'd write `scores(1)`. The subscript is the number in parentheses. In this case, you're referring to the first average in the array. To refer to the second average, you'd write `scores(2)`. The third and fourth averages are `scores(3)` and `scores(4)`, respectively. Get the idea?

If you're a little confused, look at Figure 9.1, which shows how the `scores()` array might look in memory. In this case, the four scores are 145, 192, 160, and 203. The value of `scores(1)` is 145, the value of `scores(2)` is 192, the value of `scores(3)` is 160, and the value of `scores(4)` is 203.

Programmer Lingo

An **array** is a type of variable that can hold many values rather than just one. It is actually a section of your computer's memory that contains enough room to store the number of values you specify.

Programmer Lingo

A **subscript** (also called an *index*) is the number in parentheses after an array's name. The subscript identifies which value in the array you want to access. For example, in the array name `numbers%(10)`, the subscript is 10. It refers to the tenth value stored in the array `numbers%()`.

score%(1)	score%(2)	score%(3)	score%(4)
145	192	160	203

Figure 9.1

An array in memory.

113

The Old Indirect Approach

As you've learned, most numerical literals in a QBasic program can be replaced by numerical variables. Suppose, then, you were to use the variable x as the subscript for the array scores(). Then, if the value of x were 2, the value of scores(x) would be 192. If the value of x were 4, the value of scores(x) would be 203.

Now take one last gigantic intuitive leap (c'mon, you can do it) and think about using your subscript variable x as both the control variable in a FOR...NEXT loop and the subscript for the scores() array. If you use a FOR...NEXT loop that counts from 1 to 4, you can use a single INPUT line to get all four players' averages. The following program shows how this is done:

```
CLS
DIM scores%(4)

FOR x = 1 TO 4
  INPUT "Enter player's score: ", scores(%x)
NEXT x

PRINT
FOR x = 1 TO 4
  PRINT "Score for player"; x; ": "; scores(%x)
NEXT x
```

Here is the program's output:

```
Enter player's score: 146
Enter player's score: 192
Enter player's score: 156
Enter player's score: 137

Score for player 1 :   146
Score for player 2 :   192
Score for player 3 :   156
Score for player 4 :   137
```

Programmer Lingo

The little memory boxes that make up an array are called **elements of the array.** For example, in an array named numbers%(), numbers%(1) is the first element of the array, numbers%(2) is the second element, and so on.

At the top of the program, you'll see a strange new keyword, DIM. DIM is short for "dimension" and is used to tell QBasic how much room in memory you need for your array. In this program, you've "dimensioned" the array as scores%(4), which tells QBasic that you need to store four integers in this array.

Do you understand how the program works? In the first FOR...NEXT loop, the variable x starts with a value of 1. The value retrieved by the INPUT statement is stored in scores%(x), which means that when x equals 1, the value is stored in scores%(1). The next time through the loop, x equals 2, so the value retrieved by the INPUT statement is stored in scores%(2). This continues until x has incremented from 1 to 4, becomes 5, and the FOR…NEXT loop ends. The second FOR…NEXT loop works similarly, incrementing x from 1 to 4 and printing the contents of the array one element at a time.

All arrays actually have what's called a "zeroth" element. That is, you can actually

Danger Ahead!

When you dimension your arrays, make sure you have enough room for the data you need to store. Once you dimension an array, QBasic will not allow you to store or retrieve values beyond the end of the array. For example, if you dimension an array as numbers%(10) and then try to access numbers%(11), your program will come to a crashing halt and give you a subscript-out-of-range error. Don't make your arrays bigger than they need to be, however, because this wastes your computer's memory.

start storing data in element 0 of an array. This means that an array that's been dimensioned as numbers%(2) has three elements: numbers%(0), numbers%(1), and numbers%(2). However, most QBasic programmers ignore the zeroth element of an array because it's confusing to think of element 0 as being the first element.

Yet Another Fantabulous Example of Programming Prowess

The previous program shows how handy arrays can be, but there's something missing from the program. First, there's no built-in Space Invaders game, so using this program for long periods of time is not only not exciting but also downright boring. More to the point, though, the players' names are missing. In this version of the program, you've resorted to using a player number rather than each player's name. You can get around this problem easily by creating an array to hold strings. (You can get over the Space Invaders problem by taking a Nintendo break.) The following program shows how this is done:

```
CLS
DIM scores%(4), name$(4)
```

```
FOR x = 1 TO 4
  INPUT "Enter player's name: ", name$(x)
  INPUT "Enter player's score: ", scores%(x)
NEXT x

PRINT
PRINT "PLAYERS' SCORES"
PRINT "---------------"
FOR x = 1 TO 4
  PRINT "Score for "; name$(x); ": "; scores%(x)
NEXT x
```

The program's output looks like this:

```
Enter player's name: Chris
Enter player's score: 156
Enter player's name: Stephen
Enter player's score: 176
Enter player's name: Justin
Enter player's score: 135
Enter player's name: Caitlynn
Enter player's score: 185

PLAYERS' SCORES
----------------
Score for Chris:  156
Score for Stephen:  176
Score for Justin:  135
Score for Caitlynn:  185
```

When you run this program, you're asked to enter not only the players' scores but also their names. The names are stored in a string array, and the scores are stored in an integer array. Because both arrays used the same subscript value for each player's name and score, the first name in the string array matches with the first score in the integer array, the second name matches with the second score, and so on. It's then a simple matter to use another loop to print out the names and scores.

Starting Off Right

Your game-scores program still isn't as efficient as it could be. Why, for example, should you have to enter the name of each player every time you run the program? Do you really need that much typing practice? There must be some way to store data in your programs without having to enter it from the keyboard. You could get a grease pencil, write the players' names on your computer's screen, and hope they sink in. A better (and more dependable) method is to use QBasic's DATA and READ statements.

Data is information that you manipulate or store in your program. When you want to place data into your program without having to input it manually, you can use a DATA statement. For example, the statement DATA 1,5,65,10 makes the four integers 1, 5, 65, and 10 part of your program's data. This data is saved along with the rest of your program lines. Reading data means moving the data from one place to another, usually from a DATA statement into a variable of some kind. To read data from a DATA statement, you use the READ command. For example, the statement READ x% reads the first value in a DATA statement into the variable x.

When you start a program line with the keyword DATA, QBasic knows that the values that follow should be stored with the program so that each time you run the program, that data is available for your use. To store the names of your players, you'd use the following line:

```
DATA Chris,Stephen,Justin,Caitlynn
```

Notice the commas between the names. This is how QBasic separates one piece of data from another.

Now that you have a way of storing your players' names along with the program, how can you get those names into your string array? Easy! By using QBasic's READ command. To read the first name, you might write the following:

```
READ name$(1)
```

This command takes the next value from the program's DATA statements and stuffs it into name$(1). In the DATA statement just shown, name$(1) becomes Chris. The data pointer, which always points to the next data item in the list, is then moved to Stephen. The next READ statement then reads Stephen, the data pointer is moved to Justin, and so on. When all the data items have been read, the data list is empty—until the program runs again and the cycle is repeated. (By the way, data in your program can be placed in more than one DATA statement. In fact, you can have as many DATA statements as you like.)

The following program shows how the DATA and READ statements work. It's important that you understand this program because this is the way arrays are often initialized.

```
CLS
DIM scores%(4), name$(4)

FOR x = 1 TO 4
  READ name$(x)
  PRINT "What's "; name$(x); "'s score";
  INPUT scores%(x)
NEXT x
```

117

```
PRINT
PRINT "PLAYERS' SCORES"
PRINT "-----------------"
FOR x = 1 TO 4
  PRINT "Score for "; name$(x); ": "; scores%(x)
NEXT x

DATA Chris,Stephen,Justin,Caitlynn
```

The program produces the following output:

```
What's Chris's score? 165
What's Stephen's score? 134
What's Justin's score? 187
What's Caitlynn's score? 174

PLAYERS' SCORES
-----------------
Average for Chris:   165
Average for Stephen:   134
Average for Justin:   187
Average for Caitlynn:   174
```

Cool Stuff

You don't have to use DATA and READ statements to initialize arrays. You can also initialize arrays by using assignment statements, just as with regular variables. For example, the line

```
FOR x = 1 to 10: num%(x) = 0: NEXT x
```

initializes to 0 every element of the array num%() (assuming, of course, that the array was dimensioned as num%(10)).

When you run the new version of the program, you're no longer asked to enter each player's name. Instead, the names are read by the program, using the data following the DATA statement. Each time through the first FOR…NEXT loop, a player's name is read from the data, and you're asked to provide that player's score. By the end of the loop, all four players' names and averages have been placed in their respective arrays.

You can use DATA and READ statements with any kind of data. You can even mix different types of data on a single DATA line. You just have to be sure you read each data item into the right variable type. You couldn't, for example, read a string into a numerical variable. To see how this works, suppose you now want to include each player's score and name in the program's data. The following is the game-score program with this change installed:

Cool Stuff

It doesn't matter where in your program you place your DATA statements. QBasic always starts reading from the DATA statement closest to the top of the program, wherever it happens to be. However, many programmers place their DATA statements at the end of their programs to keep them out of the way.

```
CLS
DIM scores%(4), name$(4)

FOR x = 1 TO 4
  READ name$(x)
  READ scores%(x)
NEXT x

PRINT
PRINT "PLAYERS' SCORES"
PRINT "-----------------"
FOR x = 1 TO 4
  PRINT "Score for "; name$(x); ":"; scores%(x)
NEXT x

DATA Chris,145,Stephen,192,Justin,160,Caitlynn,203
```

Here is this program's output:

```
PLAYERS' SCORES
-----------------
Score for Chris: 145
Score for Stephen: 192
Score for Justin: 160
Score for Caitlynn: 203
```

This version of the program is almost the same as the previous one. The main difference is that you no longer need to enter data from the keyboard. All the data is contained in the program's DATA statement. If a player's score changes, you need to change only the appropriate entry in the DATA statement.

The Least You Need to Know

➤ When you have many related values that you want to store under a single variable name, use an array.

➤ The number within parentheses after an array is the array's subscript, which identifies each element of the array.

➤ To process an array in a loop, you can use the loop-control variable as the array's subscript.

➤ The QBasic DIM statement enables you to set the size of an array.

➤ QBasic's DATA statement allows you to store various types of data within your programs. The READ statement reads data from a DATA statement and places it in the appropriate variables.

Fiddling with Files

To state the obvious, it does no good to edit a document and then have no way to save your changes and load them at a later time. This is why computer makers came up with disk drives and other forms of long-lasting storage. In order to access disk drives, a programming language must have commands that tell the computer what data to save and how to save it. So, if you've been trying to save data from your QBasic programs by copying the screen onto paper with a pencil, you're going to love this chapter!

Three Steps to Access a File

Simple file handling is actually an easy process once you get the hang of it. There are, however, three steps you need to perform to be sure your program's data gets properly tucked away in that binary home called a file:

1. Open the file.
2. Send data to the file or read data from the file.
3. Close the file.

In the following sections, you'll cover each of these steps in detail.

Opening a File

Probably the most complicated part of managing file I/O (input/output, remember?) is opening the file in the proper mode. You see, not only can files be used to save and load data, they also can be used to save and load specific kinds of data in specific ways. For example, there's a big difference between opening a file to read a line of text and opening a file to read a database record, even though a file must be opened in both cases. Specifically, you can open a file in one of five different ways, called modes. These modes are as follows:

➤ Append

➤ Input

➤ Output

➤ Binary

➤ Random-access

Before you reach for the Valium, let me assure you that these modes are not as confusing as they may seem to be. First, because you're just starting out, you can forget about binary and random-access files. You'll leave those puppies to a more advanced book that covers things like databases, records, and binary files. Feeling better already, right?

The remaining modes are easy to understand. To prove that claim, you're about to open a file in output mode, which makes good sense. You can't, after all, load data from a file until you've saved data to the file. Here is the QBasic statement that creates and opens a file in output mode:

```
OPEN "c:\MyFile.dat" FOR OUTPUT AS #1
```

The keyword OPEN tells QBasic that you're about to open a file. (Program lines such as Open My Mail really annoy QBasic.) The string that follows the OPEN keyword is the path and name of the file you want to open. In this case, the file is called MyFile.dat and is located in the root directory of drive C.

Now comes the part that determines the file mode. See the FOR OUTPUT part? This tells QBasic that you want to open the file in the output mode. This mode enables a program to save data to the disk file. In this case, the file is MyFile.dat. If the file doesn't already exist, QBasic creates it. If the file does exist, QBasic gets the file ready to accept output from your program, which includes erasing the current contents of the file.

Examine that last sentence carefully! What you do need to notice is the phrase "which includes erasing the current contents of the file." To state the point again, *if you use the output mode to open an existing file, QBasic erases the previous contents of the file.* Sorry. I didn't mean to get all excited, but some things have to be clearly understood, you know?

That's all there is to opening a file, except for that mysterious AS #1 tacked on the end of the line. Every time your program opens a file, the program needs a way to refer to the file. The same way your friends may refer to you as Bill, Carol, Al, or "Hey, freak!" your QBasic program must refer to the open file with a number. In this case, that number is 1. You could try writing OPEN "C:\MyFile.dat" FOR OUTPUT AS Carol, but it's unlikely to work and will annoy Al.

Saving Data to the File

Your file is now open, sitting there patiently on your disk drive like a kitten waiting for a scratch behind the ears. The file, however, will sit there waiting patiently for attention long after the kitten has wandered away in boredom. I wouldn't suggest that you try to scratch your file behind the ears, but it might be a good idea at this point to put some data into the file, something you can do with a QBasic command like this:

```
PRINT #1, "This is a test"
```

As you undoubtedly realize, the keyword PRINT tells QBasic that you want to print data to a file. QBasic knows you're printing to a file rather than to the screen, thanks to the #1 after the PRINT keyword. The number is the same number the program used to open the file. Remember the AS #1 part of the OPEN statement? That's the culprit.

After the file number, you place a comma and then follow that with the data you want to save to the file. In this case, the data is the string "This is a test". After QBasic has performed this command, your file will contain the string, no fuss or muss.

Cool Stuff

When you're typing program lines, make sure you get all the punctuation right. Leaving out something as simple as a comma can bring your program to a crashing halt. For example, don't forget the comma in the PRINT statement, between the file number and the data to save.

Closing the File

When you put your jewelry in a safe, you finish the task by closing the safe door. A file and its data are similar. After you place data into the file, you must close the file;

otherwise, you may wind up losing data. Data isn't usually the target of jewel thieves, of course, but it can still disappear mysteriously. Take it from someone who's lost enough data to fill an encyclopedia.

To close a file, you call on the ever-trusty CLOSE statement, like this:

```
CLOSE #1
```

You've probably already figured out that the number after the CLOSE keyword is the same number that the program gave the file when it opened it with the OPEN statement.

Programmer Lingo

Closing files in a QBasic program (and most programs written in other languages as well) is important because not all the data you've sent to the file has necessarily arrived there before you close the file. The reason for this anomaly is something called **buffering.** Because disk drives are so slow compared to computer memory, QBasic doesn't actually send data directly to the disk file. Instead, it saves up the data in your computer's memory until it has enough data to be worth taking the time to access the disk drive. The CLOSE statement tells QBasic not only to close the file but also to be sure to send all the data from the buffer first.

Although it's important to close your files after accessing them, the truth is that if you don't, QBasic will. However, QBasic closes all open files only when the program ends normally. This means that leaving file closing up to QBasic is dangerous. If something happens and the program doesn't end normally, QBasic can't close the file for you, and you may lose data.

Trying It Out

It's time now to see all this file stuff put to work. To do this, start a new QBasic project and type the following lines, as shown in Figure 10.1.

```
DIM msg AS STRING
CLS
msg = "This is a test."
```

```
PRINT "Opening file..."
OPEN "c:\MyFile.dat" FOR OUTPUT AS #1
PRINT "Saving text..."
PRINT #1, msg
PRINT "Closing file..."
CLOSE #1
PRINT "File saved."
PRINT
```

Figure 10.1

Your finished program should look like this.

After typing the lines, save your work and run the program. When you do, the application's main window appears, as shown in Figure 10.2.

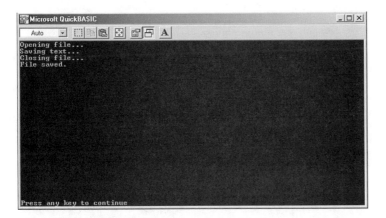

Figure 10.2

This application saves a string to a file.

Here's what's going on. The first line of the program declares a string variable:

```
DIM msg AS STRING
```

After declaring the variable, the program sets the variable to the text that'll be written to the file:

```
msg = "This is a test."
```

Next comes the old familiar OPEN statement (preceded by a PRINT statement), which opens the file for output:

```
PRINT "Opening file..."
OPEN "c:\MyFile.dat" FOR OUTPUT AS #1
```

With the file open, the program can save the contents of the variable data to the file:

```
PRINT "Saving text..."
PRINT #1, msg
```

Finally, the program closes the file and tells the user that the text was saved:

```
PRINT "Closing file..."
CLOSE #1
PRINT "File saved."
```

Loading Data from a File

Your file now has data in it. Data in a file, however, is about as useful as a hairdryer to a toad if you have no way of getting the data out again. That's where the INPUT statement comes in handy. Luckily, you're about to see how it works.

Here are new program lines that do the deed. Type these program lines right after the ones you just typed for the previous example, as shown in Figure 10.3.

```
DIM msg2 AS STRING
PRINT "Opening file..."
OPEN "c:\MyFile.dat" FOR INPUT AS #1
PRINT "Reading file..."
INPUT #1, msg2
PRINT "Closing file..."
CLOSE #1
PRINT "Your text: ";
PRINT msg2
PRINT
```

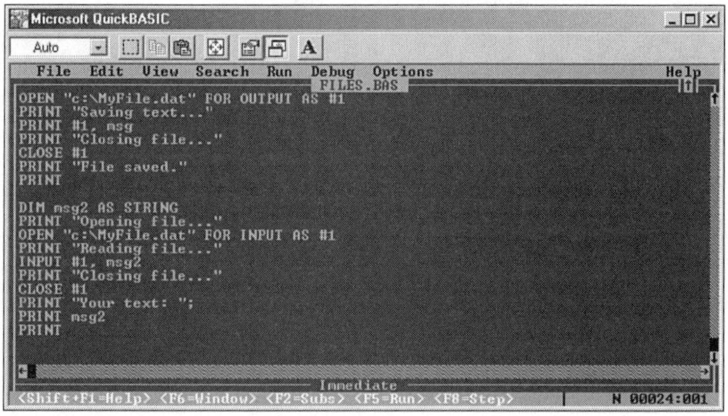

Figure 10.3

The program, after you add the new lines.

You're now ready to try the program again. Save your work and run the program. You'll see the program's window, as shown in Figure 10.4.

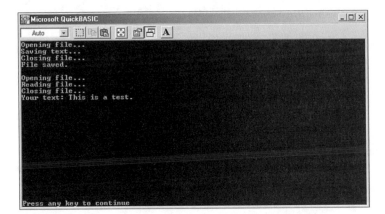

Figure 10.4

Now the program can load text, too.

How do these new program lines work? The first line declares another string variable:

```
DIM msg2 AS STRING
```

After declaring the variable, the program opens the file for input:

```
PRINT "Opening file..."
OPEN "c:\MyFile.dat" FOR INPUT AS #1
```

With the file open, the program can load the text from the file and into the string variable data:

```
PRINT "Reading file..."
INPUT #1, msg2
```

Finally, the program closes the file and displays the loaded text on the screen:

```
PRINT "Closing file..."
CLOSE #1
PRINT "Your text: ";
PRINT msg2
```

Notice that the INPUT statement looks a lot like the PRINT statement. That is, the file number, a comma, and the variable name follow the INPUT keyword. In this case, though, the variable receives the data rather than holding the data that will go to the file.

Appending Data to a File

Every time you run the preceding program and it opens the MyFile.dat file for output, the previous contents of the file get erased like a teacher's chalkboard at the end of

127

the day. This is all fine and dandy if you want to start a new file, but what if you want to add something to the file? Easy! You open the file in append mode.

To check this out, add the following new lines to your program:

```
PRINT "Opening file..."
OPEN "C:\MyFile.dat" FOR APPEND AS #1
PRINT "Appending to file..."
PRINT #1, "This is another test."
PRINT "Closing file..."
CLOSE #1
PRINT "File appended."
PRINT
```

These program lines are almost exactly like the first ones you added to this program, except they open the file in append mode rather than in output mode, and they save a string literal to the file rather than the contents of a string variable.

Because your file will have more than one line of text in it after the append, the program needs a different way to input data from the file. Specifically, the program needs to keep loading text strings until it gets to the end of the file. To do this, add the following lines to the end of the program:

```
DIM msg3 AS STRING
PRINT "Opening file..."
OPEN "C:\MyFile.dat" FOR INPUT AS #1
PRINT "Reading lines from the file..."
DO WHILE NOT EOF(1)
    INPUT #1, msg3
    PRINT "Text Line: ";
    PRINT msg3
LOOP
PRINT "Closing file..."
CLOSE #1
```

Now save your work and run the program. When you do, you see the screen shown in Figure 10.5.

How does the program know when it's reached the end of the file? The secret to this little mystery lies in the DO WHILE loop, the first line of which looks like this:

```
DO WHILE NOT EOF(1)
```

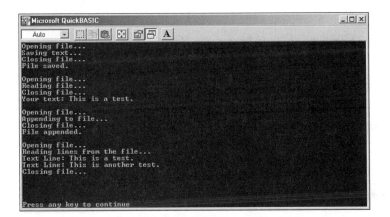

Figure 10.5

The program now reads multiple lines of text from a file.

You already know what a DO WHILE loop is, and you know what the NOT operator does, but what is that EOF(1)? EOF is a function that returns the value TRUE when the file is at the end and returns FALSE if the file is not at the end. The number in the parentheses is the number assigned to the file in the OPEN statement. Basically (no pun intended), the first line of the DO WHILE loop can be translated into English as "Do while file #1 is not at the end of the file."

Inside the loop, the program loads and displays a line of text:

```
INPUT #1, msg3
PRINT "Text Line: ";
PRINT msg3
```

Then the LOOP keyword sends QBasic back to the beginning of the loop, where the function EOF again checks for the end of the file. (Guess what EOF stands for?) If the program hasn't reached the end of the file yet, the loop loads another line of text; otherwise, the loops ends.

Cool Stuff

In this chapter, you've used files only to save text data. However, you can use the file-handling techniques you've learned to save most kinds of data to a file, including integers and floating-point values. For example, if you have an integer variable called myInt, you can save it to an open file with a line like Print #1, myInt.

129

The Least You Need to Know

➤ Accessing a file requires three steps: opening the file, saving or loading data to or from the file, and closing the file.

➤ The OPEN statement opens a file in one of five modes—append, binary, input, output, and random access. Currently, you don't need to know about binary and random-access files; they're for more advanced programmers.

➤ The PRINT # statement stores data in an open file.

➤ The INPUT # statement loads data from an open file.

➤ The CLOSE statement finalizes operations on a file and closes it to further access.

➤ Opening a file for output creates the file if it doesn't exist or opens and erases the file if it does exist.

➤ To read data from an existing file, you must open the file for input.

➤ To add data to the end of a file, use the append file mode.

➤ The EOF function returns TRUE when the program has reached the end of a file and FALSE if the program has not reached the end of the file.

Part 4
Advanced Programming

There are many things you can do with a computer program to make programming more convenient and spice up your programs once you have them running. For example, in this part of the book, you learn how to handle errors and how to break your program down into more manageable chunks known as functions and subroutines. Just for the fun of it, you'll also learn how to make computer sounds and how to draw simple graphics.

Chapter 11

Whoops! What Now?

In This Chapter

➤ Understanding runtime errors

➤ Using the ON ERROR statement

➤ Dealing with specific types of errors

➤ Displaying error messages

In a perfect world, everything you tried to do with your computer would work out exactly as you planned it. When you wanted to open a file, the file would always be on the disk. When you wanted to print a document, there would always be paper in the printer.

Unfortunately, we don't live in a perfect world. I know this because I never win the lottery, I've never been invited to lunch by Catherine Zeta-Jones, and I always—*always*—find out that I'm out of clean socks when I'm in a rush to get out the door.

Because of our less-than-perfect world, an important part of programming is learning what to do about errors when they threaten to crash your magnum opus of a program. Guess what you'll learn about in this chapter?

Two General Kinds of Errors

When writing programs, you run into two general types of errors: forgetting to refill your jar of gummy bears and not videotaping that *Star Trek* episode you never saw before. Although these errors are too horrible to even imagine, believe it or not, there are actually two other kinds of errors that are more relevant to this discussion:

➤ Logic errors
➤ Runtime errors

Logic errors are mistakes that cause the program to do something other than what you want. You make this kind of mistake while writing the program. For example, if you write x = y + z and what you really needed to write was x = y * z, you've created a logic error, by which I mean an error caused by your logic being wrong.

Runtime errors, on the other hand, which are the subject of this wonderful piece of writing that you're reading now, happen not when you're writing the program but rather when someone is running it. Suppose your program needs to load a specific data file and, for some reason—probably because you partied too hard on the night before you created the program's installation—that file is missing. When your program tries to open the file, it generates a runtime error.

The big problem with runtime errors, besides the fact that they clue everyone in to what a party animal you are, is that if you don't handle them in your program, the program comes to a screeching halt. The short form of "comes to a screeching halt" is "crashes," a word that strikes fear into the hearts of programmers and computer users everywhere.

The Art of Predicting the Future

If you think about it a minute, you'll come to the conclusion that to deal with runtime errors, you have to be able to see into the future. This is because you have to know what errors will happen before they happen.

The truth is that to handle runtime errors, you don't need to *know* what will happen. You only need to know what *might* happen. For example, when your program is about to open a file, you might think to yourself, "Well, what if the file isn't there?" If there's a chance of that happening (and because this isn't a perfect world, there's *always* a chance of that happening), you need to do something about the error before it crashes your program.

Every programming language has a way to handle these kinds of errors. The C++ language, for example, uses something called try and catch blocks. In QBasic, you handle runtime errors by using something known to all those people who know stuff that you didn't know until you started reading this book ... ahem ... as the ON ERROR statement.

The ON ERROR statement actually predicts the future for you. It does this by grabbing every single runtime error that occurs, whether that error is caused by a missing file, by dividing a number by 0, or by entering the wrong data at the keyboard because your cat just jumped into your lap with a dead mouse in its mouth and cruddy cat litter all over its paws. Once the ON ERROR statement catches an error, it's up to you and your program to figure out what to do with it.

Putting On the Catcher's Mitt

Catching an error is easy. Just add an ON ERROR statement before your program is about to do something risky. Knowing what to do with the error is a little trickier, however, and depends completely on your program and the type of error with which your program has been presented. But let's not put on the icing before baking the cake, eh?

Before you need to worry about what to do with an error, you have to catch one. Professional programmers use very expensive, high-tech nets and hooks for this task. This is because hotshot programmers like a challenge, and runtime errors—due to their many legs and their tendency to skitter rapidly from one computer to another— are glad to provide that challenge. You, however, are going to use a safer method to catch runtime errors. You may remember that I recently mentioned the ON ERROR statement. Let's see how it works.

First, start a new QBasic program and type the following lines:

```
DIM msg2 AS STRING
CLS
PRINT "Opening file..."
OPEN "c:\text.dat" FOR INPUT AS #1
PRINT "Reading file..."
INPUT #1, msg2
PRINT "Closing file..."
CLOSE #1
PRINT "Your text: ";
PRINT msg2
PRINT
```

This small program is similar to part of one you wrote in Chapter 10, "Fiddling with Files," except that the name of the file to open has been changed to text.dat. (I'm assuming that you have no file of this name on your C: drive. If you do, move it somewhere else for the moment.) Run this program, and you'll get the error shown in Figure 11.1.

When your program user sees an error like this, he's likely to freak out—and rightly so. It's your job as programmer to see that the user never gets confronted with errors he can do nothing about. In this case, the user has no idea what file is missing.

When you dismiss the error box, QBasic highlights the line on which the error occurred, as you can see in Figure 11.2.

Figure 11.1

A file-not-found runtime error.

Figure 11.2

The highlighted error line.

The following is the same program with some helpful changes. To create this program from your existing one, add the following first line (the ON ERROR line) and all the lines from the first END statement to the last END statement:

```
ON ERROR GOTO FileError
DIM msg2 AS STRING
CLS
PRINT "Opening file..."
OPEN "c:\text.dat" FOR INPUT AS #1
PRINT "Reading file..."
INPUT #1, msg2
PRINT "Closing file..."
CLOSE #1
PRINT "Your text: ";
PRINT msg2
PRINT
END
FileError:
PRINT "Please place the text.dat file"
PRINT "in the C: root directory and"
PRINT "then rerun the program."
END
```

After you finish typing, save your work and run the program. When you do, you see the screen shown in Figure 11.3.

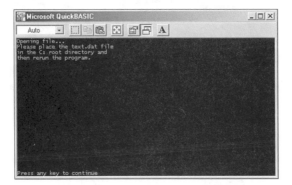

Figure 11.3

The program now uses error trapping.

Now the user doesn't get a rude runtime error from QBasic. Instead, he gets a gentle reminder from you that a file needs to be placed on this disk so that the program can find it.

Specifically what happens is this: The first line in the program tells QBasic that if a runtime error occurs, program execution should jump to the label FileError. (By the way, this is one of the few legitimate uses for the GOTO command in a QBasic program.) If you count up five lines from the end of the program, you'll see this label. When the program tries to open the nonexistent file, a runtime error occurs, and QBasic jumps to the FileError label, where the program prints a message to the user and then ends.

If the user runs the program and the file is where it should be, on the other hand, the file opens and the program runs normally. Eventually (you know, like in a thousandth of a second), the program gets to the END statement right before the FileError label and ends. If that END statement weren't there, the program would continue past the FileError label, printing the error message there. Because there really wasn't an error, you don't want this to happen.

To see that the program runs fine when it finds the file, load Notepad and type the text **This is a test.** Save the file to your C:\ *root directory* under the name text.dat. Then run the program again. When you do, you see the screen shown in Figure 11.4.

Cool Stuff

To turn off error trapping so that QBasic no longer jumps to a label when a runtime error occurs, add the line ON ERROR GOTO 0 (that's a zero, not the letter "O") to your program at the point where you want to turn error trapping off. If you don't turn error trapping off, any runtime error that occurs anywhere in the program will cause QBasic to jump to the label specified in the last ON ERROR statement QBasic encountered. This can lead to confusing results.

137

Figure 11.4

The program still uses error trapping.

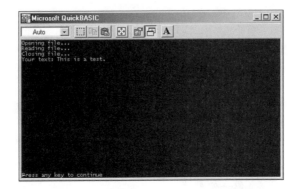

Programmer Lingo

A drive's **root directory** is the part of the drive that is not inside any other folders. In other words, when you look at drive C: with Windows Explorer and you're not inside a folder on drive C:, you see all the folders and files in the C:\ root directory.

Which Error Is Which?

Next, let's build up the program a little more, as shown in the following code. To change the preceding program to this one, add the seventh and ninth line shown here:

```
CLS
ON ERROR GOTO FileError
DIM msg2 AS STRING
PRINT "Opening file..."
OPEN "c:\text.dat" FOR INPUT AS #1
PRINT "Reading file..."
FOR x = 1 TO 10
  INPUT #1, msg2
NEXT x
PRINT "Closing file..."
CLOSE #1
PRINT "Your text: ";
PRINT msg2
PRINT
END
```

138

```
FileError:
PRINT "Please place the text.dat file"
PRINT "in the C: root directory and"
PRINT "then rerun the program."
END
```

The program now wants to read 10 lines of text from the file, but you only have one line in the file. What do you think will happen? Run the program and see. When you do, you see the screen shown in Figure 11.5.

Figure 11.5

Trying to read 10 lines of text.

Whoops! Do you see the problem here? When the program tries to read more text than is available in the file, it generates a runtime error. The error causes QBasic to jump to the FileError line, but the error message there is only good for when the file is missing, and is confusing in this case. What to do!

What you do is check and see what kind of error occurred and then print an appropriate error message. QBasic keeps around a couple of special variables, one of which holds just the info you need. This variable is called Err, and it contains a number code for the last runtime error that occurred. Table 11.1 shows the many values Err can have.

Table 11.1   QBasic Runtime Error Codes

Code	Description
1	NEXT without FOR
2	Syntax error
3	RETURN without GOSUB
4	Out of DATA
5	Illegal function call
6	Overflow
7	Out of memory

continues

Table 11.1   QBasic Runtime Error Codes   (continued)

Code	Description
8	Label not defined
9	Subscript out of range
10	Duplicate definition
11	Division by zero
12	Illegal in direct mode
13	Type mismatch
14	Out of string space
16	String formula too complex
17	Cannot continue
18	Function not defined
19	No RESUME
20	RESUME without error
24	Device timeout
25	Device fault
26	FOR without NEXT
27	Out of paper
29	WHILE without WEND
30	WEND without WHILE
33	Duplicate label
35	Subprogram not defined
37	Argument-count mismatch
38	Array not defined
40	Variable required
50	FIELD overflow
51	Internal error
52	Bad filename or number
53	File not found
54	Bad file mode
55	File already open
56	FIELD statement active
57	Device I/O error
58	File already exists
59	Bad record length
61	Disk full
62	Input past end of file
63	Bad record number

Code	Description
64	Bad file name
67	Too many files
68	Device unavailable
69	Communication-buffer overflow
70	Permission denied
71	Disk not ready
72	Disk-media error
73	Feature unavailable
74	Rename across disks
75	Path/file access error
76	Path not found

To see how to use the Err variable, it's time to add more code to your burgeoning program. The following is the complete program. To create this program from the preceding one, simply update the lines between the FileError label and the END statement:

```
CLS
ON ERROR GOTO FileError
DIM msg2 AS STRING
PRINT "Opening file..."
OPEN "c:\text.dat" FOR INPUT AS #1
PRINT "Reading file..."
FOR x = 1 TO 10
  INPUT #1, msg2
NEXT x
PRINT "Closing file..."
CLOSE #1
PRINT "Your text: ";
PRINT msg2
PRINT
END
FileError:
IF ERR = 53 THEN
  PRINT "Please place the text.dat file"
  PRINT "in the C: root directory and"
  PRINT "then rerun the program."
ELSEIF ERR = 62 THEN
  PRINT "The text.dat file contains fewer"
  PRINT "lines than expected by the program."
ELSE
  PRINT "A fatal error has occurred."
```

```
   PRINT "Please reinstall the program"
   PRINT "from scratch."
END IF
END
```

When you've finished typing, save your work and run the program. When you do, you see the screen shown in Figure 11.6.

Figure 11.6

Displaying the right error message.

Now, when any runtime error occurs, the program checks whether it's a file-not-found error (53) or an end-of-file error (62). If an error occurred other than these two, the program prints a default message, telling the user to reinstall the program.

As you can tell from Table 11.1, handling runtime errors can be a meticulous process. In fact, in professional applications, error-handling code is a big chunk of the entire program. Still, if you watch out for the errors your program may generate, you're going to have a much happier set of users.

The Least You Need to Know

➤ When writing programs, you run into two general types of errors: logic errors and runtime errors.

➤ Logic errors are mistakes you make when writing a program, and they cause the program to do something other than what you want.

➤ Runtime errors happen not when you're writing the program but when someone is running it.

➤ Every programming language has a way to handle runtime errors.

➤ In QBasic, you handle runtime errors by using the ON ERROR statement.

➤ QBasic's Err variable contains a number code for the last runtime error that occurred.

Chapter 12

Your Computer As Van Gogh

In This Chapter

➤ Understanding screen resolution and pixels

➤ Drawing shapes with dots

➤ Using the QBasic LINE command

➤ Using the QBasic CIRCLE command

Not all that long ago, the only thing a computer monitor could display was text. The idea that someday we'd be able to use our computers to display graphics, let alone photographic-quality images, was still in the realm of science fiction. But that reality is here. Of course, drawing the graphics for a 3D game or loading and displaying a photograph requires very advanced programming skills. Still, QBasic features enough graphics commands to give you a taste of what it's like to draw with your computer.

I Think I'm Seeing Spots!

Before you can become a computer artist, you have to understand one simple fact. All computer images are made of hundreds of rows and columns of little dots known as *pixels*. How many dots you can fit on your screen depends on your current screen resolution. For example, your computer is most likely (but not necessarily) set to a screen resolution of 800×600. This means your computer screen displays 800 dots horizontally (800 rows) and 600 dots vertically (600 columns). Everything you see on the screen is the result of these 480,000 dots being set to different colors.

Programmer Lingo

A **pixel** is the smallest dot that can be displayed on your computer's screen. The size of a pixel varies with the screen resolution to which your system is set.

To see how this affects the graphics on your computer screen, let's try an experiment. Close all open windows (on your computer's screen, dummy, not in your house!) and then right-click on the Windows desktop. When you do, a menu pops up, from which you should select the Properties command. A dialog box appears. Figure 12.1 shows what it looks like.

Next, click the dialog box's Settings tab. You'll see a different view of the same dialog box, as shown in Figure 12.2.

Near the bottom right of the Settings page, you'll see a box labeled Screen Area. In that box is your current screen resolution. In the preceding figure, the screen resolution is shown as 800×600.

Figure 12.1

The Display Properties dialog box.

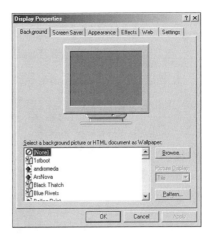

Figure 12.2

The Display Properties dialog box's Settings page.

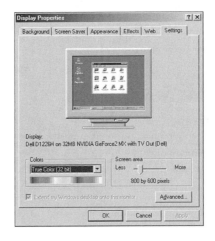

144

Now, think about this for a minute. What happens if you tell the computer to make its dots larger? Probably, people in your house will start asking why you're talking to your computer. More importantly, if the computer makes the dots on your screen larger, two related things will happen:

1. The screen will be able to display fewer dots. That is, because the dots are bigger, not as many fit on the screen.

2. Any graphics on the screen will look bigger because they're being drawn with bigger dots.

To see this in action, change the setting in the Screen Area box to a lower resolution. For example, if the resolution is currently 800×600, change it to 640×480. (If your screen is already set to 640×480, you probably won't be able to make the resolution lower. Just hang in there and wait for the rest of us. The following figures will let you see what's going on.) When you try to change the resolution, Windows gives you the message shown in Figure 12.3.

Figure 12.3

Changing the screen resolution.

Click OK to dismiss this dialog box. Windows then changes your screen resolution and asks whether you want to keep it that way. Don't answer Yes or No. Just wait 15 seconds and Windows will automatically set your screen back to the way it was.

Figure 12.4 shows what my screen looks like at 800×600.

Figure 12.5 shows the same screen set to 640×480.

Notice how everything is larger on the screen with the 640×480 resolution.

What does all this have to do with drawing graphics? Well, when you want to draw something on the screen, you obviously have to tell the computer not only *what* to draw but *where* to draw it. The rows and columns of dots create a grid you can use to locate any dot on the screen. All you have to do is refer to the dot's row and column.

145

Figure 12.4

A computer screen set to 800×600 resolution.

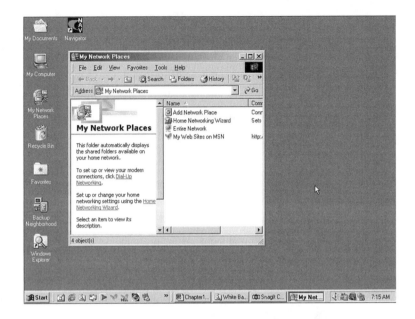

Figure 12.5

A computer screen set to 640×480 resolution.

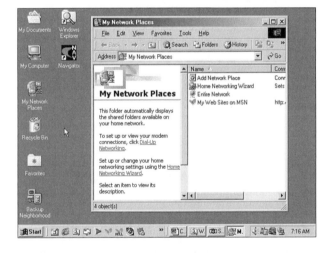

To make this experiment a little more confusing (there's an unwritten rule in computer science that nothing can be too simple), the first row and column are not numbered 1 but rather 0. This means that a computer screen set to 800×600 resolution has rows numbered from 0 to 799 and columns numbered from 0 to 599. The first dot on the screen—the one in the upper-left corner—has the coordinates 0,0, and the last dot on the screen—the one in the lower-right corner—has a coordinate of 799,599.

Graphics a la Mode

The first step in drawing graphics on the screen is to set the screen's resolution. Every programming language worth its name (and a lot that aren't) has a way to do this, and QBasic is no different. To set the screen resolution with QBasic, you use the SCREEN command. This command requires a number that specifies the screen you want. For example, a screen mode of 1 gives you a resolution of 320×200. Table 12.1 shows the many graphics modes you can set with the SCREEN command.

I should mention here that there's a lot more involved in a screen mode than just the resolution. A screen mode also specifies the number of colors you can use, how text will appear, and more. For example, some of the screen modes in Table 12.1 can show 16 colors, whereas others can show only black and white. I don't want to make things too confusing for you, however, so we'll stick to the basic stuff. If you want to know more, you can look up the SCREEN command in your QBasic help.

Point of Interest

Notice that the highest resolution available in Table 12.1 is 640×480. This is because QBasic is a very old version of the BASIC programming language, and computer monitors back then couldn't display the high resolutions we have now. If you enjoy programming, you'll probably end up switching to a language like Visual Basic, which gives you a lot more power over graphics.

Table 12.1   QBasic Screen Modes

Mode #	Resolution
0	Text mode only
1	320×200
2	640×200
3	720×348
4	640×400
7	320×200
8	640×200
9	640×350
10	640×350
11	640×480
12	640×480
13	320×200

Every Picture Is Worth a Thousand (or More) Dots

Now you know about screen resolution and how to set it. You also know that all graphics you can display on your computer screen are made up of tons of little dots called pixels. So, how do you get your computer to draw those dots? By using the PSET command. Here's a very short program that does just that:

```
CLS
SCREEN 1
PSET (10, 10)
```

The PSET command requires the column and row numbers of the dot you want to draw. That's the numbers inside the parentheses. Figure 12.6 shows what you get when you run this program.

Figure 12.6

A dot on the screen at 320×200 resolution.

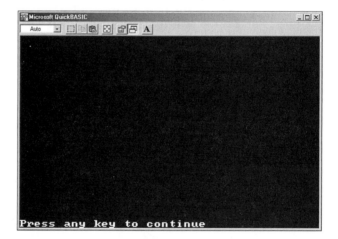

Hurray! You've actually drawn graphics on your computer screen, even if it is only a dot. A dot is a start. In fact, using only dots, you can draw a whole line. Here's a program that proves this point:

```
CLS
SCREEN 1
FOR x = 10 TO 110
  PSET (x, 50)
NEXT x
```

When you run this program, you'll see the screen shown in Figure 12.7.

148

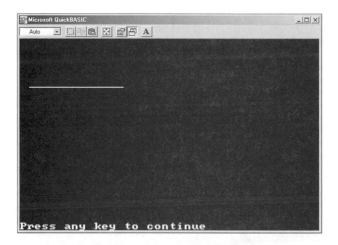

Figure 12.7

A horizontal line drawn with a series of dots.

In this case, the PSET command uses the loop variable x as the column number for each dot drawn in the loop. Placing a bunch of dots next to each other like this gives you a line. Here's how you'd modify the program to draw a vertical line:

```
CLS
SCREEN 1
FOR x = 10 TO 110
  PSET (50, X)
NEXT x
```

Now you're using the loop variable x as each dot's row number, giving you the screen shown in Figure 12.8.

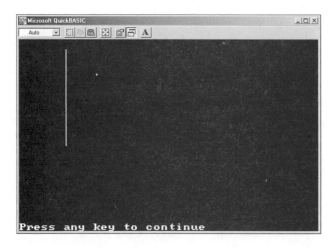

Figure 12.8

A vertical line drawn with a series of dots.

149

Suppose you want to draw a 45-degree diagonal line. Just use the loop variable for both the column and row numbers, like this:

```
CLS
SCREEN 1
FOR x = 10 TO 110
  PSET (x, x)
NEXT x
```

Figure 12.9 shows what you get.

Figure 12.9

A diagonal line drawn with a series of dots.

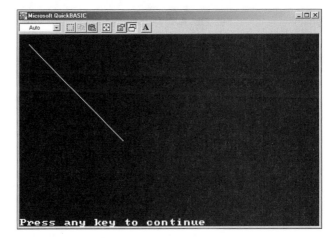

Using two loops, you can draw a solid rectangle with nothing but dots. Here's how:

```
CLS
SCREEN 1
FOR col = 10 TO 110
  FOR row = 25 TO 50
    PSET (col, row)
  NEXT row
NEXT col
```

Figure 12.10 shows what the rectangle looks like on the screen.

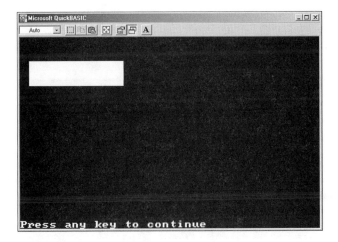

Figure 12.10

A solid rectangle drawn with a series of dots.

Dot-to-Dot the Easy Way

This all goes to show you that you can draw any shape you like using just dots. However, if this seems like a lot of work to you, the people who create programming languages agree. That's why they provide commands like LINE and CIRCLE to make things easier for you, the programmer. QBasic, unfortunately, doesn't have a lot of graphics power, so PSET, LINE, and CIRCLE are about all you get. (There's also a DRAW command, but it's very complicated to use.) Modern programming languages, however, enable you to draw tons of different shapes with a single command. That should give you something to look forward to!

Getting back to QBasic, let's talk about lines. The LINE command requires that you supply the coordinates of two points, and then QBasic draws a line between those points. Remember that first line you drew earlier with just dots? The program is a lot simpler with the LINE command:

```
CLS
SCREEN 1
LINE (10, 50)-(110, 50)
```

If you look closely at the LINE command, you can see that the coordinates for each dot are enclosed in parentheses, with the two of them separated by a hyphen. The first set of numbers in the parentheses is the coordinates where QBasic will start drawing the line, and the second coordinates are where QBasic will end the line.

Here's how you would create that solid rectangle using the LINE command:

```
CLS
SCREEN 1
FOR row = 25 TO 50
  LINE (10, row)-(110, row)
NEXT row
```

151

Point of Interest

You may think that drawing a line with the LINE command is a lot easier for your computer than drawing one using dots, and because of the QBasic FOR loop in the program, you'd be right. However, to draw a line, your computer must still draw a series of dots, so even with the LINE command, your computer is looping anyway, although it can loop faster because it doesn't have to rely on a slow QBasic loop.

QBasic's CIRCLE command is also pretty handy. Here's an example:

```
CLS
SCREEN 1
CIRCLE (100, 50), 20
```

In this example, the numbers in parentheses are the location of the circle's center point, and the last number is the circle's radius. This program produces the screen shown in Figure 12.11.

Figure 12.11

Drawing a circle.

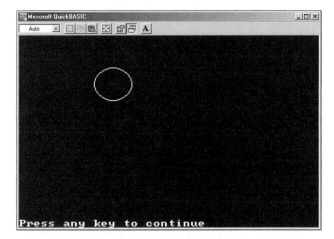

So, are you ready to try something extremely cool? Type and run this program:

```
CLS
SCREEN 1
FOR row = 25 TO 150 STEP 30
  LINE (10, row)-(310, row)
NEXT row
FOR col = 40 TO 280 STEP 30
  FOR row = 40 TO 130 STEP 30
    CIRCLE (col, row), 15
  NEXT row
NEXT col
```

This program first draws a set of horizontal lines, using a FOR loop to draw each line 30 pixels (dots) apart. Then another set of loops draws four rows of circles inside the lines, giving you the result shown in Figure 12.12.

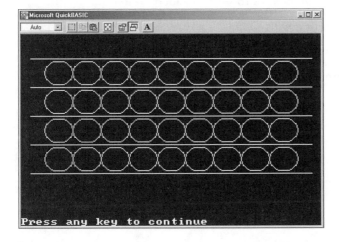

Figure 12.12

Some fancy QBasic graphics.

This chapter, of course, has only been an introduction to the art of computer graphics. We haven't talked about things like color palettes, setting colors, reading colors from the screen, bitmaps (images), and a whole lot more. Those are topics best left for when you decide to continue with programming, which I hope you will do.

153

The Least You Need to Know

➤ All computer images are made of hundreds of rows and columns of little dots known as pixels.

➤ How many pixels you can fit on your screen depends on your current screen resolution.

➤ When you want to draw something on the screen, you have to tell the computer what to draw and where to draw it.

➤ The rows and columns of pixels create a grid you can use to locate any dot on the screen.

➤ The first row and column on the screen are not numbered 1 but rather 0.

➤ The first step in drawing graphics is to set the screen's resolution.

➤ To set the screen resolution with QBasic, you use the SCREEN command.

➤ The QBasic PSET command draws dots on the screen.

➤ QBasic's LINE command draws a line between two given points.

➤ To draw a circle, use QBasic's CIRCLE command.

Chapter 13

Your Computer As Beethoven

In This Chapter

➤ Exploring the sound capabilities of today's computers

➤ Understanding sound files

➤ Creating music with your computer

➤ Programming computer sound effects

Okay, maybe using "Beethoven" and "your computer" together in a chapter title is a bit of an exaggeration. You know, like comparing the Beatles to the garage band next door that's always practicing when you're trying to catch forty winks. Actually, with a limited programming language like QBasic, it's more like comparing the Beatles to dogs barking, but let's not get too picky here. In any case, the point is that, while you may not be able to compose earth-shaking music using QBasic, you can use it to make a few interesting sounds.

Making Computers Sing

Today's modern computers have awesome sound capabilities, so awesome, in fact, that a studio can record and mix a complete, commercial-quality CD using a computer and the right software. This type of sound production, of course, requires a lot of know-how, not to mention some very expensive software. But it not only can be done, it is being done—every day.

From a professional programming point of view, to create computer sound and music, today's programmers need to master sophisticated programming libraries (such as Microsoft's DirectSound and DirectMusic) and have on hand composers, musicians, and just about all the stuff you'd find in a full-fledged studio.

A more reasonable way of handling computer music and sound is to have a program play prerecorded sound files. You have these files all over the place on your computer. They come in all different forms, but the most common is the wave file, which is sound recorded on the computer and saved into a file with the .wav file extension. I guarantee that if you do a search for files of type .wav on your computer, you'll find a bunch, as you can see in Figure 13.1.

Figure 13.1

Wave files on a computer's hard drive.

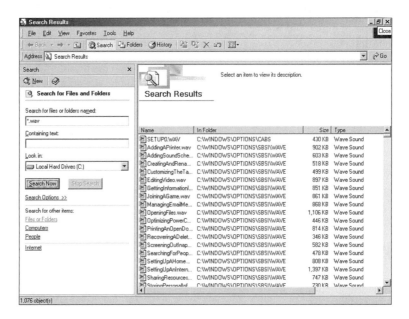

When you locate some wave files, double-click one. A piece of software on your computer should load up and play whatever sound is in the file. On newer Windows machines, that software is usually Windows Media Player, which is shown in Figure 13.2 playing a sound file.

Sound files also come in many other forms. For example, I'm sure you've heard about the infamous MP3 type of file that got Napster into so much trouble with the music recording industry. What you might not know is that MP3 is just a file format like .wav, and more often than not, MP3 files do not contain pirated music. With the right software, for example, you can record your favorite songs onto your computer in MP3 format so that you can play them while you work. This is a completely legal thing to do. (Charging your buddies, who are standing around your computer, $5 for listening to the songs isn't legal.)

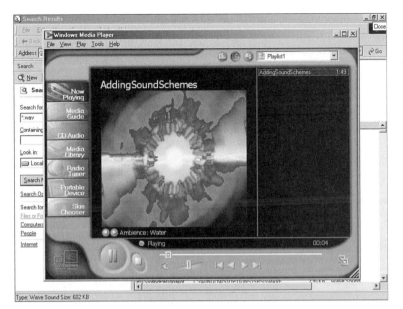

Figure 13.2

Windows Media Player playing a sound file.

Getting a Bit More Realistic

All this talk of studios, composers, and pirated top-40 hits may make you feel jittery about diving into computer sound for yourself, but you don't have to worry about that stuff for years. Making sound with your computer can actually be easy as long as you keep your expectations reasonable. For example, you can make your computer make a beep sound with one simple QBasic command, appropriately called BEEP. Here's a short program that beeps the computer five times:

```
FOR x = 1 TO 5
  BEEP
  FOR y = 1 TO 20000
    FOR z = 1 TO 2
    NEXT z
  NEXT y
NEXT x
```

In this example, it's only the BEEP command that makes the sound. The rest of the typing makes the sound happen five times with a pause between each one. If it weren't for the y and z loops after the BEEP command, the x loop would go so fast that the computer would only be able to get one sound in before the program was over.

A better and more flexible way of making sound with QBasic is with the SOUND command. To use the SOUND command, you write something like this:

```
SOUND 440, 36
```

The first number is the frequency of the sound you want, and the second number is the number of clock ticks you want the sound to last. There are approximately 18 clock clicks per second, so the preceding command plays a 440 Hz sound (the note A) for two seconds.

By placing a bunch of SOUND commands one after another, you can actually play simple songs on your computer. For example, here's a short rendition of that ol' fave "Mary Had a Little Lamb":

```
SOUND 440, 9
SOUND 390, 9
SOUND 350, 9
SOUND 390, 9
SOUND 440, 9
SOUND 0, 1
SOUND 440, 9
SOUND 0, 1
SOUND 440, 18
SOUND 390, 9
SOUND 0, 1
SOUND 390, 9
SOUND 0, 1
SOUND 390, 18
SOUND 440, 9
SOUND 520, 9
SOUND 0, 1
SOUND 520, 18
SOUND 440, 9
SOUND 390, 9
SOUND 350, 9
SOUND 390, 9
SOUND 440, 9
SOUND 0, 1
SOUND 440, 9
SOUND 0, 1
SOUND 440, 9
SOUND 0, 1
SOUND 440, 9
SOUND 390, 9
SOUND 0, 1
SOUND 390, 9
SOUND 440, 9
SOUND 390, 9
SOUND 350, 18
```

Looking at this list of SOUND commands, you can imagine how long it would take to program, say, Beethoven's Ninth! There's an easier way to play songs, though, one that requires only a single SOUND command.

What you do is take all the numbers following the SOUND commands and put them into DATA statements. Then add two –1s to the end of the data to mark the end of the song. Finally, use a loop to read the data into variables and then use those variables as the arguments for the SOUND command. Get it? Here's what the new version of the program looks like:

Cool Stuff

Notice in this program the sound commands SOUND 0, 1. Those are there to turn off the sound for just a slight moment in order to separate notes of the same frequency. That is, if you try to play several of the same notes in a row without first stopping the sound, the notes will all run together as a single note. That's a sure way to ruin a great tune!

```
DO
  READ note, duration
  IF note <> -1 THEN SOUND note, duration
LOOP UNTIL note = -1
DATA 440, 9, 390, 9, 350, 9, 390, 9, 440, 9
DATA 0, 1, 440, 9, 0, 1, 440, 18, 390, 9
DATA 0, 1, 390, 9, 0, 1, 390, 18, 440, 9
DATA 520, 9, 0, 1, 520, 18, 440, 9, 390, 9
DATA 350, 9, 390, 9, 440, 9, 0, 1, 440, 9
DATA 0, 1, 440, 9, 0, 1, 440, 9, 390, 9
DATA 0, 1, 390, 9, 440, 9, 390, 9, 350, 18
DATA -1, -1
```

Yes, even with this new method, getting your computer to play songs is a meticulous process. There's not much you can do about that unless you're a good enough programmer to create a sound editor program that can generate the DATA statements for you. If you look around on the Internet, you just might find a QBasic program that can do this.

Woops, Zoops, and Zips

Songs are just one thing you can do with the SOUND command. You can also make some wild sound effects. To do this, you again use the SOUND command inside loops. You can use the loop-control variables as notes and durations of sound, or you can use the DATA method you learned with "Mary Had a Little Lamb." (You can even do it the long way with a long list of SOUND commands, but by now, you're becoming a better programmer, and you'll want to do things the elegant way.)

As a simple example, here is a quickly rising note used as a sound effect for something like a spaceship moving across the screen. The program plays the rising note five times:

```
FOR x = 1 TO 5
  FOR y = 50 TO 500 STEP 50
    SOUND y, 1
  NEXT y
NEXT x
```

With the addition of a single line, you can make this sound effect even more interesting. Check this one out:

```
FOR x = 1 TO 5
  FOR y = 50 TO 500 STEP 50
    SOUND y, 1
    SOUND 40, 1
  NEXT y
NEXT x
```

Here's a pretty wild one that's still just a modification of the original one we wrote. In this case, the loop counts down rather than up, and there are a couple more SOUND statements in the loop:

```
FOR x = 1 TO 5
  FOR y = 500 TO 50 STEP -50
    SOUND y, 1
    SOUND 40, 1
    SOUND y * 2, 1
    SOUND 1000, 1
  NEXT y
NEXT x
```

Just for the fun of it, here's another one:

```
FOR x = 1 TO 5
  FOR y = 1000 TO 0 STEP -500
    SOUND y, 1
    SOUND y * 2, 1
  NEXT y
NEXT x
```

As you can see, even with the simple SOUND statement, you can come up with some pretty cool sounds, and you don't have to know anything about sound effects. All you have to do is experiment!

The Least You Need to Know

➤ Today's modern computers are so powerful that a studio can record and mix a complete, commercial-quality CD using a computer and the right software.

➤ From a professional programming point of view, today's programmers need to master fairly sophisticated sound programming libraries, such as Microsoft's DirectSound and DirectMusic.

➤ A common way to add sounds to a program is to have the program play pre-recorded sound files.

➤ One of the most common sound formats is the wave file, which is sound recorded on the computer and saved into a file with the .wav file extension.

➤ You can make your computer beep with the QBasic BEEP command.

➤ A more flexible way of making sound with QBasic is with the SOUND command.

➤ By placing a bunch of SOUND commands one after another, you can actually play simple songs on your computer.

➤ You can also make sound effects with the SOUND command.

161

Chapter 14

One Step at a Time

> **In This Chapter**
>
> ➤ Writing modular programs
>
> ➤ Designing programs from the top down
>
> ➤ Writing subroutines and functions

Short programs are easy to write and easy to understand. Full-size programs, however, quickly can become unwieldy, and without some form of organization, be hard to read and understand, especially when you come back to it after a few months or so. To overcome this problem, professional programmers developed something called modular programming, one of the topics you will study in this chapter.

A Programmer's Pyramid Plan

Like I said, long programs are hard to organize and read. A full-length program might contain 10 or more pages of code, and trying to find a specific part of the program in all that code can be tough. To solve this problem, you can use modular programming techniques. Using these techniques, you can break a long program into individual modules, each of which performs a specific task.

To understand how modular programming works, consider how you might organize a shopping trip. The main task might be called DO SHOPPING. Thinking about an entire shopping trip, however, can be overwhelming—just ask my wife. So, to make the task easier, you can break it down into a number of smaller steps. These steps might be GO TO GROCERY STORE, GO TO CLOTHES STORE, GO TO DRUG STORE, and GO TO VIDEO STORE.

After breaking the shopping task down into store-by-store steps, you have a better idea of what to do. But grocery shopping is also a pretty big task—especially if it hasn't been done in a while. So why not break each store step down, too? For example, grocery shopping could be broken down into BUY DAIRY, BUY BAKERY GOODS, BUY CLEANING SUPPLIES, and BUY MEAT. After breaking down each store's shopping into steps, your job is organized much like a pyramid, with the general task on the top. As you work your way down the pyramid, from the main task to the store-by-store list and finally to the tasks for each store, the tasks get more and more specific.

Of course, when shopping, you don't usually write such a list of steps (well, you might have a shopping list, but that's different). If you're an efficient shopper, the steps are organized in your mind. (If you shop like me, there are only two steps: TURN ON TV and COLLAPSE ON COUCH.) However, when writing a program, which is a more conceptual type of task, you may not have a clear idea of exactly what needs to be done. This can lead you to be overwhelmed by the project. Overwhelmed programmers are easy to spot. They stare at their computer screens blankly and often break into bouts of weeping.

Breaking down programming tasks into steps, or modules, is called modular programming. When you break your program's modules down into even smaller modules—as I did with the task of shopping—you're using a top-down approach to program design. By using top-down programming techniques, you can write any program as a series of small, easy-to-handle tasks.

QBasic provides two types of modules you can use when writing programs. The first, subroutines, is covered in the next section. The second, functions, is covered later in this chapter.

Blocks in the Pyramid

One type of program module is a subroutine. A *subroutine* is like a small program within your main program. If you were writing a shopping program (ah, if only it were possible!), the subroutines in the main module might be called GoToGroceryStore, GoToClothesStore, GoToDrugStore, and GoToVideoStore. The GoToGroceryStore subroutine would contain all the steps needed to shop for groceries (you know, buy milk, buy bread, flirt with the cashier), the GoToDrugStore subroutine would contain all the steps needed to shop for medications, and so on.

Of course, computers don't shop—not yet anyway, unless you want to count when you order stuff online. So let me focus on a more contemporary computer-oriented example. Suppose you want to write a program that draws a moving arrow onscreen. (Don't ask why.) The following program shows how to do this:

```
CLS
FOR x% = 1 TO 70
  CALL ShootArrow(x%)
NEXT x%

SUB ShootArrow (x%)
  LOCATE 5, x%
  PRINT ">>--->"
  FOR delay = 1 TO 1000: NEXT delay
  LOCATE 5, x%
  IF x% < 70 THEN PRINT "        "
END SUB
```

Here is the output from the program (except, on your screen, the arrow moves):

>>--->

Type in the first four lines of the program, which make up the main program. When you're finished, your screen should look similar to the one shown in Figure 14.1.

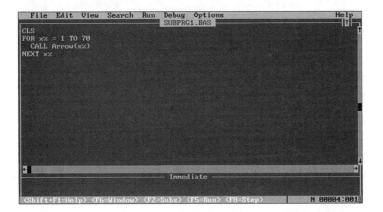

Figure 14.1

Type the main program module.

Now type the first line of the subroutine, which starts with the sub keyword. When you press Enter at the end of the line, you'll get a surprise. Your screen instantly displays the window for the program's ShootArrow() subroutine, as shown in Figure 14.2.

What happened? Did you press the wrong key on your keyboard? Did you forget to pay your electric bill? Because a subroutine is considered a separate module of your program, QBasic automatically gives it its own window. Moreover, because every subroutine must end with the END sub statement, QBasic automatically adds that statement to your subroutine. All you need to do is type the subroutine's statements between the sub and END sub lines. Do that now, so your screen looks something like Figure 14.3.

165

Figure 14.2

Starting the ShootArrow subroutine.

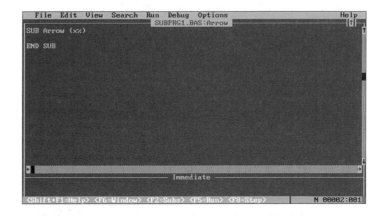

Figure 14.3

Type the ShootArrow subroutine.

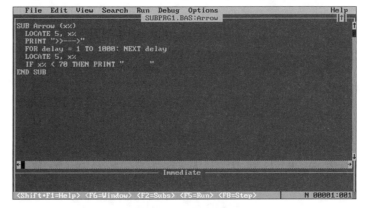

When you're finished typing, save the program as SUBPRG1.BAS, press Shift+F5 to run the program, and watch the little arrow zip across your screen.

You're probably wondering where the rest of your program went when the subroutine window appeared. You can easily get to any module of your program by selecting the SUBs entry of the View menu or by pressing F2. When you do, you see the SUBs dialog box, shown in Figure 14.4.

Figure 14.4

The SUBs dialog box.

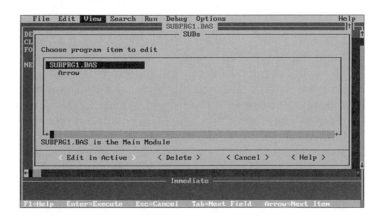

The program's main module is at the top of the module list, with other modules listed below. You can get to any module by double-clicking it with your mouse or by highlighting it with your arrow keys and pressing Enter. Notice also that this dialog box contains buttons for deleting modules from your program, should you ever need to do so.

Use the SUBs dialog box to get back to the main program. At the top of the program, you'll see this line:

```
DECLARE SUB ShootArrow (x%)
```

Talk about the ghost in the machine! Where the heck did that line come from? Every program module, except the main module, must have a DECLARE line at the top of your program. Because QBasic is such a clever little puppy, it automatically adds the necessary DECLARE statements to your program when you save it. Thank-you letters may be addressed to Microsoft.

Now for the $100-million question: How does this program work? The program is divided into two modules. The first is the main program, which comprises the first four lines you typed. This module is called the main program because it is at the highest level of your top-down design. That is, no other module uses the main program, but the main program calls modules that are lower in level.

The second module is the ShootArrow subroutine. This subroutine is run (called) by the main program, so the ShootArrow subroutine is considered to be one level down from the main program in the top-down design. The FOR…NEXT loop in the main program calls ShootArrow 70 times, once each time through the loop. When the main program calls ShootArrow, the code in ShootArrow executes. In other words, the program branches to the first line of ShootArrow and executes all the statements until it gets to the END SUB line. When it reaches the END SUB line, the program branches back to the main module, to the next line following the subroutine call. Because the line following the subroutine call is the end of the FOR…NEXT loop, the program goes back to the top of the loop, increments x%, and calls ShootArrow yet again. This continues until the loop runs out, which is when x% becomes 71.

See the x% in the parentheses in the call to ShootArrow? This is a subroutine argument. Arguments in subroutines work just like the arguments you used when calling QBasic's built-in functions. You use arguments to pass into subroutines the values those subroutines need to do their job. For example, you learned to get a string's length by calling the LEN function, like this:

```
length% = LEN(s$)
```

In this case, s$ is the function's argument, just as x% in the call to ShootArrow is ShootArrow's argument. You need to give ShootArrow this argument because ShootArrow needs to know the current value of the loop-control variable. This value determines where the program draws the arrow, as you can see when you look at the code in the subroutine.

Point of Interest

A subroutine can have as many arguments as you like, but you must be sure that the arguments you specify in the subroutine's call exactly match the type and order of the arguments in the subroutine's SUB line. To use more than one argument in a subroutine, separate the arguments with commas. For example, to add the argument y! to the ShootArrow call, you'd type this:

```
CALL ShootArrow(x%, y!)
```

Then, so the arguments match, you must change the first line of Arrow to this:

```
SUB ShootArrow (x%, y!)
```

You can use different variable names in the SUB line as long as they are the same type. In other words, using the arrow example, you can also type this:

```
SUB ShootArrow (col%, length!)
```

In the subroutine, you'd then use the variable names col% and length! rather than the original x% and y!. Subroutines don't have to have arguments. To call a subroutine that has no arguments, you wouldn't need the parentheses. For example: CALL ShootArrow.

In the first line of code in the subroutine (not counting the SUB line), you'll see a strange, new command. The LOCATE statement moves the onscreen printing position to the row and column listed after the command. The row is the first value after the LOCATE keyword and is the number of characters down from the top to start printing. The second value, in this case x%, is the column, counting from the left, at which to start printing.

The first time the subroutine gets called, the LOCATE statement moves the printing position five characters down from the top and one character to the right (because x% equals 1). The next line, which is a PRINT statement, then prints the arrow character string at the new screen position.

The do-nothing FOR…NEXT loop then keeps the computer counting from 1 to 1,000. This keeps the arrow onscreen for a while before the next LOCATE and PRINT statements erase it. (To make the arrow move faster, change the 1000 in the FOR…NEXT loop to a smaller value, which shortens the delay. To make the arrow go slower, change the

1000 to a larger value.) By calling the `Arrow` subroutine again and again, the program repeatedly draws and erases the arrow on the screen, each time one character closer to the right margin. This makes the arrow look as if it's moving.

That wasn't too tough, was it? Unfortunately, using subroutines is a little more complicated than it may appear from the preceding discussion. If you jump right in and try to write your own subroutines at this point, you'll run into trouble faster than a rabbit runs from a fox. Before you can write good subroutines, you must at least learn about something called variable scope. Coincidentally, variable scope is the next topic in this chapter.

Variable Scope

Now that you know a little about subroutines, you should know how QBasic organizes variables between modules. You may wonder, for example, why x% must be an argument in the call to `ShootArrow`. Why couldn't you just use the variable x% in the subroutine? After all, they're part of the same program, right?

Cool Stuff

Programs are broken up into small modules to make program code easier to understand. To this end, each module in a program should perform only a single task so that it stays short and to the point. When you try to cram too much functionality into a module, it loses its identity. If you can't state a module's purpose in two or three words, it's probably doing too much.

You need arguments in your subroutines because of something called *variable scope,* which determines whether program modules can "see" a specific variable. For example, if you were to change the program so that x% was not passed as an argument to `ShootArrow`, you'd get an illegal function call error when the program tried to execute the first `LOCATE` statement in `ShootArrow`.

Here's why: A variable in one module is not accessible in another (unless it's shared, which you'll learn about in a minute). So, when you don't explicitly pass x% as an argument, the `ShootArrow` subroutine can't access it. Because the variable x% in the main program is no longer visible to the `ShootArrow` subroutine, the subroutine assumes that the x% in its `LOCATE` statement is a new variable. QBasic initializes all new numeric variables to 0, so the x% in `ShootArrow` is equal to 0. There is no such screen position as 5,0; the `LOCATE` statement generates an error.

In the previous example, the x% in `ShootArrow` is local to `ShootArrow`. Just as the main program's x% cannot be seen in any module except the main program (it's local to the main program), `ShootArrow`'s x% cannot be seen in any module except `ShootArrow`. This may seem at first like a crazy way to do things, but when you think about it, it makes a lot of sense.

By not allowing a variable to be seen outside of the module in which it's used, you never have to worry about some other module accidentally changing that variable's value. Moreover, local variables make subroutines self-contained modules, as if everything the subroutine needs were put together in a little box. If the value of a variable used in a subroutine is giving your program trouble, you know exactly which module to check. You don't need to search your entire program to find the problem any more than you need to search your entire house to find a quart of milk.

The opposite of a local variable is a global variable. Global variables can be used in any module anywhere in your program. The following is a new version of the previous program. This version makes x% a global variable. Because x% is now a global variable, it need not be passed as an argument.

```
DECLARE SUB ShootArrow ()
DIM SHARED x%
CLS
FOR x% = 1 TO 70
  CALL ShootArrow
NEXT x%

SUB ShootArrow
  LOCATE 5, x%
  PRINT ">>--->"
  FOR delay = 1 TO 1000: NEXT delay
  LOCATE 5, x%
  IF x% < 70 THEN PRINT "        "
END SUB
```

The DIM SHARED line (the second line) in the program is the statement that allows x% to be used inside the ShootArrow subroutine without having to pass it as an argument. By declaring x% this way, it becomes a global variable, one that can be accessed by any module in your program.

As a novice programmer, you may think that using global variables is a great programming shortcut. After all, if you make all your variables global, you'll never have to worry about passing arguments to subroutines. However, a program with a lot of global variables is a poorly designed program—it's hard to read and hard to debug. You should write your programs to include as few global variables as is reasonable.

Still More Blocks in the Pyramid

Functions are another way you can break up your programs into modules. Unlike subroutines, however, functions always return a value to the main program. You've used QBasic functions before in this book. The LEN function is one. The value it returns is the number of characters in a string.

You write functions much like subroutines. However, function calls must assign the function's return value to a variable. Suppose you have a function named GetNumber% that gets a number from the user and returns it to your program. A call to the function might look something like this:

```
num% = GetNumber%
```

Notice that the function name includes a symbol that tells you the function's return type. Any function name that doesn't include a type symbol returns a single-precision number.

The following program illustrates how to use functions in your QBasic programs:

```
DECLARE FUNCTION GetUserInput$ ()
CLS
response$ = GetUserInput$
LOCATE 2, 1
PRINT "You typed '"; response$; ".'"

FUNCTION GetUserInput$
  LOCATE 20, 1
  PRINT "  PLEASE ENTER TEXT BELOW"
  PRINT "--------------------------------"
  PRINT " > "
  PRINT "--------------------------------"
  LOCATE 22, 3
  LINE INPUT s$
  GetUserInput$ = s$
END FUNCTION
```

Point of Interest

Remember that if you haven't declared a variable as shared, it is accessible only in the module in which it appears. This means you can have two or more variables with the same name in a program, all holding different values. Use arguments to pass variables between modules. Use global variables only when unavoidable.

The function GetUserInput$ sets the screen's printing position and prints an input box in which the user can enter his string. The LINE INPUT statement retrieves the string from the user, after which the string is returned by the function. Figure 14.5 shows the program's output.

Figure 14.5

Using the LINE INPUT *statement.*

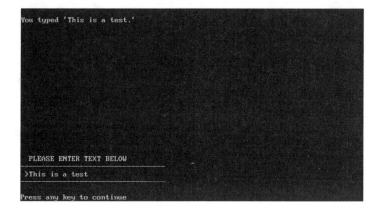

When you run the program, it prints a fancy input box on the screen (well, fancy to folks who prefer ground beef to filet mignon) and asks you to enter a string. When you enter the string, the program shows you what you typed, just in case you forget what it was—or maybe just to verify that the function did indeed return the string to the main program.

Look at the main program first. At the top, a DECLARE statement declares the GetUserInput$ function. You don't actually need to type this line. QBasic inserts the line automatically when you save the program. A little further down in the main program, you can see the line response$ = GetUserInput$, which is the call to the GetUserInput$ function. When the program gets to this point, it branches to the first line of the GetUserInput$ function. The GetUserInput$ function prints the input box on the screen and retrieves the input from the user.

The only thing in GetUserInput$ that you haven't seen before is the LINE INPUT command, which is a handy way to get strings. LINE INPUT works much like a regular INPUT statement, except you use it only to get strings and it doesn't print a question mark on the screen.

Just before the END FUNCTION line (which is how you always end a function module) is this line:

```
GetUserInput$ = s$
```

This assignment statement is where the string retrieved from the user is returned from the function to the main program. On the left of the assignment operator is the function's name, and on the right is the value to return from the function. All functions return their values this way. If, for example, you had a function called GetValue% that returned an integer, somewhere in your GetValue% function must be a line like GetValue% = value%, where value% is the value being returned from the function.

As you can see, functions are similar to subroutines. In fact, you can pass arguments to functions the same way you do to subroutines. Just add parentheses to the function's name and list the arguments, separated by commas, inside the parentheses.

172

Don't forget to match the arguments in the function's call with those in the function's FUNCTION line. For example, the function call

```
s$ = GetStr$(prompt$)
```

must call a function whose first line is

```
FUNCTION GetStr$ (prompt$)
```

(Actually, the variable prompt$ in the FUNCTION line can have any name, as long as it's the same variable type as the argument in the function call.)

The following is an example of a modular program. It also summarizes much of what you've learned so far in this book. (If that doesn't impress you, maybe the fact that it's a game will get you to type it in.) Because this program is much larger than other programs you've seen, it's a pretty big typing task. Be careful to type everything correctly. Otherwise, the program may not run properly:

```
DECLARE SUB ShowScore (score%)
DECLARE FUNCTION PlayGame% ()
DECLARE SUB EraseTarget (target.position%)
DECLARE SUB ShootArrow (a%, target.position%)
DECLARE FUNCTION ShowTarget% ()
DECLARE SUB DrawScreen ()

RANDOMIZE TIMER        'Seed random number generator.
CALL DrawScreen        'Draw the playing screen.
score% = PlayGame%     'Play the game.
CALL ShowScore(score%) 'Show the final score.

SUB DrawScreen
  CLS
  FOR x% = 1 TO 10
    LOCATE x% * 2 + 2, 1
    PRINT "-----------------------------------------------"
    IF x% < 10 THEN
      LOCATE x% * 2 + 3, 1
      PRINT x%; ">>-->"
    END IF
  NEXT x%
END SUB

SUB EraseTarget (target.position%)
  LOCATE target.position% * 2 + 3, 60
  PRINT " "
END SUB
```

```
FUNCTION PlayGame%
  score% = 0
  FOR x% = 1 TO 25
    target.position% = ShowTarget%
    start.time& = TIMER
    shot.fired% = 0

    DO
      a% = VAL(INKEY$)
      IF a% >= 1 AND a% <= 9 THEN
        CALL ShootArrow(a%, target.position%)
        shot.fired% = 1
      END IF
    LOOP UNTIL (shot.fired%) OR (TIMER > start.time& + 1)

    IF a% = target.position% THEN
      BEEP
      score% = score% + 1
    END IF

    CALL EraseTarget(target.position%)
  NEXT x%
  PlayGame% = score%
END FUNCTION

SUB ShootArrow (a%, target.position%)
  FOR x% = 4 TO 60
    LOCATE a% * 2 + 3, x%
    PRINT ">>-->"
    FOR delay = 1 TO 50: NEXT delay
    LOCATE a% * 2 + 3, x%
    PRINT "     "
  NEXT x%
  LOCATE a% * 2 + 3, 4
  PRINT ">>-->"
END SUB

SUB ShowScore (score%)
  LOCATE 20, 60
  PRINT "-------------------"
  LOCATE 21, 60
  PRINT "  Your score is"; score%
  LOCATE 22, 60
  PRINT "-------------------"
END SUB
```

174

```
FUNCTION ShowTarget%
  p% = INT(9 * RND + 1)
  LOCATE p% * 2 + 3, 60
  PRINT "X"
  ShowTarget% = p%
END FUNCTION
```

When you run this program, it draws a simple shooting gallery on your screen, as shown in Figure 14.6.

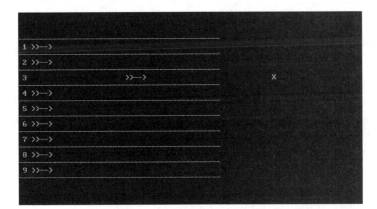

Figure 14.6

The game screen.

The gallery is made up of nine lanes, each containing an arrow. When the program starts, a target (an X) appears to the right of the lanes. Your task is to shoot the target with one of your arrows. To fire an arrow, press the lane's number. You have to be fast because the target moves quickly. After 25 targets have appeared, the game ends and your final score is displayed. If the score is not as high as you'd like, you can either throw a tantrum or try again.

There are a few things in the program you haven't seen before. First, near the top of the program is the line RANDOMIZE TIMER. This line initializes QBasic's random-number generator. The program uses random numbers to select the target's next position on the screen. Failure to initialize the random-number generator results in the same series of "random" numbers every time you run the program, which makes for a boring game. To initialize, or seed, the random-number generator, you must give RANDOMIZE a different value each time you run the program. Because TIMER represents the number of seconds since midnight—and so is different each time you run the program—it's perfect for this task.

In the main program, notice that some lines end with an apostrophe followed by a line of text. These are comments. You can use comments to document your program, like leaving notes to yourself (or whoever ends up reading your program) to explain what the program does. When QBasic sees the apostrophe, it knows that the rest of the line is a comment and ignores it. If you like, you can have an entire block of lines that are nothing but comments. QBasic won't even care if you put a letter to Uncle Henry in the middle of your program, as long as each line starts with an apostrophe.

175

Point of Interest

Most random-number generators use a seed value to get started. If you use the same seed value to initialize the generator, you'll always get the same series of numbers. Random numbers in a computer are not truly random; instead, they are calculated by a formula. Luckily, by using a different seed value every time you run a program, you can simulate true random numbers because you can't predict the series of numbers that will be created by the formula.

The rest of the main program contains nothing new. However, in the function PlayGame%, you'll see this line:

```
a% = VAL(INKEY$)
```

You already know that VAL returns the numeric value of a number string, but what the heck is INKEY$? INKEY$ checks the keyboard for a key press. If the user has pressed a key, INKEY$ returns the key's character to your program. If the user hasn't yet pressed a key, INKEY$ returns a null (empty) string.

This program uses INKEY$ to read keystrokes on the fly, without forcing the program to stop for input as it does with a regular INPUT statement. By enclosing the call to INKEY$ within a DO loop, the program constantly polls the keyboard (checks the keyboard for input) at the same time it checks to see if your time for the current target has run out. The DO loop ends if the user presses a key or if a second has passed since the loop started.

In the function ShowTarget%, you can see where the random numbers are generated. The line

```
p% = INT(9 * RND +1)
```

generates a random number from 1 to 9. The program uses this random number to determine where to print the next target on the screen. Look at this line of code carefully because it's a little tricky.

First, the QBasic function RND returns a random number between 0 and 1. To get this random number in the range you need for the program, you must apply the formula INT(N * RND + 1), which returns a value from 1 to N. In the program, you want a value from 1 to 9, so N equals 9. If you wanted random numbers from 1 to 100, you'd write this:

```
p% = INT(100 * RND + 1)
```

(Of course, p% is just a variable name; you could use any variable name you wanted.) The function INT converts the value inside the parentheses to an integer so that you don't end up with a number like 5.347324.

Everything else in the program should be familiar to you. If you have trouble figuring out a section of the code, try to think like a computer—taking the program a line at a time, making sure you know what each line does. If you do, you'll have no trouble figuring out the entire program.

The Least You Need to Know

➤ When you organize a program into subroutines and functions that perform simple tasks, you are using modular programming techniques.

➤ When you organize your subroutine and functions such that more general routines call more specific ones, you are using top-down programming.

➤ QBasic supports subroutines and functions, which are two types of modules you can use when writing a QBasic program. Functions must return values, while subroutines do not.

➤ The LOCATE statement allows you to set the screen position for the next PRINT statement.

➤ A program can access local variables only within the subroutine or function in which they appear. Global variables are accessible anywhere in a program. The DIM SHARED statement declares a global variable.

➤ The LINE INPUT statement works much like INPUT, except it can be used only to input strings and it does not display a question mark.

➤ To get random numbers, you must first use the RANDOMIZE statement to seed the random-number generator. The RND function then returns a random number between 0 and 1.

➤ The INKEY$ function checks for a key press and returns the key's character if a key was pressed or a null string if no key was pressed.

Chapter 15

Lookin' for Creepy Crawlies

In This Chapter

➤ Understanding debuggers

➤ Stepping through program code

➤ Analyzing variables at runtime

➤ Setting breakpoints

➤ Using QBasic's debugger

As your programs get longer, you'll discover that finding errors can be difficult and confusing. Often, something will go wrong with your program, and you'll have no idea where to look for the problem. This can lead to sleepless nights, a bad disposition, and the inability to eat pizza for breakfast. Luckily, most computer languages come with some sort of program debugger, which enables you to look inside your programs and find what's wrong.

Get the Raid!

Most program debuggers provide a set of basic tools for locating programming problems. Some debuggers, on the other hand, come with very sophisticated tools that enable you to do everything from looking at a variable's value to looking inside your computer's memory. Virtually all debuggers, however, provide the following basic tools:

➤ Step-into program trace

➤ Step-over program trace

➤ Variable watcher

➤ Breakpoints

Step-Into Program Trace

One of the simplest debugging tools is the line-by-line program trace, sometimes referred to as a step-into trace. A step-into program trace enables you to run your program one line at a time and watch what happens every step of the way. That is, the debugger runs the current line of code and then pauses the program. The next program line doesn't run until you tell the debugger to run it.

Using this type of program trace enables you to see which program statements are being executed and in what order. For example, what if you suspect that an IF statement is not working the way you expected it to? You can trace the program line by line, watching to see the path program execution takes as it works its way through your IF, ELSEIF, and ELSE clauses.

By the way, this type of program trace is often called step-into because, when it gets to a procedure call, it steps into the procedure and runs it line by line rather than just performing the entire procedure call. If you want an entire procedure to run without having to step into it line by line, use the step-over program trace.

Step-Over Program Trace

The step-over program trace is very similar to the step-into trace, except it enables you to run entire procedures without having to watch them execute line by line. For example, suppose you are tracing through three program lines, and one of the three is a call to a procedure named Average, which calculates the average of several numbers. You already know that the Average function works just fine, thank you very much, so all you want to do is run that function call just as if it were a single line of source code.

The step-over program trace does exactly what you want. When you get to your call to Average, the step-over trace calls the function and gets the result just as your program would. However, even though your program is executing the entire Average function, you don't have to watch it do so line by line. This is as convenient as an ice-cream truck on a hot summer day!

Use a Variable Watcher

Just as program lines don't always execute in the order you think they should, variables don't always end up with the values you think they should. This doesn't mean the computer has made a mistake. Nosireee Bob. Whether you want to hear it or not, it means *you've* made a mistake. Somewhere in your program, you're setting that variable to the wrong value. Finding this type of error would be as hard as coaxing a cat into the dog pound if it weren't for the handy-dandy variable watcher.

Using a variable watcher, you can see into any variable you like and make sure it's not going all funky on you. Suppose, for example, you're doing this awesome mathematical calculation in your programs, and all your friends would think you're a genius except for the fact that the program doesn't work. Using a variable watcher, you can fix your program before your friends discover that you're just as dumb as they are.

To find your problem, you first use a program trace (or a breakpoint, which you learn about next) to get to the program lines that are giving you trouble. Then you execute each program line one by one and watch how the values of your variables change. When you see the program set a variable to an unexpected value, you've located a problem in your program. The best part is that not one of your friends has to know that you didn't get it right the first time!

Insert Breakpoints

Breakpoints are a great way to get to a problem part of your program quickly without having to do a tedious program trace. Let's say the main section of your program has 10 lines, and you think there's a problem with line 8. You could step through the program line by line to get to line 8, but why bother if you're not interested in what's happening in the program before line 8? Instead, you can set a breakpoint on line 8 and then run the program. When program execution gets to line 8, the program stops and waits for more instructions from you. Is that cool or what? When your program stops at the breakpoint, you can do stuff like check the values of variables or start a line-by-line trace, whatever you need to do to find the problem.

Raid the QBasic Way

Luckily, you don't have to take all this stuff I've been saying about program debugging on faith. You can try it out yourself. QBasic includes a simple debugger that can help you find programming errors. The commands that control the debugger live in the Debug menu, which is shown in Figure 15.1.

In this section, you'll make QBasic's simple but handy debugger jump through some loops—figuratively and literally!

Figure 15.1

QBasic's debug menu.

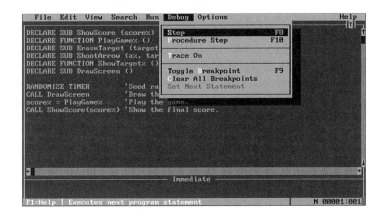

Step Into, the QBasic Way

The first command in the Debug menu is Step, which enables you to step through your program a line at a time. This is QBasic's version of a step-into program trace. Each time you select this command (the easiest way is to press F8), your program executes a single line of code and then stops.

To see how this works, type this program into QBasic. (If you already typed and saved this program in Chapter 14, "One Step at a Time," just load it.)

```
DECLARE SUB ShowScore (score%)
DECLARE FUNCTION PlayGame% ()
DECLARE SUB EraseTarget (target.position%)
DECLARE SUB ShootArrow (a%, target.position%)
DECLARE FUNCTION ShowTarget% ()
DECLARE SUB DrawScreen ()

RANDOMIZE TIMER        'Seed random number generator.
CALL DrawScreen        'Draw the playing screen.
score% = PlayGame%     'Play the game.
CALL ShowScore(score%) 'Show the final score.

SUB DrawScreen
  CLS
  FOR x% = 1 TO 10
    LOCATE x% * 2 + 2, 1
    PRINT "---------------------------------------------"
    IF x% < 10 THEN
      LOCATE x% * 2 + 3, 1
      PRINT x%; ">>-->"
    END IF
  NEXT x%
END SUB
```

```
SUB EraseTarget (target.position%)
  LOCATE target.position% * 2 + 3, 60
  PRINT " "
END SUB

FUNCTION PlayGame%
  score% = 0
  FOR x% = 1 TO 25
    target.position% = ShowTarget%
    start.time& = TIMER
    shot.fired% = 0

    DO
      a% = VAL(INKEY$)
      IF a% >= 1 AND a% <= 9 THEN
        CALL ShootArrow(a%, target.position%)
        shot.fired% = 1
      END IF
    LOOP UNTIL (shot.fired%) OR (TIMER > start.time& + 1)

    IF a% = target.position% THEN
      BEEP
      score% = score% + 1
    END IF

    CALL EraseTarget(target.position%)
  NEXT x%
  PlayGame% = score%
END FUNCTION

SUB ShootArrow (a%, target.position%)
  FOR x% = 4 TO 60
    LOCATE a% * 2 + 3, x%
    PRINT ">>-->"
    FOR delay = 1 TO 50: NEXT delay
    LOCATE a% * 2 + 3, x%
    PRINT "     "
  NEXT x%
  LOCATE a% * 2 + 3, 4
  PRINT ">>-->"
END SUB

SUB ShowScore (score%)
  LOCATE 20, 60
  PRINT "--------------------"
  LOCATE 21, 60
  PRINT " Your score is"; score%
  LOCATE 22, 60
```

```
     PRINT "--------------------"
END SUB

FUNCTION ShowTarget%
  p% = INT(9 * RND + 1)
  LOCATE p% * 2 + 3, 60
  PRINT "X"
  ShowTarget% = p%
END FUNCTION
```

When you have the program typed (or loaded) and saved, select the Debug menu's Step command or press F8. The program highlights the line RANDOMIZE TIMER and stops, as shown in Figure 15.2.

Figure 15.2

The Step command on the first program line.

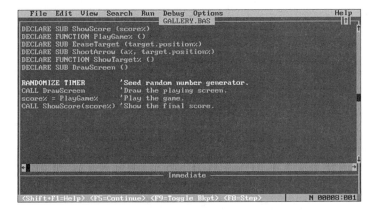

The highlighted line is the next line the debugger will execute. Press F8 and the debugger executes the RANDOMIZE line and highlights the next line in your program. Because this line is a call to the subroutine DrawScreen, the program branches to the first line of the subroutine when you press F8 again. Press F8 now and your screen will look something like Figure 15.3.

Figure 15.3

Stepping into a subroutine.

As you can see, when the debugger executes a subroutine or function call, the Step command highlights the first line of the procedure.

Press F8 until the line NEXT x% is highlighted. At this point, the program has drawn only a small part of the game's screen. But where is the screen? To see what the program has drawn so far, press F4 to switch to the output screen. Your screen should look something like Figure 15.4.

Figure 15.4

Checking program output.

Spying on Variables

When you're stepping through a program, you can do more than just examine the output screen. You can also check the values of variables. (You can even check your socks for holes, but this is unlikely to help with your programming.) For example, suppose you want to know the value of x% at this point in your program. First, press F6 to activate the Immediate window. Then type **PRINT x%** and press Enter. The output screen appears with the current value of x% displayed right below the other program output. Because the program has gone through the loop only once, this value is 1, just as it should be. Using the Immediate window this way is QBasic's version of a variable watcher.

To get a little practice with the Step command, keep pressing F8 to step through the loop. Periodically, press F4 to switch to the output screen and see what's been printed so far. Also, use the Immediate window to check the value of the loop-control variable x%, which should increase until it reaches 11.

Step Over, the QBasic Way

The next command in the Debug menu, Procedure Step, allows you to run a subroutine or function without stepping through each line of the function. This is QBasic's version of step-over program tracing. For example, if you select the Procedure Step command (pressing F10 is the fastest way) when the line CALL DrawScreen is highlighted, QBasic executes the DrawScreen subroutine, drawing the entire playing screen without stopping. After drawing the screen, the program stops on the line score% = PlayGame%.

Automated QBasic

The Trace On command in the Debug menu lets you run your program in slow motion. To use this option, first select Trace On in the Debug menu. A small dot appears next to the Trace On menu item. Now press Shift+F5 to run your program from the start. QBasic starts executing your program a line at a time, much as it did when you used the Step command, except now you don't need to keep pressing F8. To stop the trace, press Ctrl+Break. You can then check the value of any variables or examine your program's output up to that point.

Give Me a Break!

Sometimes you may want your program to run up to a certain point and then stop. For example, suppose you want to check the value of a% after the line a% = VAL(INKEY$) in the function PlayGame% executes. To do this, first bring the PlayGame% function up on your screen. Then move the window's text cursor to the line immediately following the line you want to check. (In this case, you want to place the cursor on the IF statement following the line a% = VAL(INKEY$).) Now select the Toggle Breakpoint command in the Debug menu or just press F9. The line you selected turns red, as shown in Figure 15.5.

Figure 15.5

Stopping on a breakpoint.

The line is now selected as a breakpoint. Setting breakpoints is a fast way to stop your program on a specific line.

Press Shift+F5 to run the program. Almost immediately, the program stops on the breakpoint line. You can now inspect the variable a%, which should be 0 because you haven't had a chance to press a key yet.

You can set as many breakpoints as you like in your program. To clear a breakpoint, place the text cursor on the breakpoint line and press F9 again to toggle the red highlight off. To clear all breakpoints in a program simultaneously, select Clear All Breakpoints from the Debug menu. To donate huge wads of money to my vacation fund, please check my Web site. (Just kidding.)

Next, Please

The last command in the Debug menu is Set Next Statement. This command allows you to choose any line in your program as the next line to execute. This can be handy when you want to skip over a block of code. To set the next statement to execute, place the text cursor on the line you want to execute and then select the Set Next Statement command in the Debug menu. QBasic highlights the selected line. When the program begins again, the selected line is the next to execute.

Using a debugger to trace your program's flow and to check the value of variables makes finding programming errors a lot less frustrating. Because you're not likely to ever write a perfect program, developing good debugging skills is as important as learning to program in the first place.

The Least You Need to Know

➤ As your programs get longer, you'll discover that finding errors can be difficult and confusing.

➤ Virtually all debuggers provide program tracing, variable watch, and breakpoints.

➤ A step-into program trace enables you to run your program one line at a time and watch what happens every step of the way.

➤ The step-over program trace is very similar to the step-into trace, except it enables you to run entire procedures without having to watch them execute line by line.

➤ Using a variable watcher, you can see into any variable you like and make sure it's the value it's supposed to be.

➤ A breakpoint is a program line that the debugger stops on, giving you a chance to check the values of variables or start a line-by-line trace.

➤ QBasic's debugging commands are found in the Debug menu.

➤ QBasic's Step command is a step-into program trace.

➤ QBasic's Procedure Step command is a step-over program trace.

➤ QBasic's Trace On command enables you to run your program in slow motion.

➤ QBasic's Toggle Breakpoint command sets breakpoints in your program.

➤ QBasic's Set Next Statement command enables you to choose any line in your program as the next line to execute.

Part 5

An Introduction to Object-Oriented Programming

These days, most programming languages support a new (well, relatively new) way to program called object-oriented programming (OOP). OOP is such a logical way of getting the programming job done that one has to wonder why someone didn't think of it sooner! In any case, in this final part, you leave QBasic behind and explore how Microsoft's new Visual Basic .NET language handles OOP.

Programming with Objects

QBasic is actually a pretty old programming language. If you were to think of Microsoft's latest version of BASIC (Visual Basic .NET) as a newborn babe, you'd have to think of QBasic as being that babe's great-great-great-great-great-grandfather. I wouldn't say that Neanderthal men programmed using QBasic, but it'd be close. Because QBasic represents old technology, it doesn't support many newer programming ideas. One of these ideas is object-oriented programming, which you will learn about in this chapter.

Saddling a New Horse

Because QBasic doesn't support object-oriented programming (OOP) techniques, we're going to have to switch horses in the middle of that proverbial stream. Try not to get your feet wet. These days, many languages support object-oriented programming techniques, and Microsoft's newest version of BASIC, Visual Basic .NET, is one of these. So, to demonstrate OOP, we'll say goodbye to our old friend QBasic and switch to Visual Basic .NET.

Before you climb aboard that new horse, though, you might like to know a little about it. Who knows? Maybe after you've finished this book, you'll be so enamored of programming that you'll want to run right out and buy your very own copy of Visual Basic .NET. Stranger things have happened, you know. Really. In any case, in this section, you get a quick look at Visual Basic. NET and get to see how far the BASIC language has come since the days of the Neanderthals.

Creating Projects

Ready for a tour of Visual Basic .NET? Here we go: First task: installing Visual Basic .NET. I won't go into too many details here, but when you install it, you'll find Visual Basic .NET on your Start menu. Then, to start the program, just click the Microsoft Visual Studio .NET entry in its folder, as shown in Figure 16.1.

Figure 16.1

You can run Visual Basic from your Start menu.

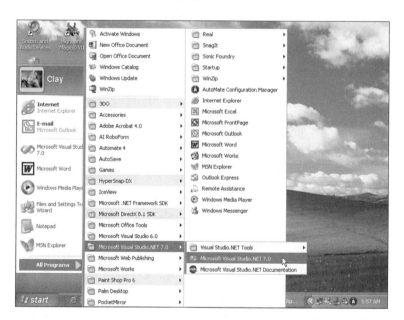

When you run Visual Basic .NET, after a short wait, its main window pops up on your screen, as shown in Figure 16.2.

The Visual Studio Home Page enables you to choose exactly the kind of Visual Basic project you want to get started on. As you can see, the window displays three choices: You can load a recent project, create a new project, or load an existing project.

When you first get started, you won't, of course, have existing projects to load. So, you'll click the Create New Project option to start a brand-new project. You should now be looking at the New Project dialog box, which looks like Figure 16.3.

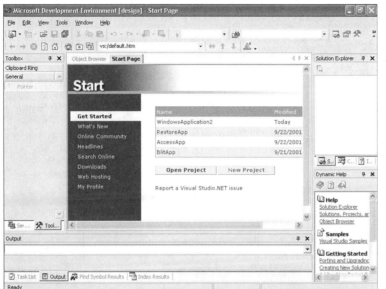

Figure 16.2

The Visual Studio main window looks like this.

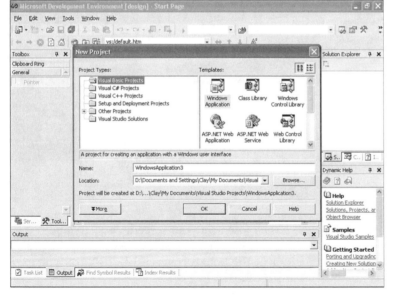

Figure 16.3

The New Project dialog box enables you to choose the type of project you want to start.

To get that new project going, you click on Visual Basic Projects in the Project Types pane and then double-click the Windows Application icon in the Templates pane. Presto!

Exploring the Visual Basic .NET Main Window

Getting a new project started cranks a lot of other stuff into action, too. First, a set of controls appears on the left side of the window. These controls are snuggled into a window called the toolbox. Also, your new program's starting window—called a *form* in Visual Basic—appears in the middle of the screen. Need some more cool stuff? Your new project's name and components appear in the Solution Explorer window, and the form's property settings appear in the Properties window. Figure 16.4 shows these wonderful new elements of Visual Basic .NET's main window.

Figure 16.4

The Visual Basic main window displays several different areas.

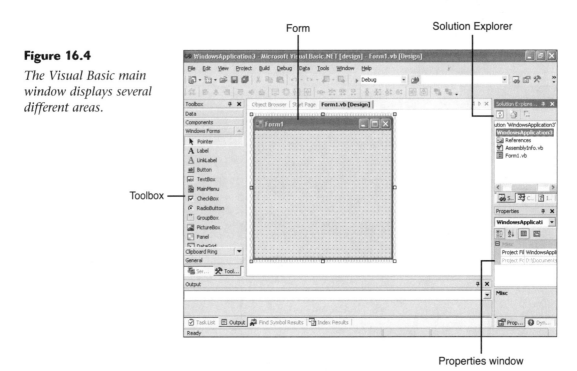

Form

Solution Explorer

Toolbox

Properties window

Now the full glory of Visual Basic .NET is exposed on your screen, curiosity about it all is probably eating you up alive. If you aren't just a teensy bit curious, you're probably reading the wrong book. Take a look at the book's cover. If it's the cover you expected, then take a look at Visual Basic's toolbox.

See all those little icons? They represent controls you can use with your program. Controls are objects like buttons, text boxes, labels, images, and shapes that you can position on your form to build your program's user interface. Awesome indeed!

The window inside the Form1.vb [Design] window—the one that reads Form1 in its title bar—is your project's window. That is, when you run your program, this is the window that appears on the screen. Logically, then, this is also the window in which you place the controls that make up your program's user interface.

The Solution Explorer window gives you an overview of the objects in the currently loaded project. Usually, a form is one of these objects. You may, in fact, have more than one form in some projects. By clicking the plus and minus signs next to folders in the Solution Explorer window, you can display more details about the project.

Finally, the Properties window displays the properties of the object currently selected in the form. You can think of properties as the attributes of an object. For example, a project's form has a property called Text, which is the text that appears in the form's title bar. If you change the text for the Text property, the text in the form's title bar changes, too, as shown in Figure 16.5.

Cool Stuff

Almost all programs have a user interface, which is the part of the application that enables the user to interact with the program. A user interface usually includes various types of buttons, menus, dialog boxes, and other kinds of objects. By using the objects that make up the user interface, the user supplies commands and information to the program. Similarly, the program accesses the user interface to display information to the user.

Changed caption

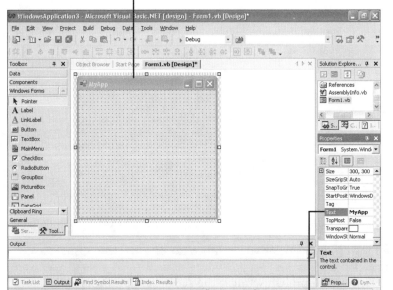

Figure 16.5

A form's title bar holds the text from the Text *property.*

Text property

195

Most controls and other Visual Basic objects have properties that determine how the objects look and act. Many of the objects in Visual Basic, in fact, share similar properties. For example, all objects have a Name property, which enables a program to refer to that object. Most objects also have properties that determine the object's size, position, text, colors, borders, and much more.

The Code Window

One of the most powerful features Visual Basic .NET is the way you can build much of your project simply by placing controls from the toolbox onto the form. Still, the controls don't do much until you tell them what to do. So, sooner or later you have to settle down to writing some program source code. In Visual Basic, you type source code into the code window.

When you first start a new project, Visual Basic doesn't display the code window. One way to bring up the code window is to double-click the form. When you do, your Visual Basic window will resemble the window shown in Figure 16.6.

Figure 16.6

The code window is a text editor into which you type your program's lines.

Code window

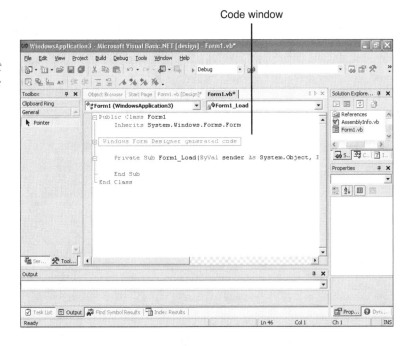

The new window that appears is the code window. As you can see, Visual Basic is pretty smart and often tries to guess what you want to do. In this case, Visual Basic has started something called a procedure—a procedure named Form1_Load. If you were actually writing a program, you'd probably finish the Form1_Load procedure by typing Visual Basic commands between the two lines Visual Basic already provided for you.

Menus and the Toolbar

Creating programs with a sophisticated programming environment like Visual Basic. NET requires that you have easy access to a ton of commands. To give you that access, the main window features a menu bar and a toolbar. The menu bar holds a series of menus, each of which contains commands you'll need to make Visual Basic do what you want. For example, if you want to add a new form to your project, you could select the Project menu's Add Windows Form command, as shown in Figure 16.7.

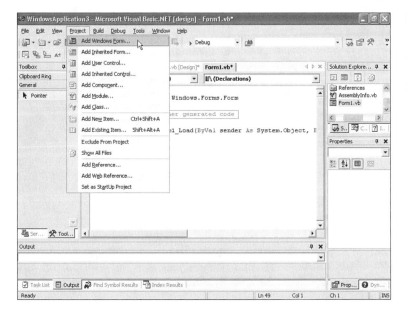

Figure 16.7

The menu bar provides a home for the various Visual Basic .Net commands.

Many of the menu commands have shortcut keys you can use to select the command directly from the keyboard. For example, in preceding figure, you can see the keystroke Ctrl+Shift+A listed after the Add New Item command. This means you can send Visual Basic the Add New Item command just by holding down your keyboard's Ctrl and Shift keys and then pressing A. You don't need to open the menu at all.

The toolbar provides access to many of Visual Basic's most commonly needed commands. Most of the buttons on the toolbar are just quick ways to select a command from the menus. For example, if you click the button that looks like a stack of floppy disks, Visual Basic saves all the files in the currently open project. Clicking this button is the same as selecting the File menu's Save All command, as shown in Figure 16.8. You can also select this command by pressing Ctrl+Shift+S.

Figure 16.8

Some menu commands, like Save All, are represented as buttons on the toolbar.

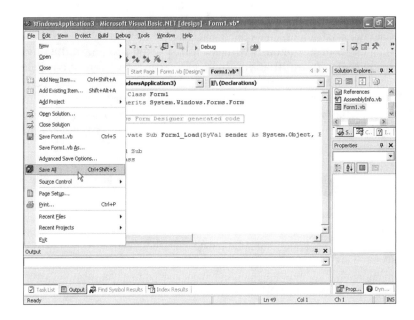

Now, wasn't that fun? Aren't you all excited about Visual Basic .NET?

Getting Back to OOP

Sorry for the side trip, but if you're interested in continuing programming, you need to know about things like Visual Basic .NET. In any case, you won't be able to run any of this chapter's programs without Visual Basic .NET, but you should be able to get a good idea of what all this OOP stuff is about just by reading this and the next couple chapters. Hopefully, you can get comfortable with object-oriented programming techniques this way. Not comfortable like with a fuzzy and warm sweater, but rather comfortable like having a general idea of what all this object-oriented stuff is about.

Object-oriented programming enables you to think of program elements—such as files, documents, arrays, and windows—as objects. Think about using a TV set. You don't have to know the details of how a TV works (thank heavens!) to watch a show. You only need to know how to get those pictures up on the screen. What's going on behind the screen is none of your business. If you try to make it your business, you may end up with a new hair style when a mess of volts passes through your body! This is also true of objects in an OOP program. To use an object, you don't need to know every detail about it. You just need to know how to make the object do what you want. For example, you can actually write a program that creates a TV object with functions named `TurnOn`, `ChangeChannel`, `AdjustColor`, `AdjustVolume`, and so on.

If this were all there was to object-oriented programming (OOP), it wouldn't be all that big of a deal. In this section, you'll discover cool techie stuff like encapsulation, inheritance, and polymorphism, the features that give object-oriented programming its true power.

The Secrets of Encapsulation

One thing object-oriented programs use that conventional procedural-type programs don't is a handy thing called *encapsulation.* Encapsulation is the OOP rule that says an object hides both the data and the functions that act on that data inside the object. When you employ encapsulation, you can control access to the object's data, forcing programs to retrieve or modify data only through the object's interface. In strict object-oriented design, an object's data is always private to the object. That is, other parts of a program should never have direct access to that data.

How is this data hiding different from a conventional programming approach? After all, you could always hide data inside of functions just by making that data local to the function. A problem arises, however, when you want to make the data of one function available to other functions. The way to do this in a structured program is to make the data global to the program, giving any function access to it. It seems that you could use another level of scope—one that would make your data global to the functions that need it—but still prevent other functions from gaining access. Encapsulation does just that.

The Secrets of Inheritance

When you have a class that's close to what you need to create an object, but you want to make a few changes, you don't have to change the original class at all. Instead, an OOP thingy called *Inheritance* enables you to create a class that's similar to that previously defined class but that still has some of its own properties and functions (called methods in a class). (A class is kind of like a blueprint for an object.) For example, suppose you want to create a TV simulation from the TV object we were talking about before. Now, though, you want the TV to have a larger screen. In a traditional program, that would require a lot of code modification. As you modified the code, you would probably introduce bugs into a tested program.

Using the object-oriented approach avoids a lot of this type of trouble: Create a new TV class by inheritance. This new TV class inherits all of the data and function members from the base class (the class from which the new class is derived). Of course, just like that chin you inherited from Grandma Linette, the new class also inherits the original class's problems. If there's a problem with a base class, however, fixing it in the base class fixes it for all the classes that inherit from the base class. Too bad you can't go back in time and fix grandma's genes, huh?

The Secrets of Polymorphism

Now here's a word and a half for you: polymorphism. Say that three times fast! Rather than being a tongue twister by design, polymorphism is another major feature of object-oriented programming. By using polymorphism, you can create new objects that perform the same functions found in the base object but that perform one or more of these functions in a different way.

For example, think of a TV. (Here we go again.) All TVs are the same type of object. They all turn on, tune to channels, manage volume, preempt your favorite sitcom with a golf tournament, and so on. However, each TV may handle these tasks in a different way. For example, the first TV may have only one speaker, while the next may have full stereo sound. Both TVs produce sound, but they do it in different ways.

In object-oriented programming, you would implement these kinds of differences using polymorphism. Yeah, it's kind of an intimidating word, but you'll feel better about it after you see a program or two that uses this technique. For now, you should be proud if you can even spell the word.

Writing a Class

While all this talk of classes and objects may be as confusing as a sweater on a lamp, creating your own classes is actually pretty easy—at least from a syntax point of view. Believe it or not, you need to know only one new keyword, Class. For example, here's the simplest Visual Basic .NET class you can write (so simple, in fact, that the class does nothing at all):

```
Class MyClass

End Class
```

About the only way to make this process easier is to hire the kid down the street to type the code in for you. This is almost exactly the same way you'd write a subroutine, except you substitute the word Class wherever you'd use Sub, and you don't hire that kid. Also, the class name isn't followed by arguments in parentheses.

Believe it or not, though, Visual Basic .NET actually *does* make the process easier because it can create the new class for you. All you have to do is select the Project menu's Add Class command, as shown in Figure 16.9.

When the Add New Item dialog box appears, you select the Class template and then type a new name for the class in the Name text box, as shown in Figure 16.10.

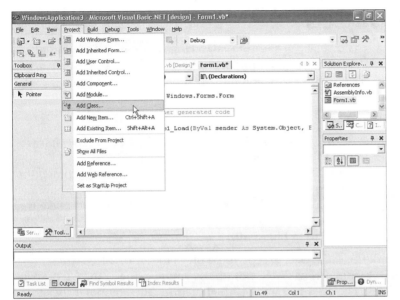

Figure 16.9

Adding a class to a project.

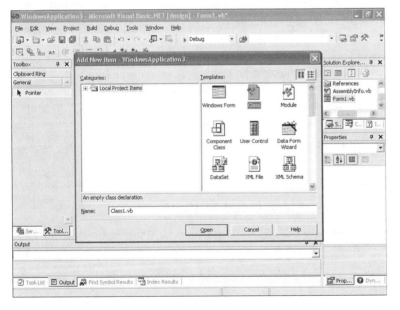

Figure 16.10

The Add New Item dialog box.

In Chapter 17, "Creating Your Own Objects," you'll learn what to put between the lines that mark the beginning and end of a class. I promise you all sorts of wonderful experiences. And ice cream. Until then, let's continue in a more philosophical direction.

Classes Versus Objects

You may remember that I said that you can think of a class as a template for an object. You can also think of a class as a room full of students, but that won't help you here. To take advantage of your new class, you must first create an object of the class. You do that like this:

```
Dim myObject As MyClass = New MyClass()
```

Here, myObject is the name of the object you're creating from the class, and MyClass is the name of the class from which you're creating the object. Dig? Think of a TV. No, just kidding. Think of a blueprint for … oh … how about a tree house? The blueprint tells you everything about how to build the tree house—except how to use a hammer and how many times you'll fall out of the tree before the project's done. You take that blueprint, and using it as a guide, you build a tree house. (If it comes out looking like a skating rink, you grabbed the wrong blueprint.)

Classes and objects work the same way, except you won't fall out of a tree when you're building an object from a class. Well, not unless you're using your notebook computer in weird places. The class you write is the blueprint the computer uses to build objects. When you ask the computer to create an object, the computer goes down to the lumberyard … whoops, I'm still thinking about tree houses. When you ask the computer to make an object from a class, the computer takes the instructions you provided (the class) and creates the object.

You can create as many objects as you like from a single class. Yep, it's true. This is just like how you can make a whole pile of tree houses from a single blueprint. Then, not only will you have a lot of great experience falling out of trees, you'll also have places for you and your friends to stay when you annoy the people who live in your real house.

In the next chapter, you continue to study OOP and classes, and you start to use classes for real.

The Least You Need to Know

➤ Object-oriented programming (OOP) is using classes to represent objects in a program.

➤ With encapsulation, you can hide both data and functions inside an object.

➤ Using inheritance, you can create a class that is similar to a previously defined class but that still has some of its own properties and methods.

➤ Using polymorphism, objects can perform the same functions found in a base object but perform one or more of the functions in a different way.

➤ You can think of a class as being a blueprint (template) for an object.

Chapter 17

Creating Your Own Objects

In This Chapter

➤ Writing a class using properties and methods

➤ Using classes in your programs

➤ Writing a base class

➤ Writing derived classes using inheritance

Now that you have some idea of what classes are and what they do, it's time to do some actual object-oriented programming. Remember, however, that because QBasic doesn't support object-oriented programming, the program examples in this chapter use the Visual Basic .NET programming language. If you don't have a copy of Visual Basic .NET (which I'm sure includes most of you), read along, anyway. The screen shots will clue you in to what's going on.

Adding Properties and Methods to a Class

In the previous chapter, you put together a simple class, albeit one that did absolutely nothing. Obviously, a class that does nothing is about as useful as a fur-lined sink. To make a class useful, you need to add properties and methods. You can think of properties as being attributes of an object. For example, in the real world, a car has attributes such as color and body style.

Methods, on the other hand, represent actions that can be performed with an object. Sticking with the car example, such actions might be starting the car and putting on the brakes. In this section, you'll learn why you need properties and methods, and you'll discover how to add them to your classes.

The Deal with Properties

When you come right down to it, a property is nothing more than a variable that's contained in a class. You've now had tons of experience with variables, so you shouldn't have any trouble with that concept. The difference is that this class variable represents an attribute of the class. For example, if you created a class named Book, you might have Title and Author properties. To create the Book class and add the Title and Author properties, you might start with something like this:

```
Public Class Book
    Private TitleStore As String
    Private AuthorStore As String
End Class
```

There are a couple of rules that deal with properties. Like most rules, you can choose to break them if you like, but I wouldn't advise you to. One of the rules is related to encapsulation, which you learned about in the previous chapter. Because of encapsulation, properties are always (or always supposed to) private to the class. This means that code from outside the class cannot access the properties directly. This may seem like a clumsy limitation at first, until you realize that limiting direct access to properties enables the class to retain complete control over them. How then, can a program get or set the values of the properties?

The words "get" and "set" are the key. The truth is that when you declared the Title and Author strings in the preceding code, you only created storage for the properties' values (which is why I added the word "store" to the variables' names). To make these variables into full-fledged properties, you have to add *property procedures,* which are special methods that enable a program to change or get a property's value. For example, here's a property procedure for Title:

```
    Public Property Title() As String
        Get
            Return TitleStore
        End Get
        Set(ByVal Value As String)
            TitleStore = Value
        End Set
    End Property
```

You need to notice the following about this property procedure:

➤ The property procedure is declared as Public because code outside of the class must be able to call the procedure.

➤ The Property keyword identifies this method as a property procedure.

➤ As far as code outside of the class goes, the name of the property is the same as the name of the property procedure: Title. The variable TitleStore cannot be seen from outside the class and simply acts as storage for the property.

➤ Between the Get and End Get lines, the property procedure returns the property's value, which in this case is the value stored in the TitleStore variable.

➤ The Set keyword is followed by a name and data type for the value that will be used to set the property's value.

➤ Between the Set and End Set lines, the procedure assigns the value received by the Set statement to the property's storage area, which in this case is the variable TitleStore.

Each property procedure is a method of the class and so must be written as part of the class. So far, then, your Book class looks like this:

```
Public Class Book
    Private TitleStore As String
    Private AuthorStore As String

    Public Property Title() As String
        Get
            Return TitleStore
        End Get
        Set(ByVal Value As String)
            TitleStore = Value
        End Set
    End Property

    Public Property Author() As String
        Get
            Return AuthorStore
        End Get
        Set(ByVal Value As String)
            AuthorStore = Value
        End Set
    End Property
End Class
```

If all this is making you as nervous as a mouse at a cat convention, don't sweat it. You'll get plenty of practice with this class stuff in this and the following chapter. So clear your head, take a deep breath, and let's move on.

Construction and Destruction Underway

Now, thanks to the property procedures you just added to your Book class, your programs can get or set the value of a property at any time. Another time you can set a property's value is when you create an object from the class. This is the job of a special class method called a *constructor*. A constructor is a method that gets called when your program creates an object of a class. You may remember creating an object like this:

```
Dim myObject As MyClass = New MyClass()
```

You probably don't remember writing a constructor for the MyClass class. That's because you *didn't* write one. In this case, the class's constructor is the default constructor provided by Visual Basic .NET for all classes. (It's called the default because if it doesn't work, it's "default" of Visual Basic. Get it?) You don't have to rely on the default constructor, though. You can create your own. When you do this, the constructor can initialize the class's properties. Here's what a constructor for your Book class might look like:

```
Public Sub New(ByVal Title As String, ByVal Author As String)
    Me.TitleStore = Title
    Me.AuthorStore = Author
End Sub
```

You should notice the following about the Book class's constructor:

➤ The constructor is declared as a Public subroutine. It has to be Public so that code outside of the class can call it.

➤ The constructor's name is New. This is the name you use for any class's constructor.

➤ The constructor accepts as arguments whatever values a program needs to pass into the class. In this case, the constructor accepts the title and author of the book.

➤ The constructor assigns the values it receives as arguments to the appropriate property storage areas.

Let's now play a game of opposites. What's the opposite of white? What's the opposite of male? Hey, you're good! What's the opposite of a constructor? Got ya! The opposite of a constructor is a *destructor*. In retrospect, that seems pretty obvious, doesn't it? A class's destructor gets called right before your program removes an object of a class from your computer's memory. You can use a class's destructor to do any kind of cleanup you need to do for the class.

By the way, there's a small technical detail we should discuss before all those Visual Basic .NET programmers out there jump all over me. I should note here that Visual Basic .NET classes don't have destructors in the sense that other OOP languages do.

However, the term "destructor" is often used in OOP discussions, so I'll stick with that term here. Here's what your Book class's destructor might look like:

```
Protected Overrides Sub Finalize()
    ' Do cleanup here.
    MyBase.Finalize()
End Sub
```

You should notice the following about the Book class's destructor:

➤ The destructor is declared as a Public subroutine. It has to be Public so that code outside of the class can call it.

➤ The destructor's name is Finalize. This is the name you use for any class's destructor.

➤ The destructor accepts no arguments.

The Book class's destructor contains nothing but a comment because the Book class doesn't need to do any cleanup chores. In this case, you probably wouldn't bother writing the destructor at all, but I included it here because I wanted you to waste your time typing. No, wait! I meant to say that I included it for demonstration purposes. Here's what the Book class looks like now:

```
Public Class Book
    Private TitleStore As String
    Private AuthorStore As String

    Public Sub New(ByVal Title As String, ByVal Author As String)
        Me.TitleStore = Title
        Me.AuthorStore = Author
    End Sub

    Protected Overrides Sub Finalize()
        ' Do cleanup here.
        MyBase.Finalize()
    End Sub

    Public Property Title() As String
        Get
            Return TitleStore
        End Get
        Set(ByVal Value As String)
            TitleStore = Value
        End Set
    End Property

    Public Property Author() As String
        Get
            Return AuthorStore
```

```
        End Get
        Set(ByVal Value As String)
            AuthorStore = Value
        End Set
    End Property
End Class
```

A Method to the Madness

Now, what the heck are you going to do with that Book class? Hmmmmmm. How about using the Book class in a program that manages computer-based electronic books? Along with the class's properties then, you're also going to need methods that perform actions on the book. What kinds of actions? Well, how about the turning of a page? You perform actions in classes by writing *methods*.

A method is very similar to the other types of procedures you've written. The main difference is that a method is encapsulated (Oooooo! Programmer speak!) in a class and therefore, unlike other parts of a program, has access to the class's properties. Here's a method you might write to turn a page of the book:

```
Public Sub TurnBookPage()
    BookPageStore = BookPageStore + 1
    If BookPageStore = 101 Then BookPageStore = 1
End Sub
```

Of course, all this method really does is update a variable called BookPageStore. There's no program code here to actually display text on the screen. That's what you have an imagination for. In fact, I'm going to stop writing right now, so that you have a chance to imagine the rest of this book.

Okay, so that didn't work very well. But the important things here are that the TurnBookPage method is declared as Public so that code outside of the class can call it. Also, notice that the Book class doesn't have a variable named BookPageStore, so what's it doing in the TurnBookPage method?

Obviously, you need to add the BookPageStore variable to the class. Did somebody say "property"? Right on! The best way to add the BookPageStore variable to the class is to create a new property. However, this time you'll create a *read-only property,* which is a property that the program can look at but not change. Here's the new property's storage variable and property procedure:

```
    Private BookPageStore As Integer

    Public ReadOnly Property BookPage() As Integer
        Get
            Return BookPageStore
        End Get
    End Property
```

This property procedure is different from the others you've written in this chapter in two significant ways:

➤ The addition of the ReadOnly keyword

➤ No Set program code, only Get

In addition to adding the BookPage property to the class, you'll also need to set it to a starting value. You can do that in the class's constructor, although you don't need to add it to the constructor's arguments because the program won't be able to set the page number when creating a book object. Why? Because you're not going to let it! So, here's the final Book class:

```
Public Class Book
    Private TitleStore As String
    Private AuthorStore As String
    Private BookPageStore As Integer

    Public Sub New(ByVal Title As String, ByVal Author As String)
        Me.TitleStore = Title
        Me.AuthorStore = Author
        BookPageStore = 1
    End Sub

    Protected Overrides Sub Finalize()
        ' Do cleanup here.
        MyBase.Finalize()
    End Sub

    Public Sub TurnBookPage()
        BookPageStore = BookPageStore + 1
        If BookPageStore = 101 Then BookPageStore = 1
    End Sub

    Public Property Title() As String
        Get
            Return TitleStore
        End Get
        Set(ByVal Value As String)
            TitleStore = Value
        End Set
    End Property

    Public Property Author() As String
        Get
            Return AuthorStore
        End Get
        Set(ByVal Value As String)
```

```
            AuthorStore = Value
        End Set
    End Property

    Public ReadOnly Property BookPage() As Integer
        Get
            Return BookPageStore
        End Get
    End Property
End Class
```

Cool Stuff

Classes can have three types of properties: read/write, read-only, and write-only. The most common properties are read/write, and they enable a program to read the property's value as well as set the value. Read-only properties, on the other hand, can only be read from outside the class and can be set only by the class itself. Write-only properties are just the opposite. They can be set from outside the class but can be read only from within the class. Frankly, I've never run into a case in which I wanted a write-only property in a class.

Reading Your Books

You've now got a full class that'll handle imaginary electronic books. Wasn't that fun? Maybe just a little? The next job on the list is to create book objects from the class and "read" them onscreen. If you happen to have Visual Basic .NET (you lucky devil), perform the following steps to create a project to test the class. If you don't have Visual Basic .NET, just read along to see how everything works.

1. Start a new Visual Basic .NET project using the Windows Application template. Name the application Classes.

2. Add the controls shown in Figure 17.1 to the application's form.

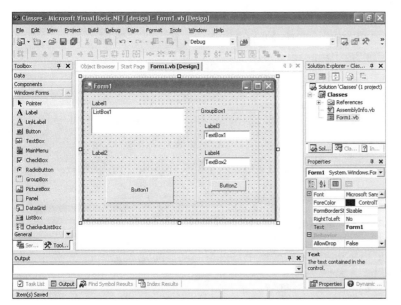

Figure 17.1

The Classes application's form.

3. Double-click the form and add the following lines to the Form1_Load procedure that Visual Studio starts for you:

```
Label1.Text = "Current Book"
Label2.Text = "You are reading page #0"
Label3.Text = "Title"
Label4.Text = "Author"
ListBox1.Text = ""
TextBox1.Text = ""
TextBox2.Text = ""
GroupBox1.Text = "Add New Book"
Button1.Text = "Turn Page"
Button2.Text = "Add Book"
numberOfBooks = 0
currentBookNumber = -1
currentBook = Nothing
```

4. Add the following lines near the top of the program, right before the Form1_Load procedure:

```
Const MAXBOOKS = 5
Dim books(MAXBOOKS-1) As Book
Dim numberOfBooks As Integer
Dim currentBookNumber As Integer
Dim currentBook As Book
```

211

5. Double-click the Button1 control and add the following lines to the Button1_Click procedure that Visual Studio starts for you:

```
If currentBook Is Nothing Then
    MessageBox.Show("Please select a book first.")
Else
    currentBook.TurnBookPage()
    Label2.Text = "You are reading page #" & currentBook.BookPage
End If
```

6. Double-click the Button2 control and add the following lines to the Button2_Click procedure that Visual Studio starts for you:

```
If numberOfBooks < MAXBOOKS And TextBox1.Text <> "" Then
    Dim bookTitle As String = TextBox1.Text
    Dim bookAuthor As String = TextBox2.Text
    books(numberOfBooks) = New Book(bookTitle, bookAuthor)
    numberOfBooks = numberOfBooks + 1
    ListBox1.Items.Add(bookTitle)
Else
    MessageBox.Show("Can't add book.")
End If
TextBox1.Text = ""
TextBox2.Text = ""
```

7. Double-click the ListBox1 control and add the following lines to the ListBox1_SelectedIndexChanged procedure that Visual Studio starts for you:

```
currentBookNumber = ListBox1.SelectedIndex()
currentBook = books(currentBookNumber)
Label2.Text = "You are reading page #" & currentBook.BookPage
```

8. Add a class module to the project. Name the class Book and complete it with the code from the Book class, as shown in Figure 17.2.

When the project is complete, save your work and run the program. When you do, the window in Figure 17.3 appears.

To use the program, type the title and author of a book into the text boxes on the right and click the Add Book button. The book then appears in the list box. You can add up to five books to the list.

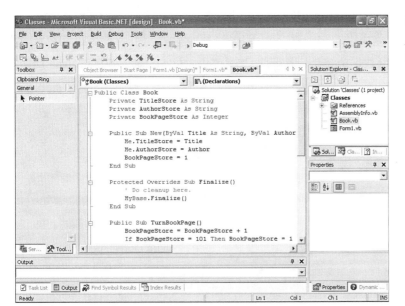

Figure 17.2

Adding the Book *class to the project.*

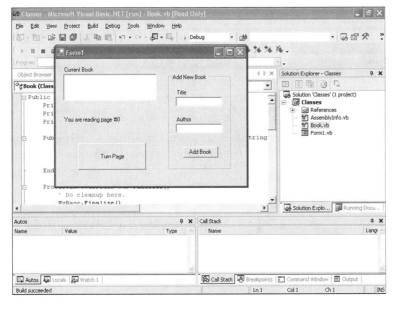

Figure 17.3

The running Classes application.

After adding at least two books to the list, select a book by clicking it. When you do, the program informs you that you are reading page 1. Click the Turn Page button to "read" the book. Each click of the button advances the book's current page. Select another book in the list and do the same. Switch between books and notice how every book remembers the last page read. Digital bookmarks are way better than the paper

213

kind, huh? You could try to save your place by folding over the corner of your monitor, but I wouldn't suggest it.

Figure 17.4 shows what the application looks like with a few books added to the list and with the current book having been read to page 15.

Figure 17.4

Reading books with the Classes application.

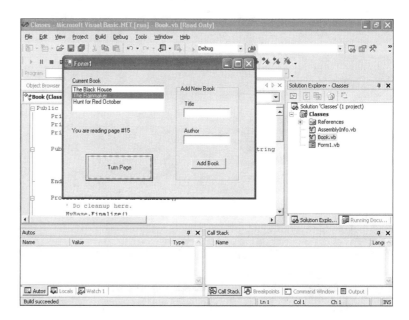

The Stuff You Need to Know

A lot of the Classes program is straightforward Visual Basic .NET programming, but there are a few points worth going over. First, notice how the program stores its Book objects in an array:

```
Dim books(MAXBOOKS-1) As Book
```

Because the program sets the constant MAXBOOKS to 5, the books array can hold five Book objects, numbered 0 through 4. The program also declares a Book object for the book the user is currently reading:

```
Dim currentBook As Book
```

When the user selects a book, the list box control's SelectedIndexChanged event handler gets called. There, the program gets the selected book's number from the list box:

```
currentBookNumber = ListBox1.SelectedIndex()
```

The program uses the book number to get the current book from the array:

```
currentBook = books(currentBookNumber)
```

214

Finally, the program displays the current Book object's last-read page, which it gets from the BookPage property:

```
Label4.Text = "You are reading page #" & currentBook.BookPage
```

Clicking the Turn Page button causes Visual Basic to call the button's Click event handler, which first makes sure that the user has chosen a book to read:

```
If currentBook Is Nothing Then
    MessageBox.Show("Please select a book first.")
```

The Nothing keyword represents the value an object has when it hasn't yet been set.

If the user has selected a book, the program calls the Book object's TurnBookPage method to advance the page count and displays the new current page in the window:

```
currentBook.TurnBookPage()
Label4.Text = "You are reading page #" & currentBook.BookPage
```

Adding a Book object to the list occurs when the user clicks the Add Book button. In that button's Click procedure, the program first makes sure that the book array has room and that the user has typed a book title into the text box:

```
If numberOfBooks < MAXBOOKS And TextBox1.Text <> "" Then
```

If everything checks out, the program creates a new Book object with the title and author supplied by the user, adding the book to the Book array:

```
Dim bookTitle As String = TextBox1.Text
Dim bookAuthor As String = TextBox2.Text
books(numberOfBooks) = New Book(bookTitle, bookAuthor)
```

After updating the book count, the program adds the new book's title to the list box:

```
numberOfBooks = numberOfBooks + 1
ListBox1.Items.Add(bookTitle)
```

The rest of the program you should be able to understand on your own. If you have trouble, take two button controls and call me in the morning. Yes, this program is a bit more advanced than what you're used to. If you're a little foggy on the details, don't worry about it. The whole point of the program is to show you how OOP works. If you've managed to get a general idea of how OOP works, you're doing great!

You've now got a good idea of what classes are and how they work. However, you wouldn't believe how much more there is to learn about classes. In fact, I could write an entire book on classes alone. You'll be glad to hear, however, that you don't have to know *that* much about classes. You do need to know about a little thing called inheritance, though—and, no, I'm not referring to that house you think Grandma Sarah is going to leave you.

Understanding the Basics of Inheritance

One of the big advantages of classes is that they provide an easy mechanism for reusing code. By that I mean, once you have created and perfected a class, you can use it again and again, knowing it'll work fine every time. But that's only half of the story. You can also use an existing class as the starting point for a new class that's similar to the starting class (called a base class) but that has new capabilities. To see how this works, look at this simple Visual Basic. NET class:

```
Public Class TestClass
    Private numberStore As Integer
    Public Property Number() As Integer
        Get
            Return numberStore
        End Get
        Set(ByVal Value As Integer)
            numberStore = Value
        End Set
    End Property
End Class
```

This class has a single property named Number that the class stores in the private class variable numberStore. The Get and Set parts of the property procedure enable a program to get and set the property's value. If you want to test this class, you could pay a big company tons of money to perform months of research, or you could just write the following program lines:

```
Dim Obj As New TestClass()
Obj.Number = 10
Dim n = Obj.Number
MessageBox.Show(n)
```

Here's what each line does, from top to bottom:

1. Creates an object of the TestClass class

2. Sets the object's Number property to 10

3. Gets the value of the Number property

4. Displays the value of the Number property in a message box

Now, want to try something really tricky? Write a new class that looks like this:

```
Public Class TestClass2
    Inherits TestClass
End Class
```

See the line Inherits TestClass? That line tells Visual Basic that you want TestClass2 to start off exactly like TestClass. What does this mean to you? It means that even though you haven't written the program lines needed to create a property named Number, TestClass2 has that property anyway, because TestClass2 inherits the Number property from TestClass. The following program lines put TestClass2 to the test:

```
Dim Obj As New TestClass2()
Obj.Number = 15
Dim n = Obj.Number
MessageBox.Show(n)
```

Here's what each line does:

1. Creates an object of the TestClass2 class
2. Sets the object's Number property to 15
3. Gets the value of the Number property
4. Displays the value of the Number property in a message box

Now both TestClass and TestClass2 are identical. The more astute among you will now be asking, "How can I have my cake and eat it too?" The even more astute will be asking, "What good are two classes that are exactly alike?"

The whole point of this inheritance stuff isn't to make classes that are exactly alike (duh!), but to start with a tested class and build new features into it. Suppose, for example, you want a class just like TestClass except you also need a property named Number2. Here's what you could write:

```
Public Class TestClass2
    Inherits TestClass
    Private number2Store As Integer
    Public Property Number2() As Integer
        Get
            Return number2Store
        End Get
        Set(ByVal Value As Integer)
            number2Store = Value
        End Set
    End Property
End Class
```

Now TestClass2 has two properties, Number and Number2. TestClass2 inherits Number from Class1 and then defines the new property Number2 within the class. Here's the proof:

Programmer Lingo

When using inheritance with classes, the starting class is called the **base class,** and the class that inherits from the base class is called the **derived class.**

```
Dim Obj As New TestClass2()
Obj.Number = 15
Obj.Number2 = 25
Dim num1 = Obj.Number
Dim num2 = Obj.Number2
```

```
MessageBox.Show(num1)
MessageBox.Show(num2)
```

Here's what each individual lines does:

1. Creates an object of the TestClass2 class
2. Sets the object's Number property to 15
3. Sets the object's Number2 property to 25
4. Gets the value of the Number property
5. Gets the value of the Number2 property
6. Displays the value of the Number property in a message box
7. Displays the value of the Number2 property in a message box

Dealing with Inheritance for Real

Okay, enough of the theoretical stuff. It's time to put object-oriented programming with inheritance to work in an actual program. As always, if you have Visual Basic .NET, you can build the sample program using the following instructions. If you don't have Visual Basic .NET, just read along to get a general idea of the process.

1. Start a new Visual Basic project named Inheritance (using the Windows Application template), as shown in Figure 17.5.

Figure 17.5

Creating the Inheritance project.

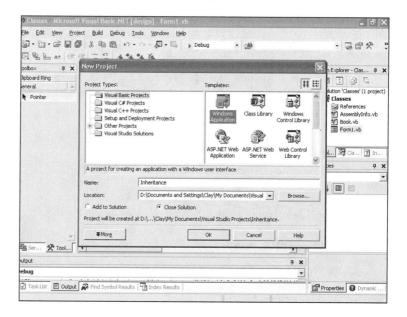

2. Add a single button to the form, as shown in Figure 17.6.

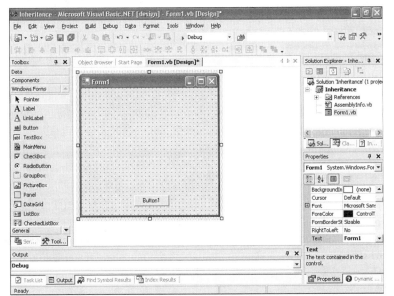

Figure 17.6

The form with its button.

Now you need to decide what kind of class you want to write. A class hierarchy, which is what programmers call classes that inherit from each other, can be a little tricky. The base class of the hierarchy should comprise all of the features that all the derived classes will have in common. After all, it doesn't make sense for a class to inherit things it doesn't need (you know, like that extra eyeball in the back of your head). It also doesn't make sense to duplicate something in all of the classes when all you have to do is put it in the base class, from which all the other classes will automatically get it. You'll probably have to read this paragraph again. It really does make sense. I promise.

3. Start with a class called Shape from which you can create more specific classes like Rectangle and Circle. Let's say that all shapes in your class hierarchy will have the following properties:

PositionX   The shape's horizontal position

PositionY   The shape's vertical position

To create this base class, first start a new class module named Shape.

4. Type these program lines into the new Shape class:

```
Public Class Shape
     Private positionXstore As Integer
     Private positionYstore As Integer
     Public Property PositionX() As Integer
          Get
               Return positionXstore
          End Get
          Set(ByVal Value As Integer)
               positionXstore = Value
          End Set
     End Property
     Public Property PositionY() As Integer
          Get
               Return positionYstore
          End Get
          Set(ByVal Value As Integer)
               positionYstore = Value
          End Set
     End Property
End Class
```

Now that you've got your base class, you can create a Rectangle class by inherit-ing from Shape.

5. Start a new class module named Rectangle and then type these program lines into it:

```
Public Class Rectangle
     Inherits Shape
     Private widthStore As Integer
     Private heightStore As Integer
     Public Property Width() As Integer
          Get
               Return widthStore
          End Get
          Set(ByVal Value As Integer)
               widthStore = Value
          End Set
     End Property
     Public Property Height() As Integer
          Get
               Return heightStore
          End Get
          Set(ByVal Value As Integer)
```

```
            heightStore = Value
        End Set
    End Property
End Class
```

As you can see from this class, a `Rectangle` object has—in addition to the `PositionX` and `PositionY` properties it inherited from `Shape`—the new properties `Width` and `Height`, which are necessary to draw a rectangle.

6. Now, how about a `Circle` class? To draw a circle, you don't need width and height. In a circle, width and height are the same value, a value called diameter. So create a new class module named `Circle` that looks like this:

```
Public Class Circle
    Inherits Shape
    Private diameterStore As Integer
    Public Property Diameter() As Integer
        Get
            Return diameterStore
        End Get
        Set(ByVal Value As Integer)
            diameterStore = Value
        End Set
    End Property
End Class
```

Now it's time to test your new classes.

7. Double-click the form's button control and add the following program lines to the `Click` event handler:

```
Dim shapeObj As New Shape()
Dim rectObj As New Rectangle()
Dim circleObj As New Circle()
shapeObj.PositionX = 15
shapeObj.PositionY = 20
rectObj.PositionX = 25
rectObj.PositionY = 30
rectObj.Width = 25
rectObj.Height = 30
circleObj.PositionX = 60
circleObj.PositionY = 80
circleObj.Diameter = 40
MessageBox.Show(shapeObj.ToString() & " : " & _
    shapeObj.PositionX & " : " & shapeObj.PositionY)
MessageBox.Show(rectObj.ToString() & " : " & _
    rectObj.PositionX & " : " & rectObj.PositionY & " : " & _
    rectObj.Width & " : " & rectObj.Height)
```

221

```
MessageBox.Show(circleObj.ToString() & " : " & _
    circleObj.PositionX & " : " & circleObj.PositionY & " : " & _
    circleObj.Diameter)
```

8. Run the program and click the form's button. When you do, the program creates objects of each of the classes and displays the object values in message boxes, as you can see in Figure 17.7.

Figure 17.7

The running Inheritance program.

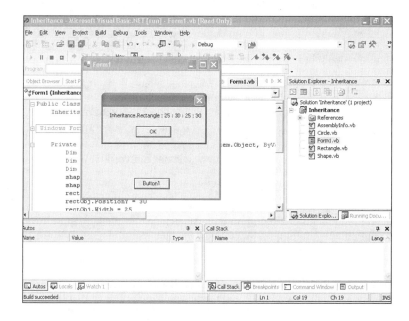

You haven't seen the end of these shape classes. In the next chapter, you'll use them to learn even more about object-oriented programming.

Cool Stuff

If you had a special type of circle you wanted to draw, you could inherit a new class from the general Circle class. For example, you might create a class called SolidCircle. In this way, you can build a circle class hierarchy with as many classes as you need, with all of those classes tracing their chain of inheritance all the way back to Shape.

The Least You Need to Know

➤ Properties are attributes of an object, much like color or model are attributes of a car.

➤ Methods represent actions that a program can perform on an object.

➤ Encapsulation dictates that property values be private to the class.

➤ A constructor is a method that your program calls to create an object of a class.

➤ You always declare a constructor as `Public` so that code outside of the class can call it.

➤ The constructor accepts whatever values a program needs to pass into the class.

➤ A class's destructor gets called right before an object is removed from your computer's memory.

➤ You can use a class's destructor to do any kind of cleanup you need to do for the class.

➤ You declare a destructor as `Public` so that code outside of the class can call it.

➤ The `Inherits` keyword specifies that you want a class to inherit the properties and methods of another class.

➤ The starting class in a hierarchy is called the base class, and the classes that inherit from the base class are called derived classes.

Chapter 18

The Strange World of Polymorphism

In This Chapter

➤ Getting a handle on polymorphism

➤ Creating classes that use polymorphism

➤ Putting class hierarchy to work

Now that you know a bit about classes and OOP, it's time to really dig in deep. Using polymorphism is probably one of the toughest parts of OOP, so once you understand the stuff in this chapter, you'll be ready to tackle the big time. If you're still confused about any of the class stuff you learned in the previous two chapters, you should probably reread those chapters before you start on this one. In this chapter, you're not only going to learn about polymorphism, but you're also going to put all your knowledge of classes to the test as you continue to build on the shape classes you started previously.

Getting Polymorphic

After that introduction, you're probably shaking in your boots. But the idea of polymorphism isn't all that hard to grasp (although putting it to work can be an intellectual process, to say the least). Polymorphism is just the capability to create objects that perform the same functions in different ways. Now, sure, there are some very technical details behind that simple sentence, but, unless you're planning writing your own compiler (good luck!), you can skip the details.

Think about the Shape, Rectangle, and Circle classes you wrote. Suppose you not only want to store data like position and size in these classes, but that you also want to draw the shapes on the screen. To do this, you plan to add a method called DrawShape to each class. However, not to state the obvious, but a circle looks nothing like a rectangle, which probably (definitely) means that you have to draw it differently. This is an example of performing the same function—in this case, drawing a shape—in different ways.

Polymorphism on the Loose

The best way to explore polymorphism is to put it to work on your own, so follow these steps (if you don't have access to Visual Basic .NET, just follow along in your head and study the figures, which show you what's going on):

1. Create a new Visual Basic project named Shapes, as shown in Figure 18.1.

Figure 18.1

Create the Shapes project.

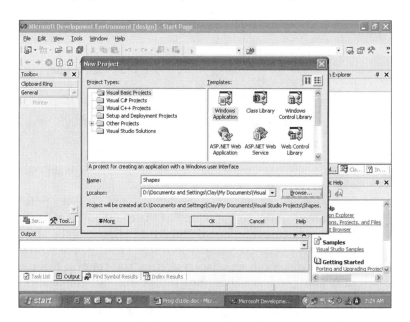

2. Add a single button to the form, as shown in Figure 18.2.

   Now, you can start writing the program.

3. Add a new class module to the program named Shape, as shown in Figure 18.3.

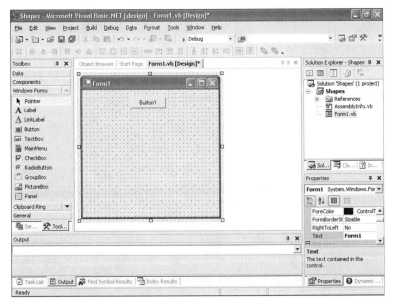

Figure 18.2

Add the button.

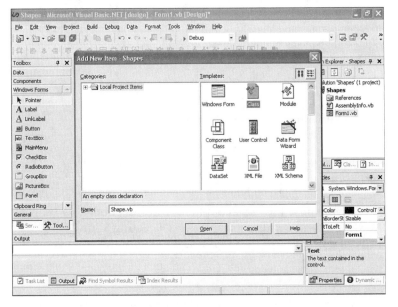

Figure 18.3

Add the Shape *class module.*

4. When the class's code window appears, complete the class so that it looks like this:

```
Public MustInherit Class Shape
    Private positionXstore As Integer
    Private positionYstore As Integer

    Sub New(ByVal x As Integer, ByVal y As Integer)
        positionXstore = x
        positionYstore = y
    End Sub

    Public Property PositionX() As Integer
        Get
            Return positionXstore
        End Get
        Set(ByVal Value As Integer)
            positionXstore = Value
        End Set
    End Property

    Public Property PositionY() As Integer
        Get
            Return positionYstore
        End Get
        Set(ByVal Value As Integer)
            positionYstore = Value
        End Set
    End Property

    MustOverride Sub DrawShape(ByVal g As Graphics)
End Class
```

When You Must, You Must

Paying attention? Then you probably noticed a couple new things about this Shape class as compared to the version you wrote in Chapter 17, "Creating Your Own Objects." For example, the first line of the class definition includes the MustInherit keyword:

```
Public MustInherit Class Shape
```

The MustInherit keyword tells Visual Basic not to allow any program to create a Shape object. Instead, programs can create objects from classes that inherit from Shape. This is because the Shape class is so general that it doesn't even represent a real object. I mean, how would you draw it? What does it look like? The only reason the Shape class exists is to provide a storage place for the properties and methods that are common to all shapes, like circles and rectangles. The MustInherit keyword ensures that the Shape class is used only in this way.

Getting That Shape Constructed

The next thing to notice is that the Shape class now has a constructor:

```
Sub New(ByVal x As Integer, ByVal y As Integer)
    positionXstore = x
    positionYstore = y
End Sub
```

You learned about constructors in Chapter 17. If you need a refresher, read this: A constructor provides a place for the Shape class to initialize itself. By providing the constructor with the x and y parameters, a program can create a Shape object like this:

```
Dim s = New Shape(15, 25)
```

Of course, thanks to the MustInherit keyword, no program can create a Shape object directly, so this program line would not compile. But you get the point. You'll soon see the right way to call the Shape class's constructor.

When You Must, You Must (Revisited)

The last new thing in the Shape class is this line:

```
MustOverride Sub DrawShape(ByVal g As Graphics)
```

See the MustOverride keyword? This tells Visual Basic that every class that uses Shape as a base class must define a DrawShape method that matches the declaration in the Shape class. By matches, I mean that the method must be called DrawShape and must accept a Graphics object as a parameter. Confused? Don't worry about it. You'll see what I mean when you write the Draw method in other classes. In fact, let's write one of those classes right now.

A Shape That Works

Add a new class module named Rectangle to your project and then complete the class with the following program lines:

```
Public Class Rectangle
    Inherits Shape
    Private wdth As Integer
    Private hght As Integer

    Sub New(ByVal x As Integer, ByVal y As Integer, _
        ByVal wdth As Integer, ByVal hght As Integer)
        MyBase.New(x, y)
        Me.wdth = wdth
        Me.hght = hght
```

```
        End Sub

    Public Property Width() As Integer
        Get
            Return wdth
        End Get
        Set(ByVal Value As Integer)
            wdth = Value
        End Set
    End Property
    Public Property Height() As Integer
        Get
            Return hght
        End Get
        Set(ByVal Value As Integer)
            hght = Value
        End Set
    End Property

    Overrides Sub DrawShape(ByVal g As Graphics)
        g.DrawRectangle(Pens.Black, PositionX, PositionY, wdth, hght)
    End Sub
End Class
```

This Rectangle class is the same as the one you wrote in the preceding chapter, except it now has a constructor and also has the DrawShape method.

Look at the constructor. To create a Rectangle object, the program needs to provide the rectangle's horizontal (PositionX) and vertical (PositionY) positions as well as its width and height. The Rectangle class inherits its PositionX and PositionY properties from the Shape class. The Width and Height properties, on the other hand, are defined right in the Rectangle class itself.

Getting Back to Base-ics

Splitting the properties between two classes this way leads to a problem. Specifically, you need a way to initialize the rectangle's PositionX and PositionY properties. The first line in the constructor of a derived class always calls the base class's constructor with the values required to initialize the base class's properties:

```
MyBase.New(x, y)
```

As you can see, you don't need to use the base class's actual name but should type MyBase.New instead. Visual Basic already knows the base class's name. Just be sure to include the right arguments, which in this case are the values for the PositionX and PositionY properties. After the call to the base class's constructor executes, the base class's inheritable properties are initialized and ready to go.

As for the properties that are unique to the Rectangle class, you initialize them in the constructor.

```
Me.wdth = wdth
Me.hght = hght
```

The Secret to Polymorphism

Now the Rectangle class's properties are ready, but the class is required to define the DrawShape method, remember? Here's what that method looks like:

```
Overrides Sub DrawShape(ByVal g As Graphics)
    g.DrawRectangle(Pens.Black, PositionX, PositionY, wdth, hght)
End Sub
```

The Overrides keyword tells Visual Basic that this function is a replacement for a function of the same name in the base class. Because this version of DrawShape is in the Rectangle class, it must draw a rectangle using the Rectangle class's properties. That, of course, is what the call to DrawShape does. The DrawShape method will get its Graphics object when the main program calls the method.

A Second Shape That Works

Now add a Circle class to the program. Create a new class module named Circle and complete the module with these program lines:

```
Public Class Circle
    Inherits Shape
    Private diam As Integer

    Public Sub New(ByVal x As Integer, ByVal y As Integer, _
            ByVal diam As Integer)
        MyBase.New(x, y)
        Me.diam = diam
    End Sub

    Public Property Diameter() As Integer
        Get
            Return diam
        End Get
        Set(ByVal Value As Integer)
            diam = Value
        End Set
    End Property

    Overrides Sub DrawShape(ByVal g As Graphics)
```

```
        g.DrawEllipse(Pens.Black, PositionX, PositionY, diam, diam)
    End Sub
End Class
```

This Circle class is just like the Circle class from the preceding chapter except, like the Rectangle class, it now has a constructor and a DrawShape method. If you're slow on the draw today, please notice that the Circle class's DrawShape method draws a circle rather than a rectangle.

From Ancestor to Ancestor

Now let's go one step further with the shape classes. Let's add a specialized circle shape called FilledCircle. A filled circle shape will be exactly like a regular circle shape, except the circle will be drawn in a solid color rather than just as an outline. Because a FilledCircle object is so much like a Circle object, you'll derive FilledCircle from Circle.

Add a new class module named FilledCircle to your program and complete the class so that it looks like this:

```
Public Class FilledCircle
    Inherits Circle
    Private brsh As Brush

    Public Sub New(ByVal x As Integer, ByVal y As Integer, _
            ByVal diam As Integer, ByVal brsh As Brush)
        MyBase.New(x, y, diam)
        Me.brsh = brsh
    End Sub

    Public Property FillColor() As Brush
        Get
            Return brsh
        End Get
        Set(ByVal Value As Brush)
            brsh = Value
        End Set
    End Property

    Overrides Sub DrawShape(ByVal g As Graphics)
        g.FillEllipse(brsh, PositionX, PositionY, _
            Diameter, Diameter)
    End Sub
End Class
```

Here are a few things to notice about the new FilledCircle class:

➤ It inherits from `Circle`.

➤ The constructor calls `MyBase.New`. In this case, `MyBase.New` refers to `Circle.New`. Inside `Circle.New`, the first line is also `MyBase.New`, but this time `MyBase.New` refers to `Shape.New`. This is how the values for `PositionX` and `PositionY` make it all the way back to `Shape`.

➤ The required `DrawShape` method draws a filled circle rather than an outlined circle.

So now you have a class inheritance tree that looks like the one shown Figure 18.4.

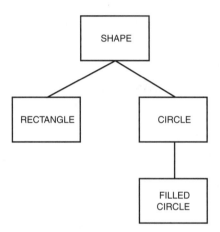

Figure 18.4

The `Shape` *inheritance tree.*

Testing Your Shapes

With all your classes in place, it's time to put them to work. Double-click the form's button and add the following program lines to the `Click` event procedure:

```
Dim ARectangle As New Rectangle(20, 25, 20, 25)
Dim ACircle As New Circle(50, 75, 50)
Dim AFilledCircle As New FilledCircle(70, 195, 40, Brushes.Red)
Dim g As Graphics = CreateGraphics()
ARectangle.DrawShape(g)
ACircle.DrawShape(g)
AFilledCircle.DrawShape(g)
ARectangle.PositionX = 200
ARectangle.PositionY = 100
ARectangle.Width = 75
ARectangle.Height = 50
ARectangle.DrawShape(g)
ACircle.PositionX = 150
ACircle.PositionY = 125
ACircle.Diameter = 100
```

```
ACircle.DrawShape(g)
AFilledCircle.PositionX = 150
AFilledCircle.PositionY = 30
AFilledCircle.Diameter = 60
AFilledCircle.FillColor = Brushes.Blue
AFilledCircle.DrawShape(g)
```

Now you can run the program. When you do, click the button. You'll see the window shown in Figure 18.5.

Figure 18.5

The running Shapes *program.*

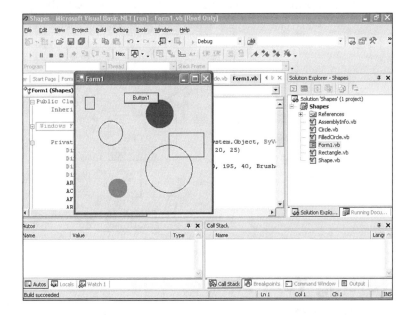

There's nothing too tricky going on in the main program. First, it creates Rectangle, Circle, and FilledCircle objects, after which the program gets a Graphics object to use for drawing. By calling each object's DrawShape method, the associated shape appears onscreen. The program then changes the shapes' properties and calls their DrawShape methods once again, displaying a new set of shapes.

To make sure you have this class stuff down, see if you can add a FillRectangle class to the hierarchy. Hint: To draw a filled rectangle, call the Graphics object's FillRectangle method. Look FillRectangle up in your online documentation to get the details.

End of the Line

This concludes your brief journey into the world of programming. I hope at this point that you're excited by the possibility of making your computer do what *you* want it to do. If so, your local major bookstore stocks tons of titles on programming. Such books will teach you everything you need to know to become a computer-programming guru!

The Least You Need to Know

➤ When you want to create objects that perform the same functions in different ways, you can use polymorphism.

➤ No program can create an object directly from a class that specifies the MustInherit keyword in its declaration.

➤ If a class declares a method with the MustOverride keyword, every derived class must define the method.

➤ To initialize a base class, the derived class's constructor should call MyBase.New().

➤ The Overrides keyword specifies that the function being defined overrides (is a replacement for) a function of the same name in the base class.

Exploring C#

In the last few chapters, you got a chance to explore object-oriented programming with Visual Basic .NET, Microsoft's latest version of the Visual Basic language. Visual Basic. NET had not been released as of this writing, but by the time this book sees print, Visual Basic will either be on store shelves or very close to it.

Visual Basic. NET is not the only new object-oriented programming language that Microsoft has created for its .NET Framework. Also included in Visual Studio .NET is the new language C#. Unlike Visual Basic, however, this is the very first version of C#. In this chapter, you get a chance to explore the powerful features that C# offers programmers.

Pronounced *C Sharp*

If you didn't know how to pronounce C#, you're not alone. C# is a brand new programming language and, until recently, was just a note you could play on a piano! Exactly what is C# like? How did it get its name? You may have heard of a language called C. If not, take my word that it exists. The C programming language is an older version of the language C++ (pronounced *C plus plus*), which is hugely popular in the world today.

So, guess where the "C" in C# comes from. That's right, C# is based on the popular C++ language. In C#, it's kind of like Microsoft took the C++ language and got rid of all the stuff that tripped people up the most, but still managed to retain most of the power of C++.

But there's even more. C# comes with a fully visual development environment, just like Visual Basic. This means you can build your application's user interface by placing controls on a form, which is a heck of a lot faster than writing the source code that creates and places controls (although you can do that, too, if you want). In short, C# takes the best parts of C++ and Visual Basic and rolls them together to create a powerful, but easier to use, development language.

Judging a Book by Its Cover

Just looking at the C# programming environment doesn't tell you a whole lot about the language, but it does give you an idea of how sophisticated the tools are. For example, Figure 19.1 shows what Visual Studio .NET (the name of the integrated development environment [IDE] that comes with C#) looks like when you first start it up.

Figure 19.1

The Visual Studio .NET IDE.

On this starting screen you see the Start page, which is where you choose the project you want to work on. The buttons enable you to open an existing project or start a new one. Another way you can load a project is by clicking on a project name in the box above the buttons.

Let's say you want to start a brand-new project, so you click the New Project button. When you do, the New Project dialog box opens, as shown in Figure 19.2. Using this dialog box, you can give Visual Studio the details of your project.

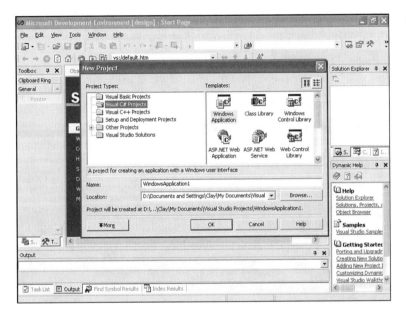

Figure 19.2

The New Project dialog box.

The types of projects available to you depend on which tools you have installed on your system. The full, professional version of Visual Studio comes with the Visual Basic .NET, Visual C# .NET, and Visual C++ .NET programming languages. Right now, though, we're only interested in C#, so you would click on Visual C# Projects in the Project Types pane of the New Project dialog box and then select Windows Application from the Templates pane. Finally, you give the project a name in the Name text box and set the project's location (where the files will be saved) in the Location box.

When you've completed filling in the dialog box, all you have to do is click the OK button, and wonderful things start to happen. What happens is that Visual Studio creates a new project for you. This includes not only setting up the source-code files you'll need but also filling those files with the minimum program code you need to produce your application's window on the screen. Figure 19.3 shows you what the IDE looks like at this point.

Want to see the source code Visual Studio created for you? Just double-click inside the Form1 form. When you do, the form's code window pops up, enabling you to explore and edit the form's source code (see Figure 19.4).

Figure 19.3

The Visual Studio IDE with a new C# project started.

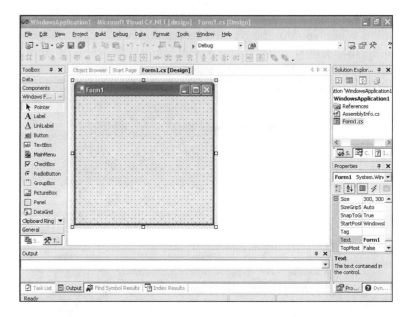

Figure 19.4

The C# source code for the project's starting form.

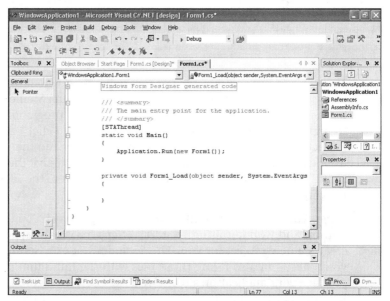

Visual Studio has done so much work for you at this point that you can actually run the program without adding another line of source code. Don't believe it? Just click the little arrow next to the word "Debug" in the toolbar and then watch and be amazed as your C# program takes off, compiling its source code and running the resultant executable file.

You then see the window shown in Figure 19.5. This window is your new C# application's window. Of course, it doesn't do anything but the most basic window stuff at this moment (such as minimizing, maximizing, and closing), but that's quite a lot considering how much (or actually how *little*) you put into writing the program.

Figure 19.5

The new application's window.

Getting Your Application to Do Something

Just like the forms you've seen with Visual Basic, a C# form doesn't do much until you add some controls and then write some source code to tell those controls what to do. Almost everything that happens in an application is the result of the user selecting some sort of command. That command may be in a menu, in a dialog box, as a result of pressing a button, or something else. To see how this works, let's add a button to your new C# application's window.

To see the toolbar, which contains the controls you can add to your window, you must first select the project's form. You do this by clicking the tab that says "Form1.cs [Design]." When the form appears, so does the toolbox.

Near the top of the toolbox (located on the far left of Visual Studio's window) is a control named Button. Just double-click that control to make a button appear on your form. You can then use your mouse to drag the button wherever you'd like inside the form. Figure 19.6 shows the button placed in the center of the form.

At this point you can run the program, and you'll see a window with a button in the middle, as shown in Figure 19.7. Go ahead and click the button. Nothing happened? That's because you haven't yet told the application what the button is supposed to do. To do that, you have to write some C# source code and associate it with the button.

Figure 19.6

Adding a button to the form.

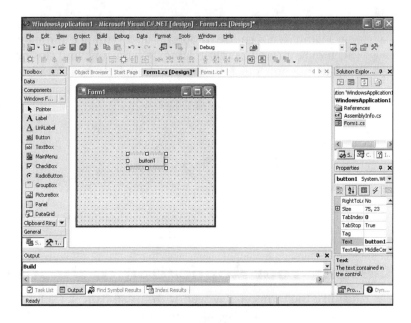

Figure 19.7

The window with its new button.

When you close the window with the button, the Visual Studio IDE puts you right back where you were, staring at your form's design window and its toolbox. Now double-click the button control you placed in the form. Presto! Visual Studio writes some more source code for you. This time, the source code is the beginning of the procedure that runs when the user clicks the button. All you have to do is write the C# source code that you want to execute when the button is clicked. To keep things simple, add a line of C# source code that makes a message box appear. Figure 19.8 shows the new button1_Click procedure.

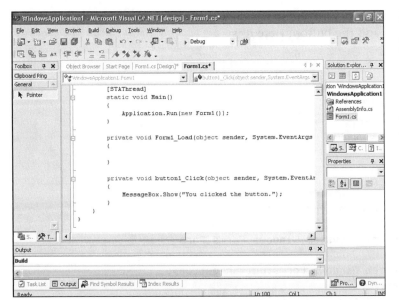

Figure 19.8

Associating source code with the button control.

Now, run the program again and, when the application's window appears, click the button. The message box appears, as shown in Figure 19.9.

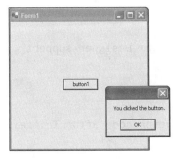

Figure 19.9

Now the button does something.

How OOP Fits In

Because this last section of the book is about object-oriented programming (OOP), you may wonder at this point how C# fits in. Well, I already mentioned that C# is a fully object-oriented language. You may not realize, however, what I mean by "fully." Not only does C# fully support the object-oriented way of doing things, you simply have no choice but to do things the object-oriented way. Why? Because even the source code that represents your application's form is a class, and all the code you add to your program (except for things like compiler instructions) must be part of a class.

To see what I mean, take a look at the source code you have so far for your application with the window and the button. Here it is:

```csharp
using System;
using System.Drawing;
using System.Collections;
using System.ComponentModel;
using System.Windows.Forms;
using System.Data;

namespace MyApp
{
    /// <summary>
    /// Summary description for Form1.
    /// </summary>
    public class Form1 : System.Windows.Forms.Form
    {
        private System.Windows.Forms.Button button1;
        /// <summary>
        /// Required designer variable.
        /// </summary>
        private System.ComponentModel.Container components = null;

        public Form1()
        {
            //
            // Required for Windows Form Designer support
            //
            InitializeComponent();

            //
            // TODO: Add any constructor code after InitializeComponent
call
            //
        }

        /// <summary>
        /// Clean up any resources being used.
        /// </summary>
        protected override void Dispose( bool disposing )
        {
            if( disposing )
            {
                if (components != null)
                {
                    components.Dispose();
                }
```

```
        }
        base.Dispose( disposing );
    }

    #region Windows Form Designer generated code
    /// <summary>
    /// Required method for Designer support - do not modify
    /// the contents of this method with the code editor.
    /// </summary>
    private void InitializeComponent()
    {
        this.button1 = new System.Windows.Forms.Button();
        this.SuspendLayout();
        //
        // button1
        //
        this.button1.Location = new System.Drawing.Point(112, 120);
        this.button1.Name = "button1";
        this.button1.TabIndex = 0;
        this.button1.Text = "button1";
        this.button1.Click += new System.EventHandler(this.button1_Click);
        //
        // Form1
        //
        this.AutoScaleBaseSize = new System.Drawing.Size(5, 13);
        this.ClientSize = new System.Drawing.Size(292, 266);
        this.Controls.AddRange(new System.Windows.Forms.Control[] {
                                                    this.button1});
        this.Name = "Form1";
        this.Text = "Form1";
        this.ResumeLayout(false);

    }
    #endregion

    /// <summary>
    /// The main entry point for the application.
    /// </summary>
    [STAThread]
    static void Main()
    {
        Application.Run(new Form1());
    }

    private void button1_Click(object sender, System.EventArgs e)
    {
```

```
                MessageBox.Show("You clicked the button.");
        }
    }
}
```

This code example isn't meant to terrify you—even though it probably does! Rather, it's meant to show you what C# code looks like and how important classes are to that code. First, look near the top of the program. See the line namespace MyApp? A namespace is nothing fancier than an area in which all symbol names are guaranteed to be unique. Okay, I know that that sounds a bit like techno speak. Basically, what it means is that any class, variable, or function name (as well as other kinds of symbols) inside the namespace cannot be seen outside of the namespace (at least, not without also adding the namespace name to the variable name, as in the example MyNamespace.MyVariable.)

This is similar to what you learned about variable scope. For example, variables defined inside a function cannot be accessed from outside the function. A namespace protects the source code for an entire application from having symbol names that accidentally duplicate names that might be defined in other modules used with the project.

A little after the namespace line, you see this:

```
public class Form1 : System.Windows.Forms.Form
```

This is the line that starts the class for your form. Remember inheritance? This program derives the Form1 class from the base class named System.Windows.Forms.Form. Everything from this line until the next-to-last closing brace belongs to the class. (The last closing brace ends the namespace.) If you look closely at the code example, you can see class methods such as Form1 (which is the class's constructor), Dispose (which acts sort of like the class's destructor), and InitializeComponent.

There's also a special method named Main. The Main method is special because that's where the program starts. That is, when you run the program, the code in the Main method is the first to execute.

Do you see how all this fits in with what you've learned about OOP? To help you visualize the class, here's the same code with all the details stripped out so that you can easily see the class's structure:

```
    public class Form1 : System.Windows.Forms.Form
    {
        private System.Windows.Forms.Button button1;
        private System.ComponentModel.Container components = null;

        public Form1()
        {
        }
```

```
        protected override void Dispose( bool disposing )
        {
        }

        private void InitializeComponent()
        {
        }

        static void Main()
        {
        }

        private void button1_Click(object sender, System.EventArgs e)
        {
        }
    }
}
```

As you can see, the class isn't as complicated as it first may have appeared. It has only two properties (the private variables button1 and components) and only five methods (Form1, Dispose, InitializeComponent, Main, and button1_Click). See? You're already beginning to understand C#. How cool is that?

The Least You Need to Know

➤ C# is a brand-new programming language from Microsoft.

➤ C# is based on the popular C++ language.

➤ C# comes with a fully visual development environment, just like Visual Basic.

➤ Visual Studio .NET is the name of the integrated development environment (IDE) that comes with C#.

➤ The full professional version of Visual Studio comes with the Visual Basic .NET, Visual C# .NET, and Visual C++ .NET programming languages.

➤ Visual Studio automatically can create the minimum program code you need to produce your application's window on the screen.

➤ The C# toolbar contains the controls you can add to your window.

➤ When you double-click a control in a form, Visual Studio generates the beginning of the control's procedure.

➤ C# is a fully object-oriented language, which means that almost everything in your programs goes into classes.

Programming Languages Overview

Programming languages follow the same life cycle as other types of technology. What's new and cutting edge today becomes outdated and unused tomorrow. With all the code out there, though, few languages completely die away. A few programmers, for example, still use FORTRAN, which is one of the first programming languages ever developed. You're not likely to run into FORTRAN code yourself, though. Another language you may never run into is COBOL, which was used extensively for business applications (it was great for creating reports) but is considered a dinosaur these days.

If I were to list every language ever used (assuming I could even do it, which isn't likely), I'd have a very long list. However, most of the languages on the list would be either outdated or applied to the types of specialized programming problems you're not likely to run into. The point is that there are only a few popular programming languages out there these days. Yes, dozens of programming languages are available, but only a few get extensive use. Those languages are Visual Basic, C++ (pronounced *C plus plus*), and Java. Another language that will probably be big is Microsoft's brand new C# (pronounced *C sharp*).

Visual Basic

Visual Basic just may be the most popular programming language in the world today. This not only is because Visual Basic derived from the immensely popular BASIC language (the only one of the older languages still used extensively today), but also because this version of BASIC features a visual editor that enables you to create windows, dialog boxes, menus, and more just by placing controls onto a form. Figure A.1, for example, shows a Visual Basic project that a programmer just started by placing a text box and a button onto the project's form.

Figure A.1

Visual Basic's visual editor.

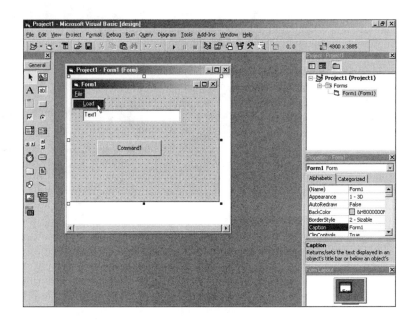

Visual Basic's visual editor and components are so powerful that you can create a complete user interface for your application in minutes. The only thing the programmer has to write is the source code that makes each component of the user interface do what it's supposed to do. For example, the programmer may use the visual editor to create a File menu with a Load command, as shown in Figure A.2.

Figure A.2

Creating a user interface with Visual Basic.

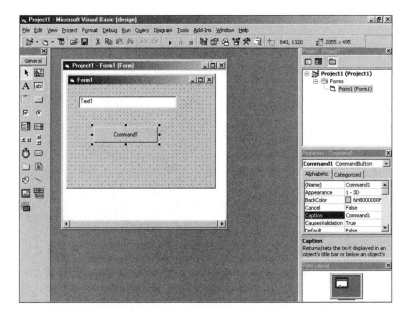

After creating the menu command, the programmer must write the code that should execute when the user selects the command. This means opening the code window and writing the event procedure associated with the menu command. Visual Basic makes this process as easy as possible; if the programmer double-clicks the menu command in the project's form, Visual Basic automatically starts the event procedure, as shown in Figure A.3.

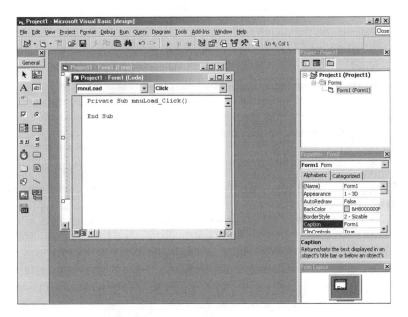

Figure A.3

Visual Basic's code editor.

At the time of this writing, the most popular version of Visual Basic is Visual Basic 6. By the time you read this, however, Microsoft will have released its next incarnation of VB, named Visual Basic .NET. This version of the language is very different from previous versions. Although the visual editor is still an important part of the development environment, all new Microsoft languages are based on the .NET Framework, which is a massive set of libraries for creating everything from small Windows utilities and applications to full-fledged Web applications.

The Visual Basic language is popular with many businesses as well as with hobbyist programmers and programmers who create shareware. Visual Basic also gets a lot of use with professional application developers, who like to use it to quickly create prototypes for their applications.

C++

Visual Basic's competitor for the most popular language in the world is C++. C++ is everywhere, and chances are, most of the applications you use on your computer were written with C++.

251

For a number of reasons, C++ is not an easy language to learn and master. First, C++ isn't really a high-level language like BASIC; rather, it falls somewhere between a high-level language and an assembly language. That is, although C++ enables the developer to write programs using high-level programming techniques like for loops, functions, and classes, the language gives the programmer an immense amount of power. When you're programming in C++, you'd better save your work often because you're almost certainly going to lock up your computer sooner or later!

Because C++ is such a powerful language, it's used for everything from application development to the development of operating systems. Windows itself was written with C++; this should give you some idea of the power behind the language.

C++ is also harder to learn than a language like BASIC because of its concise syntax, which uses many arcane symbols and constructs. Professional C++ programmers are infamous for cramming as much functionality into a single line of code as possible, yielding programs that look like a whole lot of nonsense. This, of course, is not good programming style, but C++'s concise syntax is just too much of a temptation for programmers who want to show off.

C++ comes in many forms, from freeware compilers to very expensive, integrated development environments. The free versions of C++ (the GNU compiler, for example) come with only the basic tools for converting C++ source code into an executable file. The development environments, of which Microsoft's Visual C++ is the most popular, come with scads of tools that take even professional developers months to learn to use.

As of this writing, the most popular version of Visual C++ is Visual C++ 6.0. Figure A.4 shows the development environment of this version.

Figure A.4

The Visual C++ 6.0 development environment.

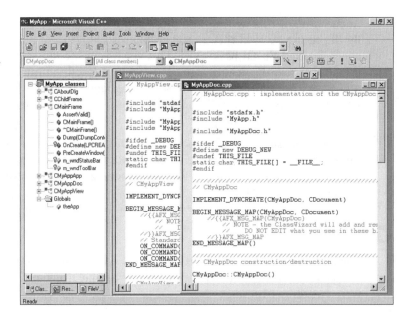

Just as with Visual Basic, Microsoft is about to release a new version of Visual C++ called Visual C++ .NET. In fact, Microsoft will probably have released this new version by the time you read this. Figure A.5 shows the Visual C++ .NET development environment.

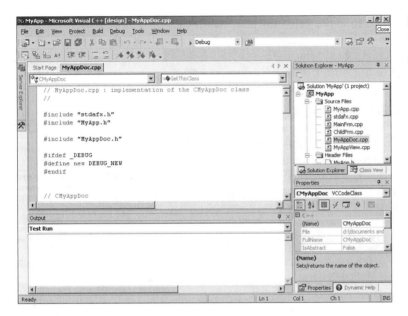

Figure A.5

The Visual C++ .NET development environment.

Java

Java is a sort of simplified version of C++. Although Java can be used to create complete applications, programmers use it mostly to provide a special kind of Web content known as applets. *Applets* are small programs that run inside a Web page, and they enable a Web page to process data or perform other program tasks that can't be managed by plain HTML. (By the way, HTML is not a programming language. It's a page description language, and it is incapable of performing any form of data processing.)

Just as with C++, you can start programming with Java by downloading freeware tools. These tools don't provide many conveniences, but they work. If you want to spend a few bucks, many software publishers sell sophisticated Java development environments. These include traditional editor and compiler suites as well as full-fledged visual environments similar to Visual Basic.

One of Java's big advantages is its built-in security features, which guarantee that Java-based Web content cannot do nasty things to your computer. Because Java is a full-featured programming language, Java applets can perform almost any kind of programming task. For this reason, Java's security features are critical, ensuring that an applet that appears in a Web page can't access your private files.

253

C#

The last language in this roundup is C#. As I'm writing this paragraph, C# exists only in beta form. By the time you read this, however, you'll probably be able to run down to the software store and pick up a copy of C# .NET.

Many people expect C# to take the programming world by storm. One reason for this is that the C# development environment combines the visual elements of Visual Basic with a powerful language similar to C++. Like Visual Basic, Visual C# .NET enables the program to build a user interface by dragging components from a toolbox. That is, a developer can prototype a complete user interface without writing a single line of code.

The C# language itself is very similar to C++, except it's based on the .NET Framework and avoids many of the pitfalls that make C++ programming difficult. Still, moving from C++ to C# is a fairly painless process due to the languages' similarities. If you program in C++, you already know most of C#, although you will have to get used to some important differences as well as learn to program with the .NET Framework. Figure A.6 shows what the Microsoft C# development environment looks like.

Figure A.6

The Visual C# .NET environment.

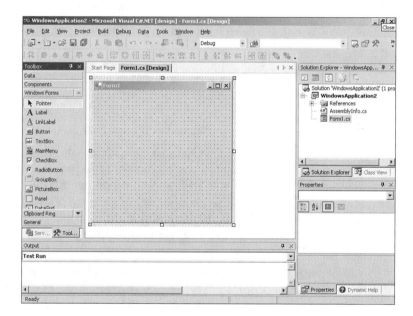

A Word About Scripting Languages

Full-featured application programming languages aren't the only ones out there. You'll also run into a whole slew of what's called *scripting languages*. In many cases, a fine line separates full-featured languages and scripting languages. The biggest difference is that scripting languages are mostly used for smaller jobs and so usually aren't as powerful as their full-featured cousins.

For example, Microsoft Word includes a scripting language that enables you to program sophisticated macros that can do just about anything you want with your Word documents. Microsoft Word's scripting language is almost as powerful as the full version of Visual Basic.

In fact, many large-scale applications feature their own scripting languages that enable the user to add new features to the application or to make the application automatically perform often-used tasks. Check your applications' help files to see whether any support a scripting language. If they do, you can customize the applications to perfectly suit your way of working.

People also use scripting languages a lot to add computational and processing abilities to Web pages. Two popular scripting languages used for this purpose are VBScript and JavaScript. If you look at the HTML for a professionally designed Web page, you'll almost certainly see some kind of scripting language being used to add abilities to the pages that HTML itself cannot handle.

HTML, by the way, is not a programming language, or even a scripting language. It's a page-description language that can do little more than specify how text and graphics should appear on a page. While a page of HTML may look even more confusing than a page of program source code, you can't use HTML to write any type of program. Another famous page-description language is PostScript, which enables PostScript printers to produce very graphically sophisticated documents.

Summary

There you have it, a short introduction to the programming languages that will probably serve you best should you decide to move on beyond QBasic. Virtually everything you learned in this book can be applied to these other languages. The syntax, however, is very different from one language to the next.

A Programmer's Quick Reference

You've covered a whole lot of information in this book, and while it would be difficult to summarize all the material in one place, I've made an attempt to put together in this appendix information that you may need to reference as you further explore programming. Take a couple of minutes to look over this material, and then come back to this appendix when you have questions about anything covered here.

Steps Required to Write a Computer Program

1. Type the program using QBasic's editor.
2. Save the program to disk.
3. Run the program and see how it works.
4. Fix programming errors.
5. Go back to step 2.

A Programmer's Tools

➤ **Source-code editor** All programs start off in the form of source code, which is the programming commands you type. In order to type these commands, you of course need some sort of editor. This editor can be as simple as Windows Notepad or can be an expensive third-party application.

➤ **Interpreter** A piece of software that executes program source code one line at a time. Because each line must be converted to machine language as the program runs, interpreters tend to run programs slowly. An interpreter performs these steps:

1. Read a line of source code.

2. Convert the line to machine language.

3. Pass the machine language instruction to the computer for execution.

4. Go back to step 1 until the interpreter has read all lines of source code.

➤ **Compiler** A piece of software that converts an entire source-code file into machine language, which is stored in an executable file. Compiled programs run much faster than interpreted programs, because the entire conversion process occurs before the user attempts to run the program. A compiler performs these steps:

1. Read a line of source code.

2. Convert the line to machine language.

3. Store the machine-language instructions in the program's executable file.

4. Go back to step 1 until the compiler has read all lines of source code.

➤ **Debugger** A piece of software that enables you to explore, in slow motion, what's going on in your program. In a typical debugging session, you would execute each line of source code one at a time and watch the results.

QBasic Reserved Words

ABS	APPEND	ABSOLUTE	AS
ACCESS	ASC	AND	ATN
ANY			
BASE	BLOAD	BEEP	BSAVE
BINARY			
CALL	COLOR	COM	CASE
COMMON	CDBL	CONST	CHAIN
COS	CHDIR	CSNG	CHR$
CSRLIN	CINT	CVD	CIRCLE
CVDMBF	CLEAR	CVI	CLNG
CVL	CLOSE	CVS	CLS
CVSMBF			

DATA	DEFLNG	DEFSNG	DATE$
DEFSTR	DATE$	DIM	DECLARE
DO	DEF FN	DOUBLE	DEF SEG
DRAW	DEFDBL	$DYNAMIC	DEFINT
ELSE	ERDEV	ELSEIF	ERDEV$
END	ERL	ENVIRON	ERR
ENVIRON$	ERROR	EOF	EXIT
EQV	EXP	ERASE	
FIELD	FOR	FILEATTR	FRE
FILES	FREEFILE FIX	FUNCTION	
GET	GOSUB GOTO		
HEX$			
IF	INSTR	IMP	INT
INKEY$	INTEGER	INP	IOCTL
INPUT	IOCTL$	INPUT$	IS
KEY	KILL		
LBOUND	LOCK	LCASE$	LOF
LEFT$	LOG	LEN	LONG
LET	LOOP	LINE	LPOS
LPRINT	LIST	LOC	LSET
LOCATE	LTRIM$		

259

MID$	MKI$	MKL$	MKD$
MKS$	MKDIR	MKSMBF$	MKDMBF$
MOD			
NAME	NOT	NEXT	
OCT$	ON	OFF	OPTION
OR	OUT	OUTPUT	
PAINT	POINT	PALETTE	POKE
PCOPY	POS	PEEK	PRESET
PEN	PRINT	PLAY	PSET
PUT	PMAP		
RANDOM	RETURN	RANDOMIZE	RIGHT$
READ	RMDIR	REDIM	RND
REM	RSET	RESET	RTRIM$
RESTORE	RUN	RESUME	
SCREEN	SQR	STATIC	SEEK
$STATIC	STEP	SELECT	STICK
SGN	STOP	SHARED	STR$
SHELL	STRIG	SIN	SINGLE
STRING	SLEEP	STRING$	SOUND
SUB	SPACE$	SWAP	SPC
SYSTEM			
TAB	TIMER	TAN	TO
THEN	TROFF	TIME$	TRON
TYPE	TIMER		

UBOUND	UNTIL	UCASE$	USING
UNLOCK			

VAL	VARSEG	VARPTR	VIEW
VARPTR$			

WAIT	WIDTH	WEND	WINDOW
WHILE	WRITE		

XOR

QBasic Suffixes for Specifying Data Types

Type	Suffix	Example
Integer	%	total%
Long integer	&	count&
Single precision	!	value!
Double precision	#	weight#
String	$	name$

QBasic's Arithmetic Operators

Operator	Name	Use
+	Addition	Sum values
−	Subtraction	Subtract values
*	Multiplication	Multiply values
/	Division	Divide values
\	Integer division	Determine the whole number result of division
^	Exponentiation	Raise a value to a power
MOD	Modulus	Determine the remainder of division

Examples of Arithmetic Operations

Operation	Result
5+8	13
12–7	5
3*6	18
10/3	3.333333
10\3	3
2^3	8
10 MOD 3	1

Operator Precedence

Order	Operator	Name
1	^	Exponentiation
2	* / \ MOD	Multiplication, division, integer division, and modulus
3	+ -	Addition and subtraction

QBasic's Relational Operators

Operator	Meaning	Examples
=	Equals	3=(4-1) or "FRED"="FRED"
<>	Not equal to	5<>(3+3) or "FRED"<>"SAM"
<	Less than	3<23 or "A"<"B"
>	Greater than	41>39 or "BART">"ADAM"
<=	Less than or equal to	5<=6 or "ONE"<="ONE"
>=	Greater than or equal to	10>=10 or "THREE">="TWO"

Examples of Using the VAL Function

Function Call	Result
VAL("34")	34
VAL("56.23")	56.23
VAL("23.6&HYG")	23.6

Function Call	Result
VAL("2 3 4")	234
VAL("-76")	–76
VAL("764,345")	764
VAL("0")	0
VAL("SJuHGd")	0
VAL("HFGYR345")	0
VAL("nine")	0
VAL("3.4D+4")	34000

File Modes

➤ **Append**   Adds data to the end of a file.

➤ **Input**   Enables a program to read data from the file.

➤ **Output**   Enables a program to write data to a file.

➤ **Binary**   Enables non-text file management. All values are treated as binary numbers.

➤ **Random-access**   Enables a program to read and write at any location within the file.

QBasic Runtime Error Codes

Code	Description
1	NEXT without FOR
2	Syntax error
3	RETURN without GOSUB
4	Out of DATA
5	Illegal function call
6	Overflow
7	Out of memory
8	Label not defined
9	Subscript out of range
10	Duplicate definition
11	Division by zero
12	Illegal in direct mode

continues

Code	Description
13	Type mismatch
14	Out of string space
16	String formula too complex
17	Cannot continue
18	Function not defined
19	No RESUME
20	RESUME without error
24	Device timeout
25	Device fault
26	FOR without NEXT
27	Out of paper
29	WHILE without WEND
30	WEND without WHILE
33	Duplicate label
35	Subprogram not defined
37	Argument-count mismatch
38	Array not defined
40	Variable required
50	FIELD overflow
51	Internal error
52	Bad filename or number
53	File not found
54	Bad file mode
55	File already open
56	FIELD statement active
57	Device I/O error
58	File already exists
59	Bad record length
61	Disk full
62	Input past end of file
63	Bad record number
64	Bad file name
67	Too many files
68	Device unavailable
69	Communication-buffer overflow
70	Permission denied

Code	Description
71	Disk not ready
72	Disk-media error
73	Feature unavailable
74	Rename across disks
75	Path/file access error
76	Path not found

QBasic Screen Modes

Mode #	Resolution
0	Text mode only
1	320×200
2	640×200
3	720×348
4	640×400
7	320×200
8	640×200
9	640×350
10	640×350
11	640×480
12	640×480
13	320×200

Debugging Techniques

➤ **Step-Into Program Trace**   A step-into program trace enables you to run your program one line at a time and watch what happens every step of the way. That is, the debugger runs the current line of code and then pauses the program. The next program line doesn't run until you tell the debugger to run it.

➤ **Step-Over Program Trace**   The step-over program trace is very similar to the step-into program trace, except it enables you to run entire procedures without having to watch them execute line by line.

➤ **Variable Watcher**   Using a variable watcher, you can see into any variable you like and make sure that it contains the value that it should. You can also watch as the variable changes values as a result of executing program lines.

265

➤ **Breakpoints**   When you set a breakpoint, program execution continues until it reaches the breakpoint. Then, the program pauses, so you can do things like check the values of variables, start a line-by-line trace, or do whatever else you need to do in order to find a problem.

Three Main Features of Object–Oriented Programming

➤ **Encapsulation**   Encapsulation enables you to hide both the data and the functions that act on that data inside a class. Once you do this, you can control access to the data, forcing programs to retrieve or modify data only through the class's interface. In strict object-oriented design, an object's data is always private to the object.

➤ **Inheritance**   Inheritance enables you to create a class that is similar to a previously defined class but that still has some of its own properties and methods. To use inheritance, you derive one class from another and then add whatever new features the new class needs.

➤ **Polymorphism**   By using polymorphism, you can create new objects that perform the same functions found in a base object but that perform one or more of these functions in a different way.

Speak Like a Geek: The Complete Archive

argument   A value that's passed to a procedure or function. *See also* parameter.

arithmetic operations   Mathematical operations, such as addition, multiplication, subtraction, and division, that produce numerical results.

array   A variable that stores a series of values that can be accessed using a subscript. *See also* subscript.

BASIC   Stands for the beginner's all-purpose symbolic instruction code, the computer language on which Visual Basic is based.

bit   The smallest piece of information a computer can hold. A bit can be only one of two values, 0 or 1.

boolean   A data type that represents a value of true or false.

Boolean expression   A combination of terms that evaluate to a value of true or false. For example, (x = 5) AND (y = 6).

branching   This occurs when program execution jumps from one point in a program to another instead of continuing to execute instructions in strict order. *See also* conditional branch and unconditional branch.

breakpoint   A point in a program at which program execution should be suspended to enable the programmer to examine the results up to that point. By setting breakpoints in a program, you can more easily find errors in your programs. *See also* debugging.

byte   A piece of data made up of eight bits. *See also* bit.

class   A special type of program module that contains methods and properties that implement an object in object-oriented programming.

compiler   A programming tool that converts a program's source code into an executable file. *See also* interpreter.

concatenate   To join, end to end, two text strings into one text string. For example, the string "OneTwo" is a concatenation of the two strings "One" and "Two".

conditional branch   This occurs when program execution branches to another location in the program based on some sort of condition. An example of a conditional branch is the IF…THEN statement, which causes the program to branch to a program line based on a condition such as IF (x=5).

constant   A predefined value that never changes.

data type   The various kinds of values that a program can store. These values include IN-TEGER, STRING, SINGLE, DOUBLE, and BOOLEAN.

debugging   The act of finding and eliminating errors in a program.

decrement   Decreasing the value of a variable, usually by 1. *See also* increment.

double   The data type that represents the most accurate floating-point value, also known as a double-precision floating-point value. *See also* single and floating point.

element   One value in an array. *See also* array.

empty string   A string that has a length of 0, denoted in a program by two double quotes. For example, the following example sets a variable called str1 to an empty string: str1 = "".

encapsulation   An object-oriented programming term that refers to a class's capability to contain all of an object's properties and methods as well as to control which of the properties and methods are visible to other parts of the program.

executable file   A file, usually an application, that the computer can load and run. Most executable files end with the file extension .exe.

file   A named set of data on a disk.

floating point   A numerical value that has a decimal portion. For example, the values 12.75 and 235.7584 are floating-point values. *See also* double and single.

function   A subprogram that processes data in some way and returns a single value that represents the result of the processing.

global variable   A named value that can be accessed from anywhere within a program.

I/O   Stands for input/output, which is the process of transferring data into or out from the computer. An example of input is when the user types something on the keyboard; an example of output is when a program saves data to a disk file.

increment   Increasing the value of a variable, usually by 1. *See also* decrement.

infinite loop   A loop that can't end because its conditional expression can never evaluate to true. An infinite loop ends only when the user terminates the program. *See also* loop and loop control variable.

inheritance   An object-oriented-programming term that refers to the capability of a new class to inherit the properties and methods of an existing base class.

initialize   To set the initial value of a variable.

input devices   Devices, such as the keyboard and mouse, that transmit information into the computer. *See also* output devices.

integer   A data type that represents whole numbers. The values 240, –128, and 2 are examples of integers. *See also* long.

interpreter   A programming tool that executes source code one line at a time, unlike a compiler, which converts an entire program to an executable file before executing any of the program's commands. *See also* compiler.

literal   A value in a program that is stated literally, meaning the value is not stored in a variable.

local variable   A variable that can be accessed only from within the subprogram in which it's declared. *See also* global variable and variable scope.

logic error   A programming error that results when a program performs a different task than the programmer thought he programmed it to perform. For example, the program line IF x = 5 THEN Y = 6 is a logical error if the variable x can never equal 5. *See also* runtime error.

logical operator   A symbol that compares two expressions and results in a Boolean value (a value of true or false). For example, in the line IF X = 5 AND Y = 10 THEN Z = 1, AND is the logical operator. *See also* relational operator.

long   A data type that represents large integer values. *See also* integer.

loop   A block of source code that executes repeatedly until a certain condition is met.

loop control variable   A variable that holds the value that determines whether a loop will continue to execute.

machine language   The only language a computer truly understands. All program source code must be converted to machine language before the computer can run the program.

mathematical expressions   A set of terms that uses arithmetic operators to produce a numerical value. For example, the set of the terms (x + 10) / (y + 2) makes up a mathematical expression. *See also* arithmetic operations.

method   A procedure associated with an object or control that represents a capability of the object or control.

modular programming   Breaking a program up into a series of simple tasks.

numerical literal   A literal value that represents a number, such as 125 or 34.87. *See also* literal and string literal.

numerical value   A value that represents a number. This value can be a literal, a variable, or the result of an arithmetic operation.

object   Generally, any piece of data in a program. Specifically, a set of properties and methods that represents some sort of real-world object or abstract idea. In object-oriented programming, objects are created from classes.

object-oriented programming   The programming technique in which the programmer thinks in terms of objects, along with their attributes (called properties) and actions (called methods). The programmer creates classes that represent objects and then creates objects from the classes.

order of operations   The order in which a programming language resolves arithmetic operations. For example, in the mathematical expression (x + 5) / (Y + 2), QBasic will perform the two additions before the division. If the parentheses had been left off, as in the expression x + 5 / Y + 2, QBasic would first divide 5 by Y and then perform the remaining addition operations.

output devices   Devices, such as the monitor or a printer, that accept data coming out from the computer. *See also* input devices.

parameter   Often means the same thing as "argument," although some people differentiate between the two. For those who differentiate, an argument is the value sent to a procedure or function, and a parameter is the variable in the function or procedure that receives the argument. *See also* argument.

polymorphism   An object-oriented-programming term that refers to the capability of derived classes to perform the same function of a base class in different ways. For example, a Shape base class may have a Draw method that draws a shape. Rectangle and Circle classes derived from the Shape class will also have a Draw method, but the Rectangle class's will draw a rectangle, and the Circle class's will draw a circle.

procedure   A subprogram that performs a task in a program but doesn't return a value. *See also* function.

269

program   A list of instructions for a computer.

program flow   The order in which the computer executes the program statements.

programming language   A set of English-like keywords and symbols that enables a programmer to write a program without having to use machine language.

property   A value that represents an attribute of an object.

relational operator   A symbol that determines the relationship between two expressions. For example, in the expression X > 10, the relational operator is >, which means "greater than." *See also* logical operator.

return value   The value that a function sends back to the statement that called the function. *See also* function.

runtime   The period when a program is running rather than being designed.

runtime error   A system error that occurs while a program is running. An example is a divide-by-zero error or a type-mismatch error. Without some sort of error handling, such as that provided by the ON ERROR statement, runtime errors often result in a program crash.

scope   *See* variable scope.

single   The data type that represents the least accurate floating-point value, also known as a single-precision floating-point value. *See also* double and floating point.

source code   The lines of commands that make up a program.

string   A data type that represents one or more text characters. For example, in the assignment statement str1 = "I'm a string.", the variable str1 must be of the STRING data type.

string literal   One or more text characters enclosed in double quotes.

subprogram   A block of source code that performs a specific part of a larger task. In QBasic, a subprogram can be either a procedure or a function. *See also* procedure and function.

subscript   The portion of an array reference that indicates which element of the array to access. For example, in the line X = array1(10), 10 is the subscript, which is also sometimes called an index. *See also* array.

substring   A small portion of a larger string. For example, the string "One" is a substring of the larger string "OneTwo". *See also* string.

top-down programming   Organizing procedures in a hierarchy in which general-purpose procedures at the top call specific-purpose procedures lower in the hierarchy.

unconditional branch   This occurs when program execution branches to another location regardless of any conditions. An example of a conditional branch is the GOTO statement.

variable   A named value in a program. This value can be assigned and reassigned a value of the appropriate data type.

variable scope   The area of a program in which a variable can be accessed. For example, the scope of a global variable is anywhere within the program, whereas the scope of a local variable is limited to the procedure or function that declares the variable. *See also* local variable and global variable.

Index